Edinburgh's Tra

D. L. G. Hunter, C.Eng., F.I.Mech.E., F.C.I.T.

The author was educated and trained in Edinburgh, qualifying as a Chartered Engineer. He lived in that city for forty years, twelve years being spent as an Engineering Assistant with the Corporation Transport Department. After periods with the Lothians Electric Power Company and the L.N.E.R. he took up dock engineering, becoming the Mechanical Engineer with the Leith Dock Commission. In 1957 he transferred to the British Transport Commission Docks Division, later the British Transport Docks Board, at Goole, where he became the Docks Engineer until his retirement in 1973, and return to Scotland.

By the same author:

Carriages and Wagons of the Highland Railway
Edinburgh Tramways Album
Scottish Electric Tramways
Edinburgh Corporation Buses Album
Scottish Buses before 1929
Scottish Motor Traction Co. Ltd. Album
From S.M.T. to Eastern Scottish
The Highland Railway in Retrospect

EDINBURGH'S TRANSPORT

Volume One
THE EARLY YEARS

D. L. G. HUNTER C.Eng.

JAMES THIN
THE MERCAT PRESS, EDINBURGH
1992

First published in 1992 by Mercat Press
James Thin, 53 South Bridge, Edinburgh EH1 1YS

ISBN 1873644027

Typeset by Polyprint,
48 Pleasance, Edinburgh EH8 9TJ

Printed and bound in Great Britain by
Dotesios Ltd, Trowbridge, Wiltshire.

CONTENTS

ILLUSTRATIONS

MAPS

INTRODUCTION

Of all the public services in any community transport has generally attracted people's interest more than other services since the individual user is inevitably more closely identified with its operations. It is surely fitting that its history should be recorded, the more especially since the pattern of transport in our lives now changes so rapidly. It is hoped that the story will interest the general reader who knows Scotland's capital and its surroundings, as well as the specialist who is interested in the subject as such and for whom some of the considerable detail is necessarily given.

The transport scene is an ever-changing one and in my lifetime there have been many changes; from when I can just recall riding on a bus of the type depicted on page 192, through cable cars, electric cars, steam trains, to the present-day motor buses and diesel and electric trains. What will the future hold?

Although clearly the motor bus will continue to have a major part to play, the steel wheel on the steel rail has always been preferred by many people as giving a more comfortable ride, and this applied to street tramways too until they were being run down for abandonment on the pretext they were the cause of traffic congestion — and what have we got now without them! So the modern street tramway has returned in Manchester; Sheffield and other cities are to follow while the Blackpool tramway continues to serve effectively. When Edinburgh's former tramway system closed down on 16 November 1956 *The Scotsman* wondered if electric traction might not return again in time. Maybe it now will. Those less than forty years of age will not remember Edinburgh's then crumbling tramway system, far less its earlier splendid years, nor the outcry the abandonment raised.

Transport has always been surrounded by a strong political flavour and lobby. The major obstacle to the provision of effective public transport on roads, by whatever method, is the priority given to the flow of other traffic. No longer does the public vehicle stop for its passengers where most of them want, but at, for example, such widely separated points as the Waverley Bridge in Princes Street and half-way up the North Bridge. If you arrive at Haymarket railway station, see how far you have to walk to get a bus to Princes Street. This cannot encourage the use of public transport; but unless the attitude in many quarters that the general traffic flow is more important than the convenience of users of public transport can be reversed (as on the continent) efforts to induce people to use the public vehicle will largely fail.

It would seem that the most effective way of securing this proclaimed objective will be the reintroduction of the street tramway, for which priority can be more readily organised. The missing factor may be the will to act, bolstered by the objection of the car user who might have to wait a little longer for his traffic light to give him a right of way. Will Edinburgh be bold enough to follow that course?

Another important aspect is, of course, that electric traction avoids the growing pollution of the atmosphere from motor vehicle exhaust fumes, already at a danger level in parts of Edinburgh.

Although much of the content of this book appeared in *Edinburgh's Transport* as published in 1964, this work must be considered as a new book since so much amplification has been added. Three chapters have been entirely rewritten, an earlier period 1830-1870 is included and the story is continued from 1957 up to 1986. As in the 1964 book no excuse is made for the extended treatment given to the tramways and buses, since the literature of railways is prolific. However, the Scottish Motor Traction Company having been the subject of a comprehensive history of its total activities (D. G. L. Hunter, *From S.M.T. to Eastern Scottish*, John Donald Publishers, Edinburgh, 1987) that chapter has therefore been suitably condensed.

The extent of the subject matter is now so large that it has been necessary to divide the book into two volumes and a chronological division at around 1919 seemed appropriate. This volume therefore covers 1830 to 1919 with some adjustments and the second volume covering 1919 to 1986 is to follow.

The material has been gathered from contemporary sources, principally the files of *The Scotsman* and other publications including the *Dalkeith Advertiser, Edinburgh Evening Dispatch, Edinburgh Evening News, Leith Burgh's Pilot, Midlothian Journal, Musselburgh News, Portobello Advertiser, Commercial Motor, Motor Traction,* the predecessors of *Passenger Transport Journal* and *Transport World,* to all of which acknowledgement is due; also the minutes of Edinburgh Town Council, of Leith Town Council, the Edinburgh Transport Department's annual reports and the Edinburgh Magistrates' licensing minutes. These sources have been supplemented by the author's copious notes, many old documents and timetables, and much information gathered from a host of individuals over many years.

These include: from Edinburgh Corporation/Lothian Region Transport, E. O. Catford, John Henderson, Alan Jamieson, W. M. Little, W. L. Russell, Alex Scott, Bob Shaw, and many others among the inspectors, drivers, conductors and staff at Shrubhill works whose names it would be impractical to list. From S.M.T.Co./Scottish Bus Group, James Amos, Robert Beveridge, Gavin Booth, Sandy Bracken, John Clark, Bill Guthrie, Robert Harrison, Roderick Mackenzie. Others whose help is much appreciated are R. M. Hogg of the erstwhile British Transport Commission Historical Records Office at Waterloo Place, C. H. A. Collyns of the South of Scotland Electricity Board, W. H. Makey lately Edinburgh City Archivist, Mrs S. Thomson who preserved a contemporary manuscript list of horse cars, J. K. D. Blair, Alan Brotchie, Willie Cheyne, John Coutts, Tom Findlater, Robert Grieves, Andrew Harper, Jack Williamson. I also thank N. D. G. Mackenzie, General Manager L.R.T., for his encouragement.

I must also thank the staffs of the Central and Leith branches of Edinburgh Public Libraries, the British Newspaper Library at Colindale, the Library of the Institution of Mechanical Engineers, Cambridge University Library, the public libraries at Birmingham and at Penicuik, and the Scottish Records Office at Edinburgh. Thomas Murray & Co. Ltd. kindly lent their record file of Murray's Edinburgh Diaries. The fleet lists of Edinburgh Corporation and of the S.M.T. Company published by the P.S.V. Circle have also been useful and those who require the more fully detailed information on the vehicles may be referred to them. If anyone has been inadvertently omitted I now offer apology.

Mention must also be made of the illustrations, for while acknowledgement is gladly given where the photographer is known, use has been made of a number of other photographs the origin of which could not be traced. For their anonymous use only apology can be offered. The tickets in the Reinhohl collection were kindly made available for reproduction at the Chartered Institute of Transport.

Finally, I am grateful to Mr Johnstone and Mr Costello at Mercat Press for their interest in the work and for undertaking its publication.

D. L. G. Hunter

1

The Early Days, 1830 to 1870

The area which this book will endeavour to cover is difficult to define, for the size of the city itself has greatly increased over the years. While it is intended to concentrate on the city and its immediately surrounding districts it will be necessary, especially in the light of modern facilities, to allude to places a good deal further away. It must be realised that the districts we regard as part of the city today, such as Colinton, Corstorphine, Liberton or Granton, were little villages right out in the country even less than a hundred years ago. To such places many an Edinburgh citizen would go for a summer holiday.

In the early years of the nineteenth century there were no really local public travelling facilities in Edinburgh. Stage coaches ran to distant places, John Croall being the principal operator, and carriers' wagons, though very slow, might take one or two travellers. There were also short-stage coaches running from Edinburgh to Leith, to Portobello, and to Corstorphine. There had been conveyances between Edinburgh and Leith a hundred, perhaps even two hundred, years previously but these appear to have been provided for only short periods before being given up for lack of demand; many years later someone else would try again with the same result. The vehicles used carried only two, or in some cases four passengers, though one of the vehicles used accommodated as many as six passengers. Furthermore they ran very infrequently and even spasmodically, though after the completion of the first North Bridge and the new road which became Leith Walk a frequent service of small stage coaches became established using that route between the High Street, near the Tron Church, and the Shore at Leith, instead of Easter Road as hitherto. Demand for conveyance was now growing, though the vehicles still accommodated only a few passengers. In June 1826 a half-hourly service of light stage coaches was put on a route from the Port Hopetoun terminus of the Union Canal, via Castle Street and Queen Street to Leith, and this proved popular for a time with passengers from the Canal fly-boats.

The omnibus, carrying rather more passengers in a perhaps less comfortable vehicle, developed from these in the 1830s, and omnibuses were soon providing a frequent service to Leith. They also ran to Newhaven and by the 1840s a route to Morningside and a cross-town service between Stockbridge and Newington had also been established: regular public transport in Edinburgh had arrived.

Another important development in the 1830s was travel by railway. A few short lines had been built in the district for the conveyance of coal in wagons hauled by horses, but the first one to concern this story was the Edinburgh & Dalkeith Railway, authorised by an Act of 26 May 1826 and opened on 4 July 1831. On this railway, a double line of 4ft. 6in. gauge, coal was brought from Craighill and vicinity to a depot in Edinburgh at St. Leonard's. The last 1,170 yards up to the depot were through a 572-yard tunnel, on a gradient of 1 in 30, the trains being hauled up by a rope wound by a steam engine. Trains descended the incline by gravity, drawing out the rope with them. Elsewhere on the line horses hauled the wagons. The line was extended three months later to South Esk on the bank of the South Esk river and a branch line added from Niddrie to Fisherrow harbour. A short branch into the town of Dalkeith was added in 1838 and also, in the same year, a longer one from the Niddrie station to Leith, where the tiny station at Tower Street was later to be known as South Leith. All these branches were single line. Most of the traffic was conducted by various carriers.

It soon became evident that the railway offered a convenient means of travel for people journeying to and from places along its route, and a converted stage coach was put on the line by one of its users, Michael Fox, to provide a passenger service on the main line to South Esk from 2 June 1832. The passenger service proved extremely popular and after a few

A relic of the Edinburgh & Dalkeith Railway's Musselburgh branch: the stone blocks on which the rails were laid near its terminus at Fisherrow. (*F. Inglis*)

Scotland Street station, originally the Edinburgh, Leith & Granton Railway. The bricked-up mouth of the tunnel up to the Canal Street station can be seen.

years these operations were taken over by the railway company itself and augmented, with connections over all the branches as well. In 1840 the railway company owned 34 passenger carriages; some were closed-in with three compartments and an outside seat at each end occupied by the driver and also by passengers; others were open carriages. On the main line three carriages usually travelled together every two hours and a single carriage travelled on the branches. They stopped for passengers anywhere as required and fares were collected by the conductor at the Niddrie junction station, tickets not being used. On holidays a much more frequent service was run.

It appears the Fisherrow carriage ran down the branch by gravity. A trace horse was required on the grade up to Niddrie from the Leith branch. Although the speed of passenger conveyance was little different to that of the road coaches it was a more comfortable journey and the fare for the 8¼ miles only 6d., in either type of carriage.

The Edinburgh & Dalkeith was perhaps better known as "The Innocent Railway". Legend has it that this was because no one was ever hurt on it, but this is not true: a number of accidents, some fatal, are recorded in the Board of Trade's annual reports. The origin of the name is found in Robert Chambers' essay (in vol. 1 of *Select Writings of Robert Chambers*, Edinburgh 1847) wherein he says a friend of his "calls it the Innocent Railway as being so peculiar for its indestructive character, and also with some reference to the simplicity of its style of management". Robert Chambers' essay offers a good portrayal of a journey on this railway. It was nevertheless a well-run concern and a considerable success.

The second railway in Edinburgh was the first part of the Edinburgh

Leith & Newhaven Railway, authorised on 13 August 1836 and opened on 31 August 1842 from a station then called Canonmills, at the foot of Scotland Street, to Newhaven near the Chain Pier from where vessels plied to Fife. Horse haulage was used and the intended tunnel up to a station at Canal Street on the site of what was until recently known as the Waverley Market was still five years away. In these circumstances the railway could hardly compete with the horse buses running from Princes Street to Newhaven. Lack of finance caused statutory abandonment of the intended branch to Leith in 1839.

A better pier for passengers and goods at Granton had been opened in June 1838 and this was soon to be the base for the ferries to Fife. Clearly the railway had to be extended to Granton, so another Act was obtained on 19 July 1844 and the company's name changed to the Edinburgh, Leith & Granton Railway. This Act also resuscitated the branch to Leith. Financial difficulties as well as constructional ones continued and when the extension to Granton was opened on 19 February 1846, competition from the horse buses still had to be met. Meantime the regular ferry service to Burntisland had commenced on 5 September 1844. The extension diverged immediately before the old terminus, a new station named Trinity being provided on the new line.

At last the branch to Leith was completed, diverging at Warriston junction and running to the erstwhile North Leith station at the Citadel with an intermediate station at Bonnington. This branch was opened on 10 May 1846. But not until the railway could be extended up through the Scotland Street tunnel to Canal Street station could it provide an effective service, and this was not achieved until 17 May 1847. Concurrently 0–4–0 locomotives were introduced instead of horses to haul the trains between

The Granton branch in later days. The original station near the Chain Pier at Newhaven lay straight ahead, but the branch was soon extended round the curve to Granton with a new station called Trinity which can be seen on the curve.

Scotland Street station and Granton and Leith. The gradient up the tunnel to Canal Street station was about 1 in 30 and beyond the capabilities of the locomotives, so a rope haulage system was installed in the tunnel driven by a steam engine at Canal Street.

The operation of the system warrants some brief description. When a train from Granton or Leith arrived at Scotland Street station the locomotive was removed and a "brake truck" coupled on behind. The train, limited to twelve passenger carriages including the "brake truck", was then attached to the wire rope and hauled up to Canal Street station where the two passenger platforms lay straight ahead just beyond the top end of the tunnel, the goods lines diverging to the right to join the Edinburgh & Glasgow Railway by a sharp curve. Shunting at Canal Street station was done by horses, the tracks being connected by small turntables. Trains were allowed to run down the tunnel under the control of one or more "brake trucks" at the front to limit the speed to 10 mph. A chock block at the top of the down line had to be opened for the passage of a train. At Scotland Street station the "brake trucks" were removed and the locomotive attached for the journey forward to Leith or Granton.

The Edinburgh & Northern Railway, which in fact ran across Fife, bought up the Granton ferries in June 1847 and on 27 July also bought the Edinburgh, Leith & Granton Railway, incorporating the whole system into a new company — the Edinburgh, Perth & Dundee Railway — as from April 1849. The world's first train ferries were introduced on the Granton-Burntisland crossing on 3 February 1850 but only goods wagons were taken across on them. Passengers continued to use the passenger boats as hitherto.

Meantime Scotland's first main line or inter-city railway, the Edinburgh & Glasgow Railway, authorised on 4 July 1838, had been opened on 21 February 1842 with its Edinburgh terminus at Haymarket. The first four stations out from Edinburgh were those at Corstorphine (later known as Saughton), Ratho, Winchburgh and Linlithgow. Gogar was added soon after. However, the passenger fly-boats on the Union Canal continued to compete with the new railway which had to set its third class fares at a low rate. By 1844 the canal passenger traffic had almost disappeared and under an Act of 26 June 1849 the canal was vested in the Edinburgh & Glasgow Railway.

The Union Canal had been opened in May 1822 with its Edinburgh terminus at Port Hopetoun which was where Lothian House now stands. The canal connected with the Forth & Clyde Canal by a flight of locks near Falkirk and carried much passenger traffic in its first twenty years. The canal was shortened to its present terminus near Leamington Terrace about 1921 and is no longer connected to the Forth & Clyde Canal at the Falkirk end.

The Edinburgh & Glasgow company were already anxious to extend their line through Princes Street Gardens to connect up with the Edinburgh, Leith & Newhaven Railway at Canal Street. This idea faced great opposition, but with the proposed North British Railway to Berwick also in view such a link became even more desirable. So the extension through Princes Street Gardens was authorised on 4 July 1844 and duly opened on 1 August 1846.

Meantime the North British Railway, authorised on 19 July 1844, had been opened between its station under the North Bridge, to Dunbar and Berwick on 22 June 1846 with stations at Portobello, Inveresk (originally called Musselburgh), Tranent (renamed Prestonpans in July 1858), Longniddry, Drem and East Linton (originally Linton), before reaching Dunbar. A single line branch from Longniddry to Haddington was opened at the same time. It was doubled in 1847 but singled again in October 1856. A station at Joppa was opened on 14 July 1847 and another at East Fortune by 1849. There was also a station at Ballencrieff but it was closed on 1 November 1847. For a brief period in the early part of 1848 there was also a station at Jock's Lodge. Another branch, authorised on 26 June 1846, was from Drem to North Berwick and opened on 17 June 1850 as a single line with an intermediate station at Dirleton, about a mile from that village.

With the Edinburgh & Glasgow extension connected to the North British the General station was established and the Canal Street station, which of course was at a right angle, connected to it by a sharp curve which could normally accommodate only four-wheeled locomotives and vehicles.

The Caledonian Railway reached Edinburgh from Carstairs and the south on 15 February 1848 with a terminus at Lothian Road, serving stations at Kingsknowe — then called Slateford — Currie, Mid Calder etc. A new station at Slateford was opened in 1871. Subsequently the Caledonian built a branch from Slateford to Granton, opened on 28 August 1861, but this did not have any passenger service at that period.

We now have to return to the Edinburgh & Dalkeith Railway. The North British was authorised on 31 July 1845 to construct a line to Hawick and to acquire the Edinburgh & Dalkeith, part of the route of which would be incorporated in the new branch. The Act provided for the conversion of the Edinburgh & Dalkeith 4ft. 6in. gauge to the 4ft. 8½in. gauge of the other railways and for the use of locomotives, but the Leith branch was excluded from these provisions. The work started in 1846 but the two-hourly passenger service seems to have been kept going until June 1847. Locomotives commenced hauling the passenger trains from St. Leonard's as far as Niddrie on 15 February 1847, the winding engine and rope through the tunnel then being abandoned. The reconstruction included diversion of the Fisherrow branch onto the North British main line instead of crossing over it, and a double line branch was built from New Hailes to Musselburgh. This was opened for passenger trains from the General station on 16 July 1847. The old line into Fisherrow harbour now became a short stub off the Musselburgh branch. A station was provided at New Hailes in 1859. The new Hawick branch started from a junction east of Portobello* to join the old Edinburgh & Dalkeith line south of Niddrie, which it used to its South Esk terminus, and beyond which it was of course new construction. Passenger service to Dalkeith now using locomotives was resumed from both the General station and St. Leonard's on 14 July 1847 but the latter was withdrawn on 1 November 1847, to be reintroduced on 1 June 1860 but withdrawn again finally on 30 September following. The Hawick branch was opened as far as Gorebridge also on 14 July 1847, to Bowland in August 1848 and throughout on 1 November 1849, with stations at Eskbank, Dalhousie (the former South Esk station), Gorebridge, Fushiebridge, Tynehead, Heriot, Fountainhall, Stow, Bowland, Galashiels etc. Dalhousie was replaced by Newtongrange on the other side of the river on 1 August 1908. A station at Millerhill was opened on 20 February 1849.

The North British Railway's Act of 1846 had authorised conversion of the old Edinburgh & Dalkeith Railway's Leith branch to 4ft. 8½in. gauge but the use of locomotives on it was still prohibited on account of its proximity to the public highway. In the following year a junction between the Leith branch and the main line at Portobello was authorised and this was opened in the summer of 1849. The horse-hauled passenger coach service was then changed to run from Leith to a separate small platform at Portobello station instead of to Niddrie, the remainder of the branch up to Niddrie and the junction station there being subsequently abandoned. Eventually the Leith branch from Portobello was improved and doubled and the use of locomotives sanctioned by an Act of 23 July 1858, although they seem to have been used on parts of it from 1856.

The Edinburgh & Bathgate Railway, which became part of the North British, was authorised on 3 August 1846 and opened on 12 November 1849, branching off the Edinburgh & Glasgow Railway at Ratho and serving intermediate stations at Drumshoreland for Broxburn, Uphall and Livingston, all being a considerable distance from their respective villages.

A look at Redpath's Edinburgh District Railway *Time Table* for December 1849 will illustrate the services then available. There was a train from Canal Street station to Leith every fifteen minutes from 8.00 a.m. to 9.00 p.m., several with portions for Granton giving approximately an hourly service with two earlier trains at 6.30 and 7.45 a.m. The 6.30, 9.45, 12.30, 4.15 and 6.15 trains connected with the passenger ferry boats. From the General station trains ran to Dalkeith at 8.45, 10.00, 2.00, 3.45 and 8.15, and to Musselburgh at 9.15, 11.15, 1.00, 3.00, 4.40, 7.00 and 9.15. Trains served stations to Dunbar at 8.00, 11.00, 4.00, and 6.00, all with connections to Haddington which had an additional train at 2.30 p.m., and with connections to North Berwick by the 8.00, 11.00 and 4.00 p.m. Only the 8.00 a.m. and 4.00 p.m. stopped at East Fortune. None of these trains called at Joppa which was served only by some of the Musselburgh trains. The Hawick line had trains at 8.15, 10.45 and 4.30,

* It was here that in 1847 the young pointsman Robert Skeldon rigged up some wire and old weights to operate his two distant signals from his hut; a basic development in signalling practice.

An early view of the east end of the Waverley station, probably in the seventies. Many of the old four-wheel carriages of which most of the trains were then formed can be seen. (*F. C. Inglis*)

Horse bus on the Stockbridge and Newington route, probably one of Croall's in the 1870s.

only the last one calling at Fushiebridge. Trains serving stations to Linlithgow ran at 7.00, 8.30, 1.30, 4.30 and 7.00, with expresses at 11.30, 4.00 and 10.00 p.m., the latter calling also at Ratho. The 8.30 did not call at Corstorphine nor at Winchburgh. There were stopping trains to Bathgate at 9.15 and 4.30. On the Caledonian line there were stopping trains at 7.00, 12.30, 3.30 and 9.15, though only the 7.00 and 3.30 called at Slateford. On Sundays two trains ran on most lines serving the principal stations only, and there were two trains to Granton, but none to Leith, Musselburgh, Dalkeith or North Berwick. There had been considerable opposition to Sunday trains but Post Office insistence on carrying the mails had prevailed. Return services were similar.

Most trains at this time conveyed first, second and third class passengers, the latter in open carriages, many of them not even provided with seats. Despite their deficiencies they were well patronised, for third class fares were cheap, usually even cheaper than the 1d. per mile rate of the seated and closed carriages which, from 1 November 1844, had to be run at least once a day in accordance with the Regulation of Railways Act. These were the so-called Parliamentary trains. Even so, in 1843, to meet canal competition, the Edinburgh & Glasgow had introduced an even lower fourth class fare in open and seatless carriages and these carriages were in due course run forward over the North British line too. On the other hand, while the Edinburgh, Leith & Granton was using horse haulage only a second class carriage was provided at a correspondingly high fare. Before long the open carriages disappeared but fourth class fares still lingered on a few specified trains for several years until all third class fares were at the 1d. per mile rate. In 1849 the first, second and third class fares to Leith were 4d., 3d. and 2d.; to Granton 6d., 4d. and 3d.; to Dalkeith 1/-, 9d. and 6d.; and Musselburgh 10d., 8d. and 6d. To Corstorphine the four classes were respectively 6d., 4d., 3d. and 2d.

The same timetable also included the coach and omnibus times, the latter being as follows: from the Tron Church to the Shore at Leith every five minutes; from the east end of Princes Street to Granton at 6.20 a.m., 9.35 a.m., 12.20 p.m., 4.5 p.m. and 6.5 p.m. to connect with the passenger ferries sailing half an hour later; from the east end of Princes Street to Morningside at 11.00 a.m., 1.00 p.m., 2.30 p.m. and 4.30 p.m.; from Minto Street, Newington to Dean Terrace, Stockbridge every half-hour from 10.00 a.m. to 9.30 p.m. There were coaches from the east end of Princes Street to Portobello every hour from 10.00 a.m. to 9.00 p.m., to Dalkeith at 10.30, 12.00, 1.30, 4.15, 6.00 and 8.00. To Lasswade at 10.00 and 8.00 and to Penicuik at 10.00 and 4.00. The coach fares to Portobello were 6d., 4d. and 3d., and to Dalkeith 9d. and 6d., while the omnibus fare to Leith was 3d. inside and 2d. outside.

Ten years later Murray's timetables show coaches to Corstorphine at 11.00 a.m. and 8.00 p.m.; to Cramond at 1.00 and 6.30 p.m.; to Dalkeith at 10.30 a.m., 1.30, 4.00 and 8.00 p.m.; to Lasswade at 10.00 a.m., 1.00, 4.00 and 8.00 p.m.; to Musselburgh at 11.00 a.m., 2.00, 6.00 and 8.30 p.m.; to Penicuik at 9.30 a.m. and 4.00 p.m.; to Portobello every hour from 11.00 a.m. to 8.00 p.m. and at 8.30 and 9.45 p.m.; to Queensferry at 7.00 a.m., 12.00 and 4.00 p.m.; and to Ratho at 4.15 p.m.

Other branch lines in the area carrying passenger trains, all of them single line and eventually becoming part of the North British system, were the Peebles Railway, from Hardengreen junction with stations at Bonnyrigg, Hawthornden (as far as which the line was double), Rosslynlee, Pomathorn (originally Penicuik), Leadburn, and Eddleston, which was authorised on 8 July 1853 and opened on 4 July 1855; the Dolphinton branch from Leadburn with stations at Lamancha, Macbiehill (originally Coalyburn), and Broomlee which was the station for West Linton, authorised on 3 June 1862 and opened on 4 July 1864; and the Queensferry branch as far as Dalmeny with an intermediate station at Kirkliston opened on 1 March 1866 and extended to South Queensferry with an intermediate station at New Halls, opened on 1 June 1868. Ferries to Fife ran from New Halls pier. The Polton branch from near Eskbank, with intermediate stations at Broomieknowe and at Lasswade, was authorised on 21 July 1863 and opened on 15 April 1867.

The North British absorbed the Edinburgh, Perth & Dundee Railway including the ferries on 1 August 1862 and the Edinburgh & Glasgow Railway on 1 August 1865. An important development which followed was the new line built from Piershill junction to join the old Granton line near Trinity, crossing on the level the old Leith branch of the Edinburgh, Perth & Dundee. A spur was also put in from the new line to join the latter at Bonnington, and another from the Calton tunnel east of the

General station, now called the Waverley station, to join the new line at Easter Road. These new lines were opened on 2 March 1868 and from 22 March the Leith and Granton passenger trains took this new route to and from the Waverley station, the Scotland Street tunnel and Canal Street station then being closed. There was an intermediate station on the new line at Leith Walk, and additional stations were subsequently opened on 1 May 1869 at Abbeyhill and at Junction Road, the latter being only 330 yards from the North Leith terminus. Accommodation at the Waverley station was augmented from about this time, with access to it being from the Waverley Bridge.

In addition to the ferries at Granton and at New Halls pier, Queensferry, mention should be made of the steamer services from Granton to Alloa and Stirling and from Leith to Aberdour and other places in Fife. The former were transferred to Leith also in 1870. Some of the steamer services were more in the nature of excursions, especially after the opening of the Forth Bridge in 1890. Nevertheless regular services increased in scope considerably in the seventies and eighties and provided useful links to Aberdour, Burntisland, Kirkcaldy, etc. at very cheap rates. Several firms were involved, some using tugboats, but well-appointed paddle vessels regularly ran the important trips. M. P. Galloway of Leith, which later, with railway interests, became the Galloway Saloon Steam Packet Company, was probably the best known concern. The opening of the pier at Portobello in 1871 gave the trade a fillip. At Leith the West Pier was the usual starting point though some used the Shore and the Inner Harbour. Sunday sailings were popular and occupied the attentions of the Sabbath Alliance whose protests were made in many quarters. The steamer services have been fully dealt with in Ian Brodie's *Steamers of the Forth* (David & Charles, 1976).

New ideas on transport have often been developed in the Edinburgh area, which was the scene of some of the earliest experiments with steam-driven carriages such as those of Burstall and Hill of Leith. James Nasmyth had successfully demonstrated his on the Queensferry Road for a few months in 1827. There was a revival of interest in the latter in the late sixties. R. W. Thomson, a Stonehaven man who had travelled abroad and then settled in Edinburgh, practising as a civil engineer, had been designing light traction engines which were built for him by Messrs Tennant and Company at their Bowershall works. These machines of six horsepower and weighing under six tons had india-rubber tyres and were being successfully used in 1870 to haul substantial loads to the docks and elsewhere. To comply with the law, a boy had to run ahead bearing a red flag, and Mr Thomson was in trouble for failing to fulfil this requirement on occasion. An omnibus proprietor, Mr A. Ritchie, thought this machine might be an improvement on his horse buses between Edinburgh and Leith, and he had a passenger carrying trailer built by Messrs Drew and Burnet. This rather cumbersome vehicle was carried on a single axle, and seated 21 passengers inside. 44 passengers could be carried on top and were protected — in some measure — by an awning. When the outfit had been tried with success, Mr Ritchie was prevailed upon to run it on the Portobello route instead, and this service started on 2 June 1870, the vehicle rejoicing in the name of "New Favourite".

Another Leith engineer, Andrew Nairn, had also produced a somewhat similar traction engine, a three-wheeler of eight horsepower with hemp tyres, and he was now at work on an omnibus incorporating his engine. This vehicle also ran on three wheels and had a three-cylinder engine and a "Field" type boiler. It weighed seven tons and carried 18 passengers inside and 32 on top. It appears to have been intended to call it the "Edinburgh", though contemporary reports refer to "Pioneer". This machine was, however, either rebuilt or replaced by a ten-ton "Pioneer" in 1871, and was hired by a bus proprietor named Johnston, who, after running some demonstration trips, put it to regular public service on the Portobello route on 2 June of that year, charging 4d. inside and 3d. outside. It ran twelve trips a day for four months, till one day it caught fire. It was thereafter purchased by David Charters who restarted a half-hourly service to Portobello in October 1871.

Another steam bus appeared in April 1872, designed by Leonard J. Todd of Leith. This was a four-wheeled machine seating 20 inside and 50 on top, and in this case an awning was provided. It seems to have been an improvement on "Pioneer" and, bearing the name "Edinburgh", was operated between the West End and Bernard Street, with ½d. "outside" fare stages.

While these steam omnibuses were fairly successful, the roads were still unsatisfactory for such vehicles and they did not survive. The legal necessity for a boy to run in front with a red flag was an impediment too. So the public were still dependent on the horse-bus services provided by a number of proprietors. John Croall was probably the biggest

A steam bus of the early 1870s which ran between Edinburgh and Portobello.

operator, but others were Robert Aitken, A. Ritchie, George Hall, T. Johnston and David Adamson, who joined forces with Mr Atkinson, and Messrs Carse and Co. Regular services were running between the High Street and Leith every twelve minutes; Newington and Haymarket every hour; the West End and Leith every seven minutes; Newington and Stockbridge every half-hour; and a circular route from Princes Street via Newington and Morningside every hour. Croall also ran coaches to Portobello and Musselburgh; to Dalkeith; and to Lasswade. Ratho and Queensferry for Dunfermline in Fife were also served. Competition was keen at this time and led to the introduction of three-horse teams instead of two and to many changes of route and frequencies.

The Edinburgh Provisional Order of 1867 was an important piece of legislation, for it authorised the magistrates to license the owners of public conveyances, their routes, stances, timetables, and vehicles etc., also their drivers and conductors, and to make by-laws accordingly. These provisions were re-enacted by the Edinburgh Municipal & Police Act 1879 and again by the Edinburgh Municipal & Police (Amendment) Act 1891, sections 64 and 65. More details of the matters involved as stipulated in the 1891 Act will be given later, but thus, in 1867, was the foundation laid of effective control of omnibus services in the city by the Corporation, an arrangement which remained in operation until the introduction of the Road Traffic Act 1930 which put these matters on a nationwide basis. Edinburgh had led the way sixty years before.

A new route from the Register House via Market Street, Lauriston Place and Greenhill to Morningside (Asylum gate) every hour was licensed to Croall from February 1869 and another started in March 1869 was run by George Hall from the Mound to Bonnington and Newhaven every hour. Croall started another new route at this time from Haymarket to Lauder Road before obtaining a licence and was prosecuted.

The new by-laws issued on 30 December 1869 specified the colours in which the buses on certain routes were to be painted and required a lamp showing the same colour on the off-side of the front footboard at night. Conductors were required to display on their coats the number of their bus. The routes, operators and numbers were then licensed as follows:

West End-Leith, green, Nos. 1-10, Croall, Carse, Dougal, Ritchie.
High Street-Leith, green, Nos. 11, 13, 14, 15, 35, 36, Croall, Carse.
High Street-Leith, green, Nos. 26, 30, 34, Adamson.
Newington-Leith, green, No. 12, Croall.
Newington-Stockbridge, blue, Nos. 16, 21, 24, Croall, Atkinson.
Newington-Stockbridge, blue, No. 22, Adamson.
Princes Street-Morningside, red, Nos. 17, 18, 25, Croall, Atkinson.
Princes Street-Morningside, red, No. 33, Adamson.
Haymarket-Grange, orange, Nos. 20, 32, Croall, Atkinson.
Mound-Newhaven, green?, No. 23, Atkinson.
High Street-Newhaven, green?, No. 27, Croall.

Soon afterwards Atkinson's No. 19 was added for Haymarket-Newington, Croall's No. 29 for Mound-Newhaven, Croall's No. 31 for High

Street-Leith, and Adamson's No. 28 for a route from Haymarket to Hamilton Place, but in May 1870 the various proprietors agreed to a measure of regulation among themselves. Two buses were taken off the Morningside circular route and one each from the Newington-Leith, Newington-Haymarket and Newington-Stockbridge routes. There were no more cut fares; 3d. inside and 2d. outside were standardised.

From 16 May 1870 therefore the services provided were as follows: West End to Leith every six minutes run by Croall, Carse, Adamson and Ritchie with buses Nos. 1 to 9 and 26. High Street to Leith each hour and at 12, 30, 42, and 54 minutes past each hour, run by Croall and Carse with buses Nos. 11, 13, 14, 15 and 31. Princes Street, Grange, Morningside circle every hour, run by Croall with No. 17 clockwise and No. 18 anti-clockwise. Register to Morningside Asylum every hour run by Atkinson's No. 19. Stockbridge to Newington, run by Croall, Atkinson and Adamson, with buses Nos. 16, 22 and 24. Mound to Newhaven, every hour by Croall and Atkinson, with Nos. 29 and 23. High Street to Newhaven, every hour, by Croall's No. 27. Haymarket to Lauder Road, every half hour, by Croall and Atkinson, with Nos. 20 and 32. Haymarket and Duncan Street, every hour, by Adamson's No. 33. In several cases operators exchanged routes with one another on alternate weeks. Ritchie sought to run his steam bus from Waverley to Strathearn Road in December 1870 but this was refused. It is of interest to note that the services did not start till about 9.00 or 10.00 a.m.; the workman could not afford bus fares and generally lived near his work if he could.

However, an important new development was afoot. In the 1860s there had been some experiments in other parts of the country with street tramways, and in 1870 "An Act to facilitate the construction and to regulate the working of Tramways" was passed. This Act was a landmark in transport history, and empowered local authorities, or, with the latter's consent, other persons or companies, to obtain Provisional Orders from the Board of Trade authorising the construction of tramways. Various rules and regulations were laid down concerning the construction and other matters, and the Orders had to be confirmed by Act of Parliament. An important point was that a local authority, having constructed or acquired a tramway, were not to operate it, but could with the consent of the Board of Trade lease to any person the right of using it.

It was thought that Edinburgh should not lag in this new system of course, and so the press, while appreciating the improvements the horse-bus proprietors had made, and also the steam buses already mentioned, urged the formation of a company to provide a tramway system.

So let us now proceed to the development of passenger travel in and around the city after 1870, in its various forms.

2

The Horse Cars and Buses

Two groups of promoters put up tramway bills in 1870. The first, styled the Edinburgh and Leith Tramways, was handled by H. & A. Inglis, W.S., and sought powers of incorporation and to lay down and work the following tramways: 1. From Donaldson's Hospital west gate to the east end of Waterloo Place; 2. Post Office to Powburn, Newington; 3. West End to Jordanburn, Morningside; 4. Post Office to Foot of Leith Walk; 5. Foot of Leith Walk to Bernard Street; 6. Foot of Leith Walk via North Junction Street to the Chain Pier at Newhaven; 7. St. Andrew Street to Picardy Place; 8. Hanover Street, Heriot Row, Howe Street to Stockbridge and Comely Bank; 9. Church Lane, Newbattle Terrace, Whitehouse Terrace and Grange Loan to Salisbury Place. Triangular junctions were proposed at the Post Office, St. Andrew Street and Hanover Street. All the routes were to be double line except the portion through Newhaven from the Whale Brae to the Chain Pier.

The other concern, the Edinburgh Street Tramways, was in the hands of Lindsay and Paterson, W.S., and Thomas Bouch, the engineer of the first Tay Bridge, was connected with it. This scheme seemed to find more favour and the Edinburgh and Leith Tramways promoters, in the interests of an agreed scheme, arranged to drop their bill. Edinburgh and Leith town councils both supported the scheme, but when the former learned that the North British Railway were not opposing the bill because they believed they would be able to use the system for goods traffic, they quickly insisted on a protective clause. The Sabbath Alliance likewise secured some protection regarding Sunday traffic. Agreement being thus reached the bill was passed unopposed.

The Edinburgh Street Tramways Company was thus incorporated on 29 June 1871 by the Edinburgh Tramways Act 1871, which authorised the company to construct the following tramways "to be worked by animal power only" in Edinburgh, Leith, and Portobello.

1. Haymarket to Portobello (Bellfield Lane).
2. Register House to Bernard Street, Leith.
3. St. Andrew Street to Picardy Place.
4. Frederick Street to Stockbridge (Kerr Street).
5. From Royal Circus via Great King Street, Pitt Street, Goldenacre, Trinity Road, Trinity Crescent, Stanley Road, Newhaven Road, Ferry Road, and Junction Street to Foot of Leith Walk. Also a loop

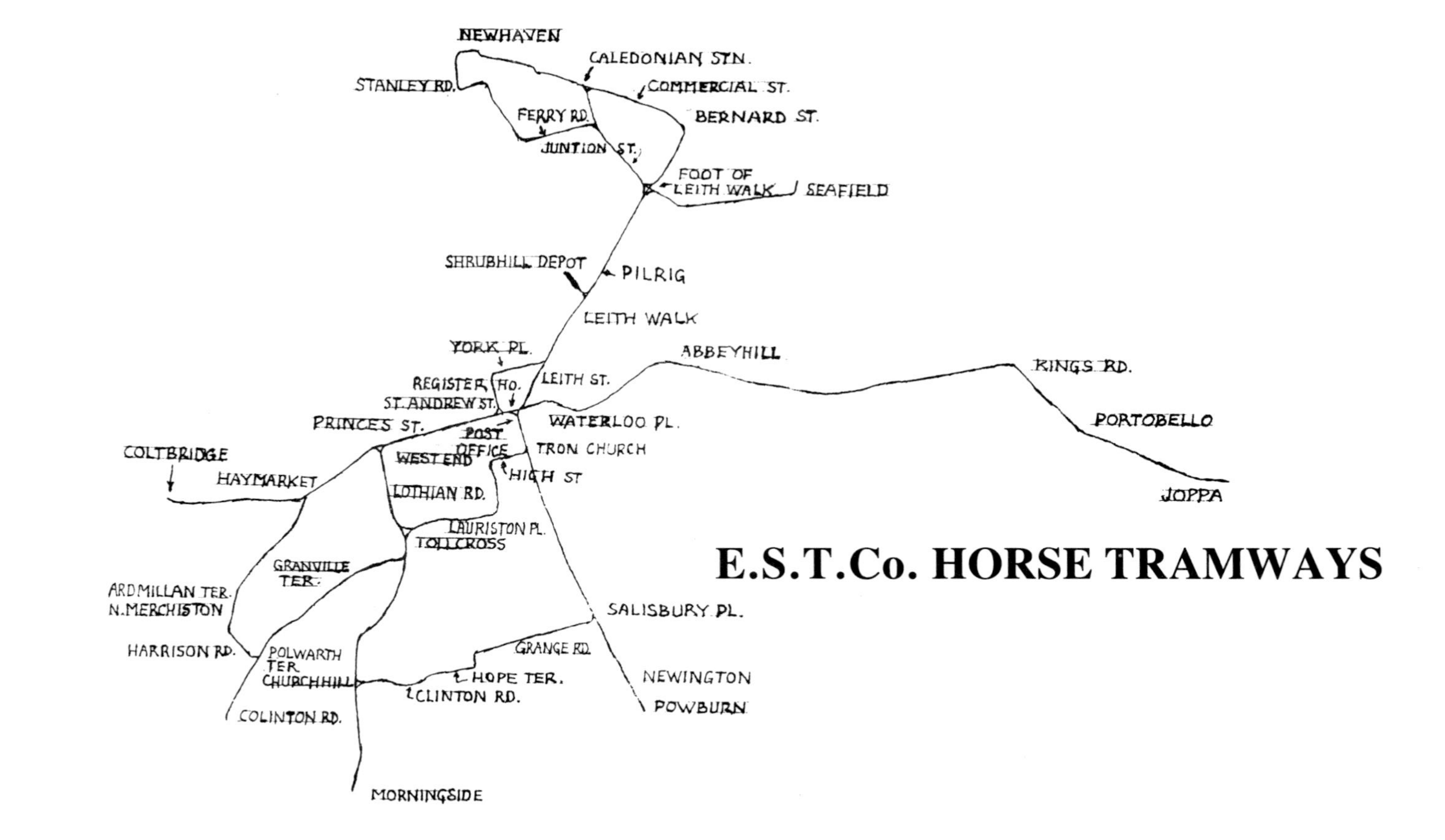
E.S.T.Co. HORSE TRAMWAYS
NEWHAVEN
CALEDONIAN STN.
COMMERCIAL ST.
STANLEY RD.
FERRY RD.
BERNARD ST.
JUNTION ST.
FOOT OF
LEITH WALK
SEAFIELD
SHRUBHILL DEPOT
PILRIG
LEITH WALK
YORK PL.
ABBEYHILL
KINGS RD.
REGISTER HO.
LEITH ST.
ST. ANDREW ST.
PRINCES ST.
WATERLOO PL.
PORTOBELLO
POST
OFFICE
TRON CHURCH
COLTBRIDGE
WEST END
HIGH ST
HAYMARKET
LOTHIAN RD.
JOPPA
LAURISTON PL.
TOLLCROSS
GRANVILLE
TER.
ARDMILLAN TER.
N.MERCHISTON
SALISBURY PL.
HARRISON RD.
GRANGE RD.
POLWARTH
TER.
CHURCHHILL
HOPE TER.
NEWINGTON
CLINTON RD.
COLINTON RD.
POWBURN
MORNINGSIDE

along East Trinity Road to Stanley Road with triangular junctions at each end.
6. Post Office to Powburn, Newington.
7. West End to Churchhill.
8. From Churchhill via Colinton Road, Hope Terrace, Kilgraston Road, and Grange Road to Salisbury Place.
9. From Earl Grey Street, Tollcross via Lauriston Place and Chambers Street (then being made) to South Bridge.
10. Haymarket to Coltbridge (railway bridge).

There were to be triangular junctions also at the Post Office, St. Andrew Street and Frederick Street. The section from the Foot of Leith Walk to Charlotte Street, Leith, was single line with one passing loop, otherwise double lines were proposed, but crossovers were to be provided in the narrow streets.

The capital of the company was £300,000 and the works were to be completed within three years. Other clauses laid down the gauge to be 4ft. 8½in. Fares were not to exceed 1d. per mile, though 3d. could be the minimum fare until three years after the opening when the Board of Trade could reduce this to 2d. Two workmen's cars were to be run on each route with ½d. per mile fares and 1d. minimum; and there were to be no Sunday services without the local authorities' consent. Attached to the Act were schedules of agreement with the local authorities which gave them power to regulate the traffic in the same manner as they did the omnibus traffic. Under one of these arrangements Edinburgh Corporation undertook to widen the North Bridge within two years and the company were to pay £2,500 towards the cost of this work. The Haymarket to Leith, Newington, and Morningside sections were to be constructed immediately and the remainder as soon as possible. The chairman of the company was Dr Alex Wood and D. W. Paterson the secretary. Some compensation was paid to some of the omnibus proprietors.

The company's engineer was John Macrae, and the construction of the lines was let to a contractor named James Gowans (later Sir) who proceeded rapidly with wrought iron rails weighing 52 lbs per yard laid on longitudinal timbers which in turn rested on a concrete bed and were tied to gauge by wrought iron tie-bars.

On Monday 6 November 1871 the first section, from Bernard Street to Haymarket, was opened to traffic without ceremony. Throughout most of the day a six-minute service was provided between Leith and the West End with alternate cars proceeding on to Haymarket. Although the loop via York Place and St. Andrew Street was also completed this was not used at that time, the cars proceeding by Leith Street and the Post Office with the aid of an extra pair of trace horses up the hill. Ten cars were operated, the horses being provided under contract by John Croall. The horses were adorned with bells on their necks and the drivers had a whistle with which to warn other traffic. The fare from the Register House to either terminus was 2d. inside and 1d. outside. The whole journey cost 3d. inside and 2d. outside.

The cars were kept in a shed entered off Shrubhill Lane by a single line with both facing and trailing connections to the down line in Leith Walk.

The service quickly proved very popular and by the end of the year most of the omnibuses on the route had succumbed: only three were left. Croall had withdrawn theirs from the route immediately. The branch from the Foot of Leith walk to Junction Bridge was now laid, and cars commenced to use it on 3 February 1872. There was no intimation of this and the public were now beginning to have doubts about the management. It appears that the service was looked after by an Inspector and that the "management" was in the hands of D. W. Paterson, the secretary. The cars were heavy and therefore slow, and the service unreliable. The press, especially in Leith, voiced the complaint of the lack of experienced men to direct the company's operations. The level of the rails was causing difficulty in some places and the St. Andrew Street-York Place curve had to be relaid. Even the oil used in the lamps had a bad smell!

In April 1872 the company advertised the service as follows: between Bernard Street and Haymarket via Leith Street every 16 minutes; between Junction Bridge and Haymarket via Leith Street every 16 minutes; from Bernard Street to St. Andrew Street via York Place and returning via Leith Street every 8 minutes.

But from 1 May this was altered to a five minutes service between Leith and Haymarket via Leith Street, most of the cars running to Bernard Street. The York Place line thus dropped out of use again.

Gowans the contractor had started on the Newington line at the end of January 1872 and this was nearly finished by the spring, when objection was raised that the North Bridge — still unwidened — was too narrow for a double line, and interdict was threatened. This was overcome, however, and the line was completed and advertised to be opened on Saturday 25 May 1872. (This had to be cancelled and the new service actually started on 29 May.) Four cars provided a ten minutes service from the Post Office to Duncan Street, it being announced that they would continue on to the foot of Minto Street and back to the Duncan Street stance if time permitted, which proved to be the case. The fare was 2d. inside and 1d. outside. 3d. inside transfer tickets could also be bought.

Another complaint arose over the narrowness of the top of Leith Street, and from 10 June the street was closed and the cars diverted to the York Place loop for a fortnight or so while adjustments were made. Similar complaints were made in respect of the Grange route, then under construction. This route was opened as far as the top of Marchmont Road on 6 July, alternate cars being diverted from the Newington line thus giving a twenty minutes service. At the same time the Newington cars made Mayfield Loan their terminus and returned to Salisbury Place "wrong line".

The Board of Trade also raised complaint regarding the level of the rails, and improvements were applied in the construction of the Morningside section, including clasp plates instead of bolts and nuts to secure the rails to the sleepers. Later, Gowans introduced a new rail, 21ft. long with a wide bottom resting on soleplates direct on the concrete bed, the wooden sleepers being eliminated.

With the opening of the new line from the West End by Churchhill to the Grange Road on 11 November, the company revised their services, announcing that sixteen "light and commodious cars" had been added to their stock. A ten minutes service was now provided over three routes: Bernard Street and Haymarket, Leith and Powburn and the Princes Street-Churchhill-Grange-Bridges circle. The cars carried coloured destination boards, and coloured lights at night, respectively red; green and red; and green. Some cars ran to Junction Bridge instead of to Bernard Street. New 2d. inside and 1d. outside fares were given between Post Office and Grange; Salisbury Place and Churchhill; Churchhill and West End; Tollcross and Post Office; while 3d. inside and 2d. outside applied between Post Office and Churchhill. A ride right round the circular route cost 6d. inside and 4d. outside.

While the superior comfort of the cars was generally admitted the service that the system offered was a growing diappointment. There were other complaints. The car wheels were unguarded and thought to be dangerous; they ran too close to the pavement in some places; the horses were overworked, and so on. There were a number of accidents, some fatal, and many court cases on charges of furious driving, of obstruction both by and to the cars, of overcrowding, touting, bad timekeeping and other misdemeanours. Furious riding of trace horses also came before the court, and the omnibus crews did not escape either. Town councillors and baillies who were alleged to be tramway shareholders were accused of putting their own interests first. The rails in Princes Street were laid well to the north side and many wanted them relaid nearer the other side so that carriages had room to reach the shops. The parking and waiting problem was with us then! Mechanical power, such as steam engines, was suggested in place of the poor horses. The city authorities urged the company to put the earlier tracks in order in compliance with the Board of Trade complaint.

Thus encouraged, the omnibus proprietors had drifted back and proclaimed a 1d. fare inside or out between Register House and Newington, and a "fast bus" every ten minutes from Hope Park to Leith cutting the car's journey time by ten minutes. The Edinburgh and Leith General Omnibus Co. (Ltd.) was formed on 23 October 1872 to take over Adamson's business (five buses and sixty horses) and buy new buses, and to run extended services beyond the city. The Hope Park terminus was extended to Duncan Street. The Edinburgh and Leith General Omnibus Co. had Nos. 22, 26, 28, 30 and 34 on the route, and Atkinson had a share with Nos. 20, 23 and 24. Croall's Stockbridge bus now ran from Waterloo Place every fifteen minutes, but Atkinson still ran half-hourly from Duncan Street now using his No. 19. From 21 April 1873 the Edinburgh and Leith General Omnibus Co. put on new Nos. 1 and 2 giving a half-hour service from West End to Leith, but in August concentrated their seven new buses on the Newington to Leith route. The crews were resplendent in scarlet coats and caps. So for a while, up till the summer of 1873, the buses enjoyed something of a comeback, but in the end they had to give up.

Late in November 1872 the company gave notice of their intention to promote a Parliamentary Bill the next year. The main provisions of this Bill were: an extension of time, limited to one year, for the construction of the Portobello route, the Stockbridge route, the route through Trinity and Newhaven to Leith except for the part in Ferry Road between Junction Bridge and Newhaven Road and the route from Tollcross to Chambers Street; power to make additional crossings, sidings, and connections; authority to use other than animal power provided the local authority agreed; and authority to buy and run omnibuses. Many regarded the extension of time as an attempt to abandon the construction of the aforementioned routes, and indeed the junction which had been laid in the Princes Street tracks for the future Stockbridge route was taken out at this time. While this found favour in some quarters, particularly in Leith and Trinity, the Edinburgh Town Council eventually decided to oppose the Bill, although the company offered to withdraw the provision for "other than animal power". The provision for additional sidings and connections worried many citizens for it was recalled that railway companies wanted to use the tramway tracks to gain access to various parts of the town, and the sight of a railway wagon being pulled along Princes Street — even by a horse — was unthinkable. It should be remembered that at that time many of the railway facilities to Leith had not been constructed, and the Caledonian Company was at a disadvantage in the keen competitive conditions of the times. A Committee of Owners and Occupiers of Property on the Tramway Lines in the City of Edinburgh was appointed at a public meeting and took steps to oppose the Bill. Charles Jenner was chairman.

Nevertheless the Edinburgh Street Tramways Act 1873 was passed on 5 August, though the provision for additional sidings and connections had been struck out, as also were the clause to use other than animal power, and authority to buy and run omnibuses. Parliament added three new clauses. The routes were to be laid with a single track if the local authority or road authority so decided. The latter also had power to approach the Board of Trade if they found a line to be dangerous, and the Board of Trade could, after enquiry, call for alterations, to a single track if necessary, though the local authority or road authority were to meet the cost of such alterations. A penalty of £50 per day up to a total of 5 per cent on the total estimated cost of their schemes, viz. £156,220, was to be imposed in the event of non-completion of the works unless arising from accident etc. Both the company and the opposition expressed themselves to be satisfied! The threat of goods traffic was removed. This was common enough elsewhere in the country but the nearest approach to it in Edinburgh was the temporary sand car in 1937.

Meanwhile, construction inwards to Haymarket of the Coltbridge extension was commenced in February 1873 and opened on 29 May, the route being covered by a sparse service between Coltbridge and Powburn. It was proposed to start work on the Ferry Road and Newhaven route in April but this appears to have been deferred on account of the opposition to a double line. Leith Town Council tried to persuade the company to arrange a bus service instead, but in October the company agreed — in accordance with their new Act — to lay this route as a single line with passing loops.

On 23 April 1873 a trial was made with a spring wire guard before and between the wheels of cars No. 23 and 24, but this was not very successful. On the other hand, an increase in the diameter of the cars' wheels from 2ft. 6in. to 3ft. 6in. proved beneficial, as might be expected. A few months later, Henry Shiels, the company's Carriage Superintendent, evolved a more successful life guard, although apparently of similar pattern.

Accidents continued to occur however, and it appears there was difficulty in winding on the brakes in emergency. A sprag could be dropped to prevent a run-back, and a similar arrangement fitted with a pneumatic cushion was proposed as an emergency brake. The effectiveness of the brakes as such was also in question, as there was sometimes difficulty in controlling a car, for example on Leith Street. There was a particularly nasty occurrence on 24 September 1873, when one of the last cars at night overcame brakes and horses descending the hill. The horses tried to get clear and fell near the Theatre Royal. The harness gave way and left them aside, the car, No. 20, careering on down Leith Walk unchecked until it crashed into the back of a preceding car at Shrub Hill, resulting in a number of injuries.

The overworked horses still aroused indignation, and the company, too, was not very happy about the position and their contract with Croall's who kept increasing their charges. According to D. K. Clark (*Tramways: Their Construction and Working*, Second Edition, 1894) the type of animal used was not suited to the arduous duty. So the following year, 1874, the company terminated Croall's contract and acquired the horses at a valuation of only £28 each, from 16 May providing the horses themselves. The car shed at Shrub Hill had been extended and stables etc. provided for the horses. During the following two years the stud was replaced by sturdier beasts, and a rota was arranged whereby they worked a few months on the heavier sections and then had a spell on the easier parts of the system where they recovered their strength. This was an improvement, but even so the system was probably the most difficult in the country to work. In 1876 the horses could average only 5.8 miles per day and the average cost was 7¾d. per mile. But the powers that be had rejected "other than animal power".

In July 1873 alterations to the tracks at the foot of Constitution Street were carried out and the cars turned short at Charlotte Street for a few days. In October a proposal to provide loop sidings for waiting cars at the

Waverley Market and at Haymarket was rejected. Then on 8 November a new timetable and fare schedule was introduced. Details are lacking but the *Scotsman* indicated the fare changes were "towards an increase". Both Edinburgh and Leith Town Councils protested and the company agreed from 12 November to reintroduce the 2d. inside and 1d. outside fare between Waterloo Place and Bernard Street or Junction Bridge. From the Foot of Leith Walk to either of the termini was 1d. outside or in. Discount tickets were withdrawn. Then on 25 December 1873 the Register House to Bernard Street or Junction Bridge became 2d. both outside and in, but two cars either way at 5.10 p.m. and 6.10 p.m. were announced to carry workmen outside for 1d.

Work was now proceeding on the Ferry Road and Newhaven line and this was opened on 17 January 1874, cars running from the new terminus at the west end of Stanley Road every half hour to St. Andrew Street via York Place and returning via Leith Street. After turning into Ferry Road the extension was single line with three passing loops in Ferry Road and another three in Newhaven Road. A short siding curved southwards into Craighall Road at the terminus. There was a facing crossover east of Junction Bridge. A new timetable commencing 17 January 1874 shows four cars on this service, four on the Bernard Street-Newington line, eight on Bernard Street-Haymarket, three on Coltbridge-Powburn, and six each way round the Morningside circle. In the summer of 1874 two cars were run between Coltbridge and Newhaven via York Place. The Stanley Road cars were extended to the West End in the summer of 1875.

Early in 1874, after considerable discussion, and resulting from some influential pressure as to its desirability in the interests of the animals, the Corporation concluded that it had power to license drivers and trace boys, and this measure of control was put into effect. The staff were provided with new dark blue uniforms in May 1874. Drivers' coat collars were green and the conductors' red. Their cap bands corresponded to the colours of the route on which they served. These colours, as already mentioned, were displayed on the cars, but two more have now to be added, viz. Post Office to Newhaven green and Coltbridge to Powburn buff. However, by 1876 the colour scheme seems to have fallen into disrepute. Some trace boys from Harris were accommodated in a dormitory at Shrub Hill from July 1875, but by the end of the year they had been sent home.

The widening of the North Bridge under the agreement between the Corporation and the company scheduled to the 1871 Act had also been started on 11 November 1873, but the stipulated two-year period for its completion had, of course, already expired. A further Act was therefore called for, and in this the company obtained important changes in its commitments.

Passed on 30 June 1874, the Edinburgh Tramways Act, 1874, provided a three years' extension of time for the widening of the North Bridge by the Corporation. On completion of the work the company were to lift their tracks and lay a single line in the middle of the roadway. They were also empowered to construct the Portobello route as a single line. It also allowed the company to abandon the construction of the routes from Frederick Street to Stockbridge and through Trinity to Stanley Road, and also the Tollcross to South Bridge route. The company, however, were required to pay the Edinburgh Road Trust within twelve months sums totalling £3,000, to be applied to causewaying the sides of streets in which tracks were laid. They were further bound, when required by the local authority, to arrange for a "good and sufficient conveyance by means of omnibuses" between Princes Street and Stockbridge and between the Royal Institution (at the Mound) in Princes Street and such point in Trinity as the local authority of Leith might fix. A minimum of fifteen minutes service was stipulated for the former and on the latter a twenty minutes service between 9.00 a.m. and 9.00 p.m. from June to September and a half-hourly service between 9.00 a.m. and 8.00 p.m. for the rest of the year. The company was accordingly empowered to buy horses and buses for this purpose. A fare not exceeding 2d. per mile for first class passengers was authorised on these routes, and on "any tramway routes worked in connexion therewith", but the through bus and car fare between Stockbridge and Newington was not to exceed 3d. first class and 2d. second class. The words "any tramway routes worked in connexion therewith" were soon to give rise to great trouble.

Horse-hauled tramcars were clearly impracticable on these steep northside routes, and the buses plying between Stockbridge and the Register House and the Mound and Trinity continued to run. The Trinity terminus was at Stanley Road. Croall's Nos. 1 and 2 ran to Stockbridge and Nos. 3 and 4 to Trinity.

Construction of the Portobello route was commenced at Bellfield Lane terminus in October 1874, and in accordance with the provisions of the 1874 Act, was made a single line with passing loops.

A small car shed and stables were built at Rosefield Place, not far from the Portobello terminus. The service from Waterloo Place was opened on 14 May 1875, but did not immediately crush the omnibuses running on this route. This now completed the company's system as then authorised, and amounted to 13⅜miles.

In 1874 the company again enjoyed a monopoly on Leith Walk, and at this period adopted a most uncompromising attitude towards the public. The most serious complaint arose over their action in charging inside passengers 3d. from Bernard Street to the Post Office. In November 1874 Leith Town Council decided to test the matter in court as the distance was less than two miles. On instructions therefore, Leith's Town Officer, Alex Torbain, made the journey and sued the company for the penny overcharge. The case was heard in the Sheriff Court on 4 December when the company argued that by section 4 of their 1874 Act they were empowered to charge up to 2d. per mile for first class passengers, i.e. inside, on their Stockbridge and Trinity buses "and on any tramway routes worked in connexion therewith"; and claimed that their whole tramway system was "in connexion therewith"! The sheriff gave his decision in favour of the pursuer and the company appealed to the Court of Session. This would take some time, so a notice was displayed in the cars stating that until the final decision was given the fare was 3d. inside. Many passengers refused to pay and several had their names and addresses taken. It seems conductors accepted two pennies but if change was required retained 3d. The Leith folk complained the fare was now the same as it had been on the buses: where was the promised advantage? On the other hand passengers who sought to pay only one penny for short journeys — under one mile — were successfully sued by the company for their 2d. minimum fare.

In November 1875 Lord Shand also decided against the company in the Court of Session, whereupon the company appealed to the House of Lords. There was of course a further long delay and meanwhile the company continued to be awkward with passengers. When some residents in Ferry Road asked the correct fare to Forth Street Mr Paterson referred them to the timetables displayed on the cars. On pointing out that the information was not there given, Mr Paterson wrote to say he had no more information to offer! The workmen's cars had apparently been dropped after only a few weeks' operation and now both Edinburgh and Leith Town Councils had to prod the company into running them again. They had already had to insist on the company meeting its obligations regarding the frequency of the Trinity bus service.

The inconvenience of the single line scheme for the North Bridge had now become apparent, and an amending Act — the Edinburgh Tramways Act, 1875 — was passed on 19 July 1875, which permitted the double line to remain except between the Tron Church and the south end of the actual bridge. The North Bridge was closed for the track relaying from 23 September to 19 October 1875, during which period the services were cut between the Post Office and the Tron Church. Heavy snow in December of that year disrupted services severely and this happened in some subsequent winters too. A temporary siding was laid at Tollcross in June 1876 to cater for traffic from the exhibition in the Meadows.

In 1876 the company promoted a Bill to extend their Portobello route to Musselburgh terminating at Pinkie Dykes, and to enable them to work the route with mechanical or other than animal power. There had already been another proposal for a roadside steam tramway from Portobello, through Musselburgh, Tranent and Haddington to East Linton. The House of Lords had not heard the company's fares case yet, but as the tide seemed to be against them the company sought to make sure of their increased fare by including a clause in this new Bill authorising a 3d. fare between Edinburgh and Leith.

The Musselburgh people supported the Bill wholeheartedly and Portobello Town Council's support was also secured in return for certain financial agreements. Edinburgh and Leith, on the other hand, strongly opposed it on account of the fares clause. When the Bill came before the Parliamentary Committee it was found that it did not comply with Standing Orders in respect of the extension. The company endeavoured to have the other parts in the Bill considered, but with Edinburgh and Leith opposition, the committee decided otherwise and the Bill had to be dropped.

The fares appeal was at last heard by the House of Lords on 2 and 3 July 1877. It was dismissed with costs, Lord Chancellor Cairns expressing himself as "unfavourably impressed" and referring to the company's arguments as "audacious" and "unfounded". So, the matter was settled, and the company apparently realised it would be better to adopt a more public-spirited policy.

Trials with a kind of portable cash register were made on various routes in April 1878. This locally devised apparatus was in the form of a box carried by the conductor. The passenger inserted his pennies which were then recorded on a dial, at the same time sounding a bell. A turnstile arrangement for recording passengers had been tried on a Morningside car in November 1877 but this was deemed a nuisance. Eventually, from 2 February 1880, rolls of tickets showing the fare value and the car number were issued. A parcel delivery service was introduced in April 1878.

Widening of Princes Street had commenced in 1877 and in September 1878 a new track was laid for west-going cars; the old west-going track was then relaid and used for east-going cars and the old east-going track lifted so that the tracks were now laid more centrally. The new rails were brought into use at the end of November except in front of the Royal Institution where a slight deviation towards the north side was eventually agreed and completed in April 1879.

At the same time two additional passing loops were provided on the Portobello route at the Royal High School and at Craigentinny Farm.

By this time the earlier tracks were calling for reconstruction, and considerable expenditure was incurred by this work in which 106lbs per yard rails were used in most cases.

Although the company had as yet no general authority to operate buses, they put on a bus between the Coltbridge car terminus and Corstorphine on 1 April 1878. On 11 September 1878 the Loanhead and Lasswade route and stables at Loanhead of Mr Johnston, which latterly had run from the car terminus at Powburn via Greenend and Liberton, was taken over and was then again run through to and from the Waverley Steps. In December 1878 the company started another bus service between Tynecastle Toll and the Tron Church running via Dalry Road, Morrison Street, Tollcross, Lauriston Place, George IV Bridge and High Street. The fare was 2d. inside and 1d. outside, but these were increased in March 1880 on the grounds that the service did not pay. This service was withdrawn early in 1882 as many horses were at that time afflicted by influenza and a disease known as "pink eye", necessitating some reduction in car services for a month or so. As the tram rails were then laid on most of this bus route it was not restored.

A law case arising from an accident between Liberton and Greenend on 13 September 1879, in which two passengers were killed and ten injured when a bus overturned after its forewheels struck the kerb when descending the gradient, tells us something of the vehicles used on these bus services. At first a "brake" was used on this Loanhead route, as the buses used in the town were considered unsuitable for country roads. It would seem, however, that a bus originally built by a John Brabner in 1869 for Mr Adamson and seating 14 inside and 18 outside, with the licence No. 7, was involved in this accident. A rather smaller bus No. 4, originally built by the Edinburgh & Leith Omnibus Co., is also mentioned, and it seems that "new" horses were used in the middle of a three-horse turnout. In August 1880 there was another alarming accident involving the Trinity bus at Queen Street. Large horse-drawn vehicles were provided with a "shoe" attached by a chain: before descending a steep grade, the shoe was placed on the roadway before a wheel so that the wheel was carried down the hill with the shoe sliding on the road surface, thereby ensuring a considerable braking effect. On this occasion, however, the shoe became displaced and the driver could not hold back his bus going down North Hanover Street. He attempted to turn it into Queen Street but the bus overturned and the horses fell into the gardens. One person was killed.

In the early hours of Sunday 23 February 1879 there was a big fire at the Shrub Hill stables and provender stores. The 150 horses were got out through the narrow entrance before the flames reached the stables, and although most of them just waited around in Leith Walk some went off on their own and were rounded up later in the day from such distances as Seafield and Granton. The cars were further from the seat of the fire but a few were charred and the total damage was estimated at over £2,000. The car service was operated as usual on Monday.

Reconstruction of the premises in 1879-1880 included an extension as far back as the line of the as yet unmade part of Dryden Street, so enabling the company to rationalise their horsing arrangements and to dispose of various other small stables in Leith Walk and elsewhere in the town that they had been using to accommodate their growing number of horses. Premises on the south side of Shrub Hill lane were also demolished to allow a new single line entrance direct from Leith Walk to be provided instead of the inconvenient narrow access from Shrub Hill lane. New offices were also built against the north wall inside the new entrance and these remained in use until the whole depot area was demolished in 1962.

All this led to running costs being reduced by over 3d. per car mile and in September 1879 the company introduced a new fare scale which included several penny "outside" fares and other reductions.

In 1880 the company put forward a big scheme of expansion, including the doubling of the Portobello route which was doing well in the summer. A lengthy Bill was promoted which on 11 August 1881 became the Edinburgh Street Tramways Act, 1881. The following new routes were authorised, and all were duly constructed: 1. From Haymarket to Ardmillan Terrace, double line to near Caledonian Road, thereafter single line with a passing loop at the railway bridge. 2. A single line continuation from Ardmillan Terrace by a new private road — what is

Horse cars and buses at the Post Office. The bus turning round in Waterloo Place is running from the Post Office to Stockbridge. Note the horses trying to take car 36 into the North Bridge and the man pulling the car to the right track. "Points" were open, i.e. without blades. (*F. C. Inglis*)

now Harrison Road — into Polwarth Terrace with a passing loop at the railway bridge. 2. A single line from the end of Polwarth Terrace at Colinton Road joining the latter line in Polwarth Terrace. 4. A single line continuation of this inwards to join the Morningside line in Home Street with passing loops on the town side of the trailing junction with the line from Ardmillan, near Merchiston Avenue, and at Upper Gilmore Place. 5. From Home Street via Lauriston Place, George IV Bridge and High Street to join the Newington line in North Bridge. Between Portland Place and the curve into Forrest Road this was single line with passing loops at Lauriston Street and at Graham Street. The rest was double. 6. A double line connection into the Lauriston Place route from Earl Grey Street. 7. A double line connection between Shandwick Place and Lothian Road, thus forming a triangular junction at the West End. 8. A double line branch from Junction Bridge to the foot of North Junction Street. 9. A branch from the foot of Leith Walk to Restalrig Road. This was single line with passing loops at Easter Road and at Lindsay Place. No. 10 covered the doubling of the Portobello route from Waterloo Place to the Figgate Burn, with removal of the old passing loops and a realignment at Jock's Lodge. A proposal for an extension to Musselburgh was dropped.

There were 37 Sections in the Act and five Schedules. These covered the usual financial and technical details and interests of other parties. The tramways were to be used for passenger traffic only, though small parcels could be carried if the local authority agreed to such use. Passenger's luggage was to be accepted. Two years were allowed for the completion of the new works except for the Ardmillan-Polwarth line in which case the period was three years. Section 34 was, however, important, for by it the company at last secured general power to acquire, build and operate omnibuses. They were of course subject to the licensing conditions of the magistrates, including stances.

Meanwhile in 1881 important changes in the company's personnel took place. D. W. Paterson, the secretary, resigned and Dr Wood took his place, being in turn succeeded in the chair by Thomas Hill. Dr Wood was also appointed general manager and the company's office moved to 54 North Bridge. Richard Goodyear was now in charge of the rolling-stock. There were further changes. In March 1883 James Clifton Robinson became general manager. He had been in at the very beginning of tramways, having, as a youngster from Birkenhead, joined G. F. Train twenty years earlier. His appointment seems to have given rise to much discontent among the staff, but soon a "new deal" was arranged which included some increase in wages, arrangements for meal reliefs and also some alterations in the services. He did not remain long in Edinburgh however, departing early in the following year for the Highgate Hill Cable Tramway in London. Later he was to take a leading part in the development of the London United Tramways system and received a knighthood.

We must now deal with an interesting phase regarding haulage. It will be remembered that by their Act the company were to work their tramways by animal power only. This stipulation also applied to tramway companies elsewhere, but experiments were taking place with steam power. Such experimental journeys, of course, could not be used for public traffic.

The Edinburgh Street Tramways Company were interested in the idea and a 12 hp steam tramway engine made by Henry Hughes of Loughborough was put on the Portobello line. It had 2ft. diameter wheels and 7in. x 13in. cylinders. On 9 September 1876 it journeyed about a mile before a condenser fault halted it. On 13 September the Board of Trade inspector visited some additional passing loops which had been constructed on this route and he was given a demonstration of the engine, which continued to run trial trips daily before breakfast time for the next week or two. It then departed to show its paces on the Vale of Clyde Tramways, returning to Edinburgh in April 1877, when a further week's trials were run between Portobello and Waterloo Place and along Princes Street to the West End, culminating on 27 April with a large official party aboard, they being also entertained to a champagne lunch in Portobello's Royal Hotel. Passing horses seem to have given the engine a mixed reception and although otherwise it was apparently considered very satisfactory the authorities do not seem to have been persuaded to agree to its regular use. However, there were some further trials in May when it was used for depot shunting and its use as a kind of bank engine on Regent Road instead of trace horses was suggested. Another machine described as a steam car arrived at Leith from Greenock in December 1877 and was put on the rails at Junction Bridge. This car was then tried out on the Ferry Road line. It was a "Grantham" type car designed by Robertson and Henderson of Glasgow and built by Dickenson & Co., Birkenhead. The boiler was at one end and the three-cylinder engine, which was below the floor, could be worked either simple or compound as required. On 28 December it ran a demonstration trip from Shrub Hill to the Post Office but had to wait at the foot of Leith Street for pressure to be recovered. In March 1878 it ran demonstration trips on the Portobello route and many people travelled on it, as, being unlicensed, no fares could be charged. At the end of the month it did a demonstration run with Col. Hutchison of the Board of Trade in attendance, proceeding round the Morningside circular route before returning to Portobello. Subsequently it was sent off to Stirling.

At this time there was a proposal to build a new bridge across the harbour at Leith and continue the Bernard Street line via Commercial Street and North Junction Street and so form a circular route to the Foot of Leith Walk which could be operated at a penny fare with steam engines. Leith Town Council were not at all in favour and the matter was dropped.

Yet another engine ran a trial on the Portobello line on 2 July 1880. This machine was said to be made by Messrs Duncan and Wilson of Liverpool.

However, in 1879, in the Tramways Orders Confirmation Act (11 August 1879), power was given to the Board of Trade to license the public use of steam engines on a tramway as an experiment, notwithstanding an "animal power only" clause in a company's Act, and provided the local authorities responsible for two-thirds of the route approved. Such licences were valid for a year if not revoked, and could be renewed for a second year. So, in 1881, the Edinburgh Street Tramways Company persuaded the Corporation to let them have a real trial on the Portobello line. Portobello Town Council were receptive to the idea.

A Kitson steam tramway engine was therefore obtained and started trial runs on the Portobello route on 9 February. This engine proved very successful and even tackled Leith Street without any difficulty. The Board of Trade inspector attended on 12 April and duly approved its use on the Portobello route. This commenced on 23 April 1881, the engine working from each end approximately every hour, and being accommodated at the Portobello stables. It was reported as having had the morning "workmen's car" attached as well as the ordinary one. It appears that Portobello Town Council had not then given their permission for the use of the steam engine, but this was forthcoming in October. Although there were a number of mishaps, the Kitson engine worked quite consistently, and was deemed a success. Another one was therefore ordered, but it was March 1882 before this could be supplied and put to work on the route. These Kitson engines were small four-wheeled machines, the boiler etc. being enclosed in a casing resembling a small tramcar body. The 2ft. 4½in. diameter wheels, 8in. x 12in. cylinders and driving gear were screened from view by a metal vallance round the sides and ends, extending to within a few inches of the ground. The exhaust steam was turned into a condenser mounted in the roof, and so they were normally quiet in operation.

The Corporation renewed their licence for the steam engines for a further six months in March 1882, but meanwhile the company, wishing to continue the use of the steam engines, sought to ensure their freedom of action by promoting a Bill to give them specific powers to use mechanical traction without reference to the Board of Trade or the local authorities. The Bill was not well received, and while Portobello's opposition was withdrawn in consideration of some street paving concessions, both Edinburgh and Leith opposed it. In the event Parliament did not mind the Edinburgh Street Tramways Company being authorised to use mechanical power, but felt Edinburgh and Leith should have the usual safeguards of licensing regarding the number and type of engines, their speed and the routes to be worked. So, the Edinburgh Street Tramways (Mechanical Power) Act of 1882 (passed 12 July 1882) really did no more than continue the existing system of operation by licence from the Corporation. This Act limited the number of cars to be drawn by an engine to two. Consent or revocation by the local authority required a majority of at least two-thirds of the votes. The attached Schedule required the engines to be numbered, fitted with effective braking, a bell or whistle, speed indicator, fender, and a seat for the driver affording a full view. They were to be free from noise and clatter, and the fire and machinery were to be concealed to within 4in. of the rails. Maximum speed was to be 8 mph. When the company applied in September 1882 to continue steam traction on the Portobello route, Edinburgh Corporation now had the last word and on 12 September declined to renew their licence, so the engines were withdrawn. However, as no reply to their application had yet been received from the Portobello authorities, a steam car service on the route was reintroduced outside the city boundary on 23 September. Passengers changed to horse cars for the Edinburgh portion of the route, but two or three days later the cars were taken right through, hauled by horses within the city boundary and by the steam engines beyond. The company then realised their existing licence did not expire until 27 October and so, on 6 October, they recommenced steam working through to Waterloo Place. The Portobello authorities now also declined to renew the licence for the steam engines and so 27 October was the last of them. There had been the usual complaints of smoke and noise and so on, and Edinburgh would not contemplate for its street transport that which might be, and indeed for several years was, accepted in the industrial areas of England and elsewhere.

Before we leave this matter mention must be made of other possibilities which were tried too: Moncrieff's compressed-air car, using an Edinburgh Street Tramways Company car for a trial which apparently took place in Govan; and even a machine assisted by a form of spring-wound device. These were far from satisfactory. In October 1884 a small electric car which had been shown at a local exhibition was also demonstrated, but this was not much more than a toy. A further approach to the Corporation to allow steam engines to be used was made in July 1886. This time the company hoped to use a "Greens" improved noiseless engine on the Portobello route. The ratepayers objected, and although the Edinburgh council voting was 18 for and 15 against, the two-thirds majority approval required by the Act was thus not attained and approval could not be given.

Now let us return to 1882.

Work on the various extensions authorised by the 1881 Act was commenced early in 1882 and pushed ahead vigorously, the doubling of the Portobello route having been completed on 12 December 1881. Girder rails with Mr Lindsay's patent cast-iron hollow blocks replacing alternate setts on both sides of the rail to prevent wear of the paving were used on the Portobello line and subsequently became normal practice. Gowans was the contractor for much of the works but another contractor, Andrew Waddel, was responsible for those in Leith. Both contractors were also engaged on relaying much of the older tracks, and a number of other sections of rail and fastenings were used including one where the groove was provided only by the edge of the cast-iron blocks.

At the same time another act was obtained, the Edinburgh Street

Edinburgh Street Tramways Company horse car No. 15 with knifeboard outside seats, on the Bernard Street to Haymarket route at the West End. A "brake" coming in from the Forth Bridge is also seen. (*A. W. Brotchie*)

Tramways Act, 1882 (3 July 1882), authorising construction of another single line branch, from Churchhill as far as Morningside Drive with a passing loop just short of the terminus. Three years were allowed for its completion.

There was also further extension of the Shrub Hill depot premises beyond Dryden Street with new stables, stores and workshops, most of which buildings were still in existence until recently. A siding was put in from the North British Railway with a connection to the tramway track, though this was eventually removed.

The first of the new extensions to be opened to traffic was the Foot of Leith Walk to Restalrig Road on 1 May 1882, the service running to the Waverley via York Place. Junction Bridge to the foot of North Junction Street was opened early the next month, and the services from both these new termini were then run to Haymarket. The other extensions authorised in 1881 with the exception of the line between Ardmillan Terrace and Granville Terrace were completed the following month, and the Board of Trade inspection took place on 11 July. It seems some cars may have already been running on some of the new lines, but the new services were advertised to commence on 1 August 1882 as follows: Tynecastle and Powburn; Granville Terrace and Post Office via Lothian Road returning via High Street and Lauriston, both ways round. The service from North Junction Street now ran only to West End instead of Haymarket.

Construction of the Morningside extension commenced in August 1882, but because of the building of the new railway bridge, the line had to terminate for the time being near the old toll gate just short of the bridge. This length was opened in November 1882 with a shuttle service of light single-deck cars from and to Churchhill with transfer fares to Tollcross and West End. The rest of the extension to Morningside Drive was completed and inspected by Major-General Hutchison of the Board of Trade on 26 May 1883. The services then ran from and to West End where their terminus was on the new line linking Lothian Road and Shandwick Place.

In the spring of 1883 a single sharply curved connecting line was laid from Junction Street to join the Constitution Street line before the junction leading into Duke Street, and on 30 April 1883 the two services from Restalrig Road and North Junction Street were replaced by a penny fare shuttle service from North Junction Street to Restalrig Road. This was decidedly unpopular and following protest from Leith Town Council the old services were restored within a few weeks, but running only as far as the Waverley from both termini.

Work was also now proceeding on the extension from Granville Terrace to Colinton Road and the line from Polwarth Terrace to Ardmillan Terrace. These were completed by 15 September and inspected by the Board of Trade, this time by Major Marindin, on 11 October. Gowan's 40ft. rails of 73 lbs. per yard with cast-iron blocks were used. The new line was served from 1 November by extending the Tynecastle route to a new terminus at the canal bridge near Polwarth Terrace, while the extension to Colinton Road was served by a half-hourly service from the Tron Church.

It will be recalled that the 1881 Act also authorised the company to run buses, and they lost no time in expanding their activities in that direction. Stables were acquired in the summer of 1881 at Corstorphine on the south side of the main road a little way beyond Manse Road. There was also a grazing field for the horses which thus became known as Tramway Park. From August 1881 the Corstorphine bus was run to the Waverley Steps every hour. On 1 February 1882 the Dalkeith "coach" was taken over, together with stables at Dalkeith, and the company then ran their bus four times a day from the Waverley Steps. In the summer of 1882 a bus was run to Roslin at a fare of 9d. On 1 May 1882 another bus was put on between the Portobello car terminus and Levenhall at a fare of 3d., but this did not do so well. Musselburgh traffic had long passed to the railway, and the old Edinburgh-Musselburgh coach had made its last run in February 1878. Fares, times and stances for the new service were revised in July 1882 in an attempt to popularise it, but it had to be withdrawn a few weeks afterwards.

Then in September 1882 it was proposed to divert the Mound-Newhaven bus from Goldenacre via Granton to Newhaven; but instead, a separate service was run from Granton to Newhaven and continued on to the Custom House at Leith. The other obligatory service from

Waterloo Place to Stockbridge continued too, of course. The vehicles used were of orthodox pattern, seating about 12 inside and with either a "knife-board" seat or "garden seats" for 14 on the roof, reached from a small rear platform by a narrow curved stair. Three horses were used to haul them.

With all this development and the increase in their establishment, the Edinburgh Street Tramways Company drew up their first rule book which was approved by the directors on 25 September 1882 and printed and issued to the staff in 1883. The services quoted were:

Post Office to Newhaven
Haymarket to Bernard Street
Powburn to Coltbridge
Post Office-Grange-Churchhill circle
Newington to Bernard Street
Waterloo Place to Portobello
Bernard Street to Tollcross
Post Office to Morningside
Granville Terrace to Princes Street and Post Office, and back by High Street and Lauriston Place, both ways round
Post Office-West End-Tollcross-Lauriston-High Street, circle
Bernard Street to Tollcross via High Street and Lauriston
Post Office to Commercial Street
Post Office via High Street, Lauriston, Lothian Road, and West End to Ardmillan
Tollcross via West End to Ardmillan
Restalrig Road to Haymarket

It is probable that some of these services were not worked regularly. Each route was divided up into quarter-mile distances for the purpose of calculating fares, to which a special page was devoted: "The fare chargeable by Act of Parliament by car or omnibus is 2d. either inside or outside for the first two miles or any part thereof, even a fraction of one mile". There were, however, as already noted, a considerable number of "special" penny fares. These were, outside only: Junction Bridge and Stanley Road; Leith Walk Station to Junction Bridge, or to Bernard Street; Post Office and Haymarket, or Tollcross, or Salisbury Place; West End and Coltbridge; West End and Barclay Church; Tollcross and Churchhill; Churchhill and Salisbury Place; Salisbury Place to Powburn; West End and Ardmillan; Tollcross and Granville Terrace. (Note the one-way downhill stages.) Inside penny fares were limited to: Foot of Leith Walk to Commercial Street, or Bernard Street, or Restalrig Road; Haymarket and West End, or Coltbridge, or Ardmillan; Waterloo Place and Norton Place. There were also a few 2d. and 3d. "bargains".

The conductors carried, in a "distributor", rolls of tickets of the "cloakroom" style, numbered consecutively and showing also the car number. There were 1d., 2d. and 3d. values, the 1d. ones being blue and 2d. ones white. Fares above 3d. were met by issuing more than one ticket. The flat fare on the Leith-Granton bus was 3d. inside or 2d. outside, while the other local buses charged a 2d. fare. The Loanhead bus was 6d., outside or inside, as was the outside fare to Dalkeith. Inside fares to Gilmerton were 7d. and to Dalkeith 8d. Gilmerton-Dalkeith was 4d. outside and 6d. inside. To Greenend was 6d. outside or inside. "From Stockbridge to Newington or vice versa by omnibus and car 3d. inside and 2d. outside, available only on day of issue and by next car or omnibus only. Passengers pay whole fare to conductor of car or omnibus in which they first travel, and will have their tickets checked with the date of issue, by the checker at the Register House. This fare carries to Salisbury Place or Blackett Place only, — Powburn and Grange not included."

There were eight "sections" for the inspectors as follows: No. 1 got the cars out in the morning — workmen's cars — relieved the Register House "checker" at midday, and finished early "about 2.00 p.m.". No. 2 took North of Pilrig and the Granton bus. No. 3 Waterloo Place to Coltbridge, and Corstorphine, Stockbridge and Trinity buses. No. 4 Post Office to Newington and George IV Bridge, also Loanhead and Dalkeith bus stance. No. 5 West End to Morningside and Grange. No. 6 Portobello route. No. 7 Merchiston, Dalry and Lauriston; and No. 8 was the checker at the Register House. In those days, while there was a considerable number of fixed stopping places, cars normally stopped anywhere when hailed, but exceptions were made for some of the up grades, viz. between Pilrig and Leith Walk station, then to Annandale Street; to London Road; to Picardy Place; to foot of Leith Street; and to Post Office. Similarly between Bright Crescent and Mayfield; to Blackett Place; and to Salisbury Place. Also between No. 77 South Bridge and Surgeons' Hall, Waterloo Place and the Calton Hill stairs, Abbeyhill to Abbeymount, and Barclay Church to Bruntsfield Terrace. Cars would not stop between these points. Further, cars were to be "walked" (i.e. the horses were not be allowed to trot or gallop) at the following places: Register House down to Nottingham Place; Foot of Leith Walk into Junction Street; curves at either end of Newhaven Road; Register House to St. Andrew Street; Salisbury Place; Clinton Road; at Crosscauseway, Causewayside, and Whitehouse Loan; from Tron Church to Post Office; Abbotsford Park to Morningside School; and on the passing loops on the Portobello route.

The first rule book merits further notice. From it we learn that drivers and conductors were appointed by the general manager and applicants had to be under 35 years of age, with extension to 40 years in the case of ex-police or ex-railway applicants as conductors. Conductors had to deposit £1 as security, and "must possess and constantly wear a good timekeeping watch". Fares were to be collected before starting from termini, and thereafter "as far as possible from passengers on entering".

They were not to be off the platform when the car was travelling. No standing passengers were allowed. There were, of course, stringent rules regarding sobriety, cleanliness, and improper language while it is intimated that "the Company is determined to render every possible assistance to conductors in resisting the fraudulent demands of drivers and others". "Any driver soliciting money from a conductor is liable to instant dismissal." Trace boys were to walk their horses back and if they rode them "at a walking pace" they did so at their own risk. Inspectors were to "look after the trace boys . . . and see that the horses are properly treated". A driver, too, "shall be careful and considerate in the treatment of his horses". There was a carmen's shelter at Morningside which could be used between 11.00 a.m. and 7.00 p.m. All sections of the establishment were covered. Those relating to "Workmen in the Car-Making, Smith, Farrier, Saddlery, and Lighting Departments" make strange reading today. Let us be content with the working hours, viz. Monday to Friday 6.00 a.m. to 9.00 a.m., 9.45 a.m. to 1.00 p.m., and 1.45 p.m. to 5.00 p.m. Saturdays 6.00 a.m. to 9.00 a.m. and 9.30 a.m. to 1.00 p.m. It is interesting to note, however, that in the summer of 1883 a hinged stool was provided for car drivers. The cars were now further distinguished by painting them in colours to represent the route on which they ran, the old coloured light for use at night being correspondingly amended. From 29 April 1883 red cars ran on the Bernard Street to Haymarket service, blue cars on the Bernard Street to Newington service, and white cars on the Morningside routes. Subsequently, green cars and yellow cars were introduced for other services, as will be noted. Hitherto the cars do not appear to have been themselves numbered, but carried a detachable plate bearing the number corresponding to their route licence number on the lower side panel. Soon after this time this "car" number was painted on the dashboards in the orthodox manner. In the case of those on the circular service the number was, for a time, enclosed in a circle. The open "toast-rack" cars seem to have been used for the early morning "workmen's cars", which gave rise to some complaint in the winter.

In January 1884 the timetables showed tramway services as follows: Bernard Street to Haymarket; Bernard Street to Newington; Grange-Morningside Circle, each every 10/15 minutes. Newhaven to Register House; Portobello to Register House every 20 minutes. West End to Morningside Drive; Coltbridge to Powburn; Polwarth Gardens via Dalry to Powburn; Tron Church to Colinton Road, every 30 minutes (every 15 minutes between Tron Church and Granville Terrace). North Junction Street to Register House; Restalrig Road to Register House, every hour. The Morningside Drive and Colinton Road services did not run in the late evening. The bus services were as already described. There were now 18½ miles of tramway route and 88 cars and buses.

Clifton Robinson, who went off to London early in 1884, was succeeded by the first of the really "well kent" managers. John Erskine Pitcairn came from the North British Railway where he had been in the Traffic Manager's Department. The Edinburgh Street Tramways

Company's undertaking was now thriving and under "Johnee" Pitcairn it continued to flourish.

About May 1884 there were some alterations. The services from Restalrig Road and from North Junction Street to the Register House were extended both to Haymarket and to Salisbury Place, then described as Newington; while the Morningside Drive to West End service was extended to the Register House. Other services were increased in frequency. About October the Restalrig Road and North Junction Street services were again extended from Haymarket to Coltbridge, and an additional hourly service given between Granville Terrace and Post Office via Lothian Road. The following month the Restalrig Road-Coltbridge service was diverted to North Merchiston, and the North Junction Street-Salisbury Place service ceased. The Restalrig Road-Salisbury Place service ceased too, early in 1885.

To revert to the bus services, John Player of Dundas Street was taking up this business, and in May 1883 bought a small ten-seater bus, six inside and four outside, which had been in use at an establishment at Craiglockhart. With this he ran a half-hourly service from the Mound to Howard Place at a twopenny fare. In February 1884, in spite of some opposition, his route was extended to Newhaven in competition with the Edinburgh Street Tramways Company which had to provide a statutory service on the route. Player was finding plenty of traffic too for his "brakes" to Roslin in the summers of 1883 and 1884, and in August and September 1885 he also ran excursions further afield such as Carlops, Hopetoun, and Dirleton. Meanwhile in 1884 George Hall was running to Queensferry, to be joined by the Edinburgh Street Tramways Company in 1885, and later Croall's. One of the latter's vehicles rejoiced in the name "Chevy Chase". Another route running in January 1884 was from the east end of Princes Street to Cramond, three times daily, with fares of 9d. and 6d. Sam Johnston also had two buses running to Roslin and in 1886 another run by Fred Glass was competing on this route.

On 1 June 1885 the Edinburgh Street Tramways Company started a new service from Waverley Steps to Bonnington Toll via York Place and Broughton Street, but it was taken off again early in the following year.

In 1886 the Edinburgh International Exhibition of Industry, Science and Art was held in the Meadows and drew big crowds. To cater for the traffic the North Junction Street-Coltbridge service was run to Tollcross instead during August, and diverted at the other end to Bernard Street in September. The service to Colinton Road was now run to Post Office via Lothian Road, and a ten-minute service provided between Tron Church and Tollcross via Lauriston Place. North Merchiston to Powburn was replaced by a North Merchiston to North Junction Street service. The Glasgow Omnibus & Hiring Co. secured a licence to run a bus between Waverley Market and the Meadows for the exhibition. The electric light was a feature of the exhibition and a short demonstration electric tramway was also laid down on the north side of the grounds, upon which two cars supplied by the North Metropolitan Tramway Company ran.

The Edinburgh Street Tramways Company also exhibited their latest car, fresh from the Shrubhill works, seating 16 inside and 18 outside, weighing two tons, and fitted with a special life-guard, emergency brake, and railcleaner.

Mr Pitcairn favoured long routes, and with the exhibition over some reorganisation was effected about December 1886. The services and their colours were:

Portobello to Colinton Road	Yellow	every 20 minutes
Newhaven to Morningside Drive	White	every 20 minutes
Bernard Street to Tollcross	?	every 20 minutes
Bernard Street to Newington	Blue	every 10 minutes
Morningside Circular	White	every 10 minutes
Tron Church to Tollcross	?	every 10 minutes
Coltbridge to Powburn	Blue	every 15 minutes
North Merchiston to North Junction Street	Red	every 30 minutes
North Merchiston to Restalrig Road	Green	every 30 minutes

Also some journeys from Bernard Street to Haymarket. No regular service was given on Harrison Road. There were no material changes in the bus services. The Bernard Street-Tollcross service was dropped soon afterwards, but apart from frequency changes the foregoing remained the pattern for a long time.

In accordance with Section 74 of their original Act the Edinburgh Northern Tramways Company took over the Edinburgh Street Tramways Company's obligations to run buses on the Trinity and Stockbridge routes and the latter company's buses were replaced by the Northern

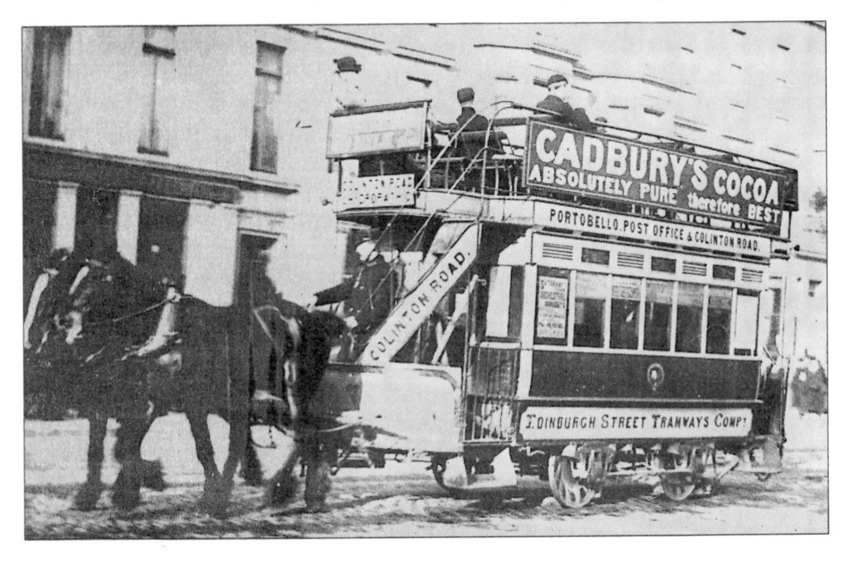

Edinburgh Street Tramways Company horse car No. 47 with the knifeboard seat replaced by garden seats, running on the long through route from Portobello to Colinton Road. The horses are evidently trotting merrily along. (*A. W. Brotchie*)

Company's on 1 December 1886. These buses were eventually superseded by the Edinburgh Northern Tramways Company's cable cars to Goldenacre and to Stockbridge, but that company had still to continue to run a bus from their Goldenacre car terminus to Newhaven. This was a small bus with no outside seats and ran every twenty minutes. For a week in February 1888 it was extended to the Custom House, Leith, except in the evenings. Another bus was put on every half-hour from Goldenacre to Granton, and at the beginning of 1889 a further one was run every half-hour from Goldenacre to Trinity Crescent.

Player's Newhaven bus was taken off early in 1887, but in that summer a bus was being run in from Penicuik in the morning and back out in the afternoon.

In 1888 an independent group of promoters proposed to lay a tramway from Coltbridge to Corstorphine. The Town Council agreed to support their projected Bill but nothing came of it.

The working conditions of the Edinburgh Street Tramways Company's employees were improved in 1889, the weekly hours being reduced from 76 to 68. Drivers were then paid from 21 shillings to 26 shillings per week and conductors from 20 shillings to 25 shillings per week.

In the summer of 1890 the International Exhibition of Electrical Engineering, General Inventions and Industry was held at Meggetland on a site on both sides of the Suburban railway north of Craiglockhart station and the Union Canal. The main entrance was from Polwarth Terrace between Ashley Terrace and Colinton Road, and a large loop line was laid in past the gate, just short of the Colinton Road terminus. For this traffic the Restalrig Road-North Merchiston service was extended up Harrison Road to the Colinton Road terminus, to which the Tron Church-Tollcross service was likewise extended.

Bernard Street to Salisbury Place was at this time extended to Powburn and new services run from North Junction Street to Powburn, and Bernard Street to Colinton Road. All routes ran at twelve minutes frequency, though this was soon altered to fifteen minutes, and the North Junction Street to Powburn service diverted along Grange Road to Marchmont Road. This carried blue colours. A bus service was also tried from Churchhill to the exhibition at a fare of 2d., but did not pay and was taken off. The bus licence numbers were 103 and 104. After the exhibition the Bernard Street-Colinton Road service was cut back to North Merchiston, and the service from Tron Church reduced, and later abandoned. The Restalrig Road-North Merchiston service was altered to Gorgie Road about August 1891.

But now the company's first twenty-one years were drawing to a close, and we must leave the development of the services meantime to deal with the coming important political phase. The company could afford no more experiments or expansion. Instead they sought from Edinburgh, Leith, and Portobello town councils an indication of their intentions. Edinburgh Town Council, in August 1890, announced their intention of taking over the system within the city. Leith were in favour of discussions with the company. In fact they did not like Edinburgh's unilateral action, for a unified system was clearly desirable. There was a meeting between Leith Town Council and the Edinburgh Street Tramways Company in November 1890, and another between Edinburgh and Leith town councils in May 1891. The company offered substantial wayleave payments, revised fares, mechanical power, and profit sharing above 6 per cent in return for a further twenty-one years lease. But Edinburgh wanted to own the tracks and on 1 December 1891 decided to buy them up, expressing the hope that Leith Town Council would do the same.

Leith, of course, wanted to know what arrangements would be made for joint control of the whole system if they bought their part, and suggested the whole undertaking be bought jointly, but Edinburgh refused to discuss these aspects of the matter, and insisted on going ahead alone. This was an awkward situation, which Portobello was meantime watching. Leith Town Council were not at that time keen to buy up the system and resented Edinburgh's high-handedness. So on 7 June 1892 Leith Town Council entered into an agreement with the Edinburgh Street Tramways Company for their continued operation in the burgh. At the end of the year Portobello Town Council likewise decided not to purchase the lines in their area.

The Edinburgh Street Tramways Company of course hoped they would be able to lease the Edinburgh part of the system from Edinburgh Corporation when the city acquired it, as local athorities still had no power to operate tramways. If this had materialised the running of the whole system would have remained with one company, with obvious advantages to all parties. But it was not to be. In any event a new Act was called for, enabling the company to enter into leases, contracts, or agreements for working the tramways, to introduce mechanical or electric power, etc. These objects were secured in the Edinburgh Street Tramways Act 1892 — passed 27 June 1892 — which also provided for alterations in the company's capital and other matters. The agreement with Leith Town Council was scheduled to the Act and provided for the following: the company undertook to promote a Bill in the next Parliamentary session to cover extensions from Restalrig Road to Seafield Place, and from North Junction Street along Commercial Street to the Custom House; also additional connections at Junction Bridge and at Foot of Leith Walk. They undertook to continue through services to Edinburgh and if Edinburgh introduced mechanical power on Leith Walk not later than 1 June 1899 (other than experimentally), promised to do likewise. Penny outside fares were to be available, and penny inside fares too, within three-quarters of a mile of termini (or up to one mile if mechanical power was introduced). They also agreed to pay a wayleave of £500 per year for seven years and £600 per year thereafter. In return, Leith Town Council promised not to exercise their option of purchase for fourteen years from the date of the Act, and for twenty-one years if mechanical power should be introduced on Leith Walk.

Accordingly the Edinburgh Street Tramways Act 1893 (passed 9 June

1893) authorised the construction of the aformentioned two extensions, and connections from Ferry Road into North Junction Street, and from Great Junction Street to Constitution Street. It will be recalled that the latter had been laid as a single line ten years previously. There was a trailing crossover in Junction Street and a facing one near the Foot of Leith Walk. Two years were allowed for completion and the extensions were duly opened well within that period.

Meanwhile, on 12 August 1892, Edinburgh Corporation had given statutory notice to the Edinburgh Street Tramways Company and to the Board of Trade of their intention to exercise their powers of acquisition in terms of Section 43 of the general Tramways Act 1870, of that part of the system within the city boundaries, but excluding the line from Waterloo Place towards Portobello. The Edinburgh Street Tramways Company asked the Board of Trade not to sanction acquisition by Edinburgh Corporation, pointing out the advantages of the through routes which the company provided. They quoted the routes as follows, giving also the numbers of cars and horses, including trace horses, employed on each route:

	Route	Cars	Horses
1.	Newhaven to Morningside Drive	9 full day cars	117 horses
	Newhaven to Morningside Drive	4 half day cars	24 horses
2.	Commercial Street to Marchmont Road	3 full day cars	36 horses
3.	Bernard Street to Marchmont Road	3 full day cars	36 horses
4.	Bernard Street to Powburn	6 full day cars	78 horses
5.	Bernard Street to North Merchiston	6 full day cars	72 horses
6.	Seafield to Gorgie Road	6 full day cars	72 horses
7.	Powburn to Coltbridge	6 full day cars	72 horses
	Powburn to Coltbridge	3 half day cars	18 horses
8.	Morningside Circular	8 full day cars	96 horses
	Morningside Circular	4 half day cars	24 horses
9.	Tron Church to Tollcross	2 full day cars	24 horses
10.	Portobello to Colinton Road	9 full day cars	117 horses

The company also stated that in addition to the above 786 horses there were 89 resting or spare, and that they also had 13 closed, ten canopy and six open cars used for workmen in the morning, or as football or holiday extras. The morning workmen's cars ran, except Sundays, from Leith to Morningside Drive via Lothian Road, to Churchhill via Grange Road, and to Dalry. An accompanying map showed Gorgie at the foot of Ardmillan Terrace and North Merchiston at the top. The bus services were also listed as will be detailed later. Despite protest also from Leith Corporation the Board of Trade duly gave its approval to Edinburgh Corporation, so the Edinburgh Street Tramways Company as "sitting tenants" endeavoured to negotiate with Edinburgh Corporation for a lease of the system and offered as much as £10,000 a year. But Edinburgh would not accept the company which now had an agreement to continue operations in Leith, and so thirty years of inconvenience at Pilrig was precipitated.

Edinburgh Corporation were also deliberating on what form of mechanical traction to adopt. Clearly the days of horse haulage were numbered. Although experiments were taking place with electric traction in various parts of the world, cable haulage was acknowledged to be the cheapest method so far devised, and its future was considered bright. The Edinburgh Northern Tramways Company's system — to be described in the following chapter — was operating successfully and economically, although it comprised only fairly short and reasonably straight routes not complicated by numerous junctions etc. There really was little option, for steam engines had been found ineffective and unpopular, and overhead wires for electric traction would have been quite unacceptable in Edinburgh at that time. No one would have dared to try to install such a system.

So the Corporation promoted their Edinburgh Corporation Tramways Act 1893, which was passed on 29 June 1893. Section 4 authorised the use of cable power with the consent of the Board of Trade who were also empowered to make various bylaws. Other sections referred to borrowing powers for money, and duties regarding road levels, water and gas mains and such matters. Local authorities, of course, still had no general power to work their tramway systems, and the Board of Trade had to approve the terms of such leases as were arranged. In this case provision was made for the Board of Trade to license the Corporation to work the system themselves, temporarily, should no satisfactory offer to lease it be forthcoming.

So offers to lease the system on certain terms were then sought. These provided for a rental of 7 per cent per annum on the purchase price to be paid by Edinburgh Corporation to the Edinburgh Street Tramways Company, plus taxes and feus etc. The lessees were also to maintain and renew the system. It was provided that the Corporation could acquire or build other lines and convert the lines to mechanical traction, and the lessees were to pay the 7 per cent rental on the capital cost of these works also. The staff's working week was to be reduced to 54 hours.

Three offers were received, namely from the Edinburgh Street Tranways Company, Messrs Dick Kerr & Co. Ltd., and the Glasgow Tramways Company. Messrs Dick Kerr & Co. Ltd. accepted all the Corporation's terms and also offered to introduce penny fares when cable traction was brought into operation.

The Edinburgh Street Tramways Comnpany preferred to offer a sum of £13,000 per annum initially, which was rather more than the Corporation would have received on the 7 per cent basis. They also agreed to pay 7 per cent on the cost of cabling certain specified main routes, but, prudently, would not bind themselves to this in respect of other routes or new routes without their prior consultation and agreement. They also urged that it would be better not to interfere with the men's working hours. The Glasgow company's offer was not disclosed.

The council met on 11 October 1893 when Messrs Dick Kerr & Co.'s offer was accepted, and it was arranged they should enter on the property on Monday 20 November. Approval of the Board of Trade was then sought, but as the terms of the lease made no mention of through running to Leith, Leith Town Council petitioned the Board of Trade to insist on such a clause.

There was thus some delay, and at the last minute a judicial factor had to be appointed to run the system, in law, from 20 November until approval of the new lease was forthcoming. This was duly given by the Board of Trade on 24 November, but with the added clause requiring the company to arrange for the interchange of traffic between the Edinburgh and Leith systems.

The Corporation thereupon took possession of the Edinburgh Street Tramways Company's system within the city, with the exception of the section from Waterloo Place to Jock's Lodge, on 9 December 1893. This amounted to about 11¾ miles. Seventy cars and some 600 horses were taken over at a valuation of about £40,000 and immediately resold to Messrs Dick Kerr & Co. Ltd., who took over the working for twenty-one years from that date.

However, there was another problem still to be resolved. The price to be paid to the Edinburgh Street Tramways Company was still unsettled. Section 43 of the 1870 Act provided for the appointment by the Board of Trade for an arbiter, who was to consider "the then value (exclusive of any allowance for past or future profits of the undertaking, or compensation for compulsory sale, or other consideration whatsoever), of the tramway, and all land, buildings, works, materials, and plant of the promoters suitable to and used by them for the purposes of their undertaking". The arbiter appointed by the Board of Trade was Mr Henry Tennant, the well-known general manager of the North Eastern Railway, then recently retired. He held this to mean the cost to construct the lines, less an allowance for depreciation, and on 13 November 1893 had announced a figure of £185,000. The company disagreed with this reasoning, holding that they were entitled to a value which took account of the rental which the property would command, and they appealed, seeking interdict in the meantime.

The arbiter's decision was, however, upheld in both divisions of the Court of Session and the company then appealed to the House of Lords. A similar action by the London Street Tramways Company was proceeding through the English courts at the same time. The cases excited much interest in tramway circles, the Edinburgh one opening first on 8 June 1894. On 30 July the decision was given upholding the arbiter's decision. While this was doubtless legally correct it did not commend itself as fair to tramway companies.

In the meantime, in January 1894, the Edinburgh Street Tramways Company had bought some property in the Leith part of Leith Walk near Smiths Place to make a new depot and stables. Until these were ready they continued to occupy part of the depot and stables at Shrubhill, now leased to Messrs Dick Kerr and Co. Ltd. Of course at this stage the tramways were still functioning as one undertaking with the same staff. Mr Pitcairn, the manager, and Mr Adam, the treasurer, had the unenviable task of serving two masters, i.e. both companies. At the staff annual dinner in March 1894 the two owning companies were jointly toasted with enthusiasm! There was a kind of "common purse" arrangement and the old company received a quarter of the receipts taken on the Leith part of the system by the Dick Kerr cars. Then, on 9 June 1894, the 29 cars and 298 horses remaining with the Edinburgh Street Tramways Company were moved down to their new premises on the site of the later Leith depot. The operating arrangements continued as before, but as the owning companies still could not reach any permanent agreement regarding through traffic, the Board of Trade appointed an arbiter in the matter in August. Again it was Mr Henry Tennant, and it was some time before he gave his decision.

In the interval another problem arose. Shortly after Messrs Dick Kerr & Co. Ltd. concluded their lease of the Edinburgh system, they approached the Corporation for permission to sub-lease the undertaking to a new company which they proposed to form. This was with a view to raising additional capital for their Edinburgh activities, and they deemed it sound to attract this capital locally and invite some prominent local gentlemen to join the board. They had indeed already registered the Edinburgh Tramway Co. Ltd. on 8 November 1893 (dissolved in June 1895), but this never functioned at all, since for some reason or other the Corporation would not entertain this apparently quite reasonable scheme. After a few months' discussions the company withdrew their request and the council were left wondering what all the bother had been about. Then, as a more sensible attitude became evident, the matter was raised again and in July 1894 the Corporation agreed to the existing lease being determined, and entered into a new lease jointly with Messrs Dick Kerr & Co. Ltd. and their new Edinburgh & District Tramways Co. Ltd., which had been incorporated on 6 March 1894. The first directors were B. Hall Blyth (chairman), Alex. Fleming, G. H. Geddes, John Kerr and F. Manuella. Part of this bargain was that inside fares on a penny per mile basis would be introduced on 1 September 1894 instead of within a month of the introduction of cable cars, as provided for in the original lease. The rolling-stock henceforth carried the name of the Edinburgh & District Tramways Co. Ltd. in place of Dick Kerr & Co. Ltd., the latter company remaining liable to the Corporation for the financial affairs. Mr Adam now became manager for the Edinburgh Street Tramways Company while Mr Pitcairn remained with the new Edinburgh & District Tramways Co. Ltd.

The new fares were introduced on 3 September 1894, and some service changes were also effected. The Commercial Street and Marchmont Road service was extended to Churchhill, while the Newhaven-Morningside Drive, and Seafield or Bernard Street to Gorgie and North Merchiston services were diverted from Leith Street to the York Place line. The new company continued to use the same type of tickets but without the car number and now headed Edin. & Dist. Tram. Co. Ltd.

Adjudication on the through services had still not been given, but on this same date the companies decided to discontinue the through service over the Portobello route, and the cars from Portobello and from Colinton Road were turned back to Waterloo Place and the Register House respectively.

At last, on 4 December 1894, the arbiter announced his interim award in the through services question. To avoid passengers having to change cars, the cars were to be taken through from the one system to the other, but in order to avoid any suggestion of running powers, horses, drivers and conductors were to be changed at the boundary at Pilrig. There was in fact no crossover at Pilrig by which the cars could have been turned back. To meet the terms of the original Act, certain through fares were to be made available, and he went on to specify these and other fares adjustments. Some of these new fares were less favourable than the current ones and Leith Town Council objected to the Board of Trade that such matters were outside the arbiter's terms of reference. The Board of Trade however claimed they could not interfere.

Nevertheless, the companies announced that on Monday 24 December 1894 through working in terms of the arbiter's award would commence. Twopenny through tickets would be issued for journeys between Post Office and Bernard Street, Junction Bridge, or the Seafield terminus, for which the second conductor would give an exchange ticket. In Leith, penny fares applied from Pilrig to the aforementioned points, while to Stanley Road was twopence. Other penny fares were Stanley Road-Junction Bridge; Bonnington Terrace-Smiths Place; and Fort Street or North Junction Street to Lorne Street. A halfpenny fare was made available between Pilrig and Smiths Place or Annandale Street. There was no longer any distinction between inside and outside fares. Some workmen's cars with a halfpenny fare were run in Leith, but the Edinburgh Street Tramways Company pointed out that they would not be able to run through workmen's cars, and could not run connecting cars to Pilrig as there was no crossover there. They asked Leith Town Council's approval for laying in one, but were refused. On the same date the through working between Portobello and Colinton Road was resumed on the same basis. From 1 January 1895 a flat rate 1d. fare was available to letter carriers under 16 years of age or 1½d. if older, except on the Portobello route. A general range of halfpenny fares was introduced in Leith on 1 July 1895.

The traditional animosity between Edinburgh and Leith now reached new heights. Contemporary tentative proposals by Edinburgh for annexation of the port did not help matters. Conditions at Pilrig were chaotic. The Edinburgh Street Tramways Company on their relatively level routes in Leith could manage with two horses per car; the Edinburgh & District Tramways Company needed four from Pilrig to the Register House. The crews got muddled up: a car would set off with the wrong conductor — or even two — leaving the next car without any. The press complained bitterly and were at pains to point out the stupidity of it all and indicate the culprit. It was observed that Dick Kerr & Co. had undertaken to pay 7 per cent on the cost of any new route for which Edinburgh would borrow the money at 3 per cent.

Edinburgh Corporation were now seeking the Board of Trade's approval of the new Edinburgh & District Tramways Company lease, and so Leith sent a public petition to the Board of Trade demanding the insertion of a clause to end "The Muddle". The matter was, however, put so clearly and pointedly at a meeting of Leith Town Council on 4 January 1895, that from the following Monday, 7 January 1895, the companies at any rate reverted to the old fare scales. The Lord Provost now held out an olive branch and sought a meeting with Leith, though apparently with little support from his colleagues. Meetings were duly held and it was suggested Leith might now buy the system in the burgh and lease it to Dick Kerr & Co. Leith might have agreed to this arrangement if they could have bought on the statutory bargain terms which Edinburgh had secured. But this sale could now only be a voluntary one on the part of the Edinburgh Street Tramways Company, who refused to sell under their own valuation of £155,000. Leith of course declined. Then Dick Kerr & Co. offered to buy up the Edinburgh Street Tramways Company's system in Leith, but the latter refused to sell unless their whole undertaking, including the Portobello line and their buses, was included, and this Dick Kerr & Co. would not undertake to do. So in June 1895 Leith Town Council resolved to proceed no further with the question.

Meanwhile, Edinburgh Corporation withdrew their application to the Board of Trade for approval of their new lease to the Edinburgh & District Tramways Company. This action of course prevented Board of Trade intervention in the through running dispute as sought by Leith, but gave rise to the charge that Edinburgh was not complying with the law. The Edinburgh Street Tramways Company then pressed Mr Tennant for a revised award regarding through services. Much ridicule was poured on the legal quibble of what constituted running powers. Mr Tennant met the parties in Edinburgh on 24 May 1895 after spending some time at Pilrig, and decided to seek legal advice in the matter, but in the end he felt unable to pronounce any more useful ruling and his interim award still stood.

Another anomaly had arisen. Dick Kerr & Co. had undertaken to reduce the crews' time to a nine-hour day as stipulated by Edinburgh Corporation. But the men's wages were then correspondingly reduced, and so the Edinburgh Street Tramways Company's men had seven shillings or so more per week. Probably Edinburgh Corporation did not foresee this aspect of their effort to ease the men's lot.

On 26 December 1894 the first staff "Rules and Regulations" for the new organisation were approved by the company's directors and issued under the joint names of the Edinburgh & District Tramways Company and Dick Kerr & Co. Ltd. Its contents were little different from the earlier Edinburgh Street Tramways Company's book.

Proposals for a tramway to Corstorphine had again been aired in the summer of 1893 — this time by an electricity company who announced their intention of seeking authority for an electric line — but the Corporation opposed it.

Notwithstanding the terms of their 1893 Edinburgh Corporation Tramways Act, several Edinburgh councillors were still not happy about cable haulage and the question of whether or not to go ahead was still being hotly debated. It was not until March 1895 that a decision was reached, and in July they appointed Mr W. N. Colam and Mr John Cooper as engineers. The latter was burgh engineer at the time. Tenders were invited and that of Dick Kerr & Co. accepted to carry out the work of conversion. Mr Colam appears to have become engineer for the company also, though this was denied in the press. The original intention was to use the existing rails but it was later agreed that it would be preferable to reconstruct the track entirely, and to compensate for the additional cost on which they would have to pay the 7 per cent rent, the company were relieved of their future obligation to renew the tracks.

It was also decided that some extensions to the system should be made, and these were provided for by the Edinburgh Improvement and Tramways Act of 1896. Passed 7 August 1896, this contained an important section, 26, authorising the use of electric power, or mechanical power (other than steam locomotives), on the Corporation's tramways. No doubt this pacified the anti-cable element, who were now no longer bound by the 1893 Act if a change of plan became possible later. The new lines authorised were:

1. A double line extension from the Powburn terminus to Lady Road.
2. A double line extension from the Morningside Drive terminus to the Braid Burn.
4. A double line branch from Dalry Road along Gorgie Road as far as Robertson Avenue.
5. A double line extension from the Coltbridge terminus to Murrayfield Avenue.
6. A new double line from Earl Grey Street, through Brougham Street, Melville Drive, and Marchmont Road to join the Grange route towards Salisbury Place.
7. A single line from Home Street round Thornybauk to the proposed new Tollcross cable power station and car shed.
8. A similar single line from Earl Grey Street by Wellington Street to the new car shed.
9. Doubling of the single line track in North Bridge, together with street widening.
10. Doubling the existing Churchhill-Morningside branch.
11. Doubling the single line parts of Dalry Road.

There was difficulty over No. 3 and this was dropped, but it came up again as No. 6 in the following year's Act, which is dealt with below. There had also been a proposal to seek a route via the Middle Meadow Walk to Warrender Park Road with automatic barriers to exclude other vehicles from the Meadows, but this was not pursued.

Meanwhile twenty-one years had now elapsed since the Portobello route had been completed, so the Corporation gave notice on 8 January

1895 of their intention to purchase the line from Waterloo Place to Jock's Lodge. The company contended that this was premature, arguing that the twenty-one years should be counted from when the double line was constructed under their Act of 1881. Again Henry Tennant was called to arbitrate and found for the Corporation, who duly took over the line on 31 January 1896 whereupon it became part of the system leased to the Edinburgh & District Tramways Company. The changing of horses and men at Jock's Lodge, which of course followed, was not such an inconvenience as at Pilrig, there being only a relatively sparse service. As at Pilrig the cars were taken through, but in this case there was no through booking. The arbiter awarded the company £13,615.

Another Act of 1896, the Edinburgh Extension Act, brought the burgh of Portobello within the city's boundaries. By this Act Edinburgh had sought also to annex Leith, but the Leithers still would have none of it, and secured the rejection of that part of the Bill. While Leith's insistence on her continued independence was quite natural, her council's attitude to the tramway situation now became somewhat difficult to understand.

The Edinburgh Improvement & Tramways Act of 1896 has already been dealt with, but one of its proposals which did not materialise sought power for Edinburgh Corporation to purchase the Edinburgh Street Tramways Company's system in Leith, subject to the company's willingness to sell, and to certain rights reserved to Leith Corporation. Both the Edinburgh Street Tramways Company and Leith Corporation petitioned against the Bill, and the Select Committee examining it would not agree to this power without Leith Corporation's agreement, which was not forthcoming. The Select Committee then went on to examine another Bill promoted by the Edinburgh Street Tramways Company which contained a counter proposal seeking running powers for them over the whole of the Edinburgh system, again with the object of providing through services and avoiding changing horses and men at Pilrig. Mr John S. Adam, the Edinburgh Street Tramways Company's secretary and manager, and others, made much of the delays at Pilrig. Of course the Edinburgh & District Tramways Company objected to this proposal, and the committee rejected it too, so that neither side gained any advantage.

The Edinburgh Street Tramways Act 1896, passed 7 August 1896, did however provide for the company selling their undertaking by arrangement, and with Board of Trade approval, at any time, notwithstanding the terms of the agreement attached to their 1892 Act. Section 27 provided for the winding up of the company in this event. Some further extensions were also authorised, however:

1. A double line extension from Portobello to Joppa. This was to be completed by 1 September 1897, and if the Portobello tracks were acquired by the local authority this extension was to be included.
2. A short single line linking up the Bernard Street and Commercial Street termini.
3. An extension, partly double and partly single, from the Stanley Road

terminus, down through Newhaven and along Annfield and Lindsay Road to join the Commercial Street line.

4. A double line junction from the foregoing into North Junction Street.

Although the Bernard Street and Commercial Street termini were quite close there was of course the harbour between, spanned by an old narrow drawbridge. The need for a new bridge was in any case generally accepted. It belonged to the Dock Commission; the Tramways Company wanted to use it; who was to pay? The result was that the Dock Commission agreed to build a new swing-bridge, with Leith Corporation and the Edinburgh Street Tramways Company each to contribute £1,500 towards the cost. The foregoing tramway extensions in Leith were to be completed within three years of the completion of the new bridge.

The Edinburgh authorities were still continuing their overtures for the extension of the cable system into Leith, but notwithstanding the undertaking in the 1892 Act, Leith Town Council seem now to have made up their minds to keep the cables out of the burgh. Nevertheless, when the plans for the new bridge were put before them in January 1897 they refused to approve them on the grounds that they did not appear capable of accommodating a cable system, and argued against paying their contribution to the Dock Commission. On the other hand the Edinburgh Street Tramways Company approved the plans. Sir William Armstrong's tender for the new bridge was accepted in February 1897 and on 24 May the old bridge was closed. Construction of the new bridge proceeded slowly and there was much complaint at the delay. A newspaper leader referred to the presence of "occasionally two men and a boy" and "the clang of a hammer may even be heard". However, early in February 1898 the new bridge was at last ready. It had cost £8,000, and when the Dock Commission sought their £1,500 the Tramways Company declined to hand over the money till they were satisfied of its suitability by actual use. This quibble caused a further week's delay and the bridge was then opened for ordinary traffic on 17 February. It was worked by hydraulic power from the Bernard Street side.

Preparation of the plans for the haulage cables in Edinburgh was now under way, and eventually, in March 1896, Dick Kerr & Company's tender for the work was accepted from among fourteen offers. Soon afterwards a start was made on the construction of the two new power-houses at Shrubhill and Tollcross, and on the laying of the aforementioned extensions as cable tracks, the policy being to work from the termini inwards towards Princes Street. Temporary tracks were laid through James Street and Dryden Street to enable the horse cars to reach the stables north of Dryden Street, which continued in use for the time being. These were lifted again in 1903.

But again the plans were amended as further extensions were thought desirable. Accordingly the Edinburgh Corporation Act 1897 (3 June 1897) provided for the following new tramways:

1. A further extension from Lady Road to Liberton Dams.
2. A further extension from the Braid Burn to the city boundary.

3. A further extension from Robertson Avenue to the city boundary.
4. A further extension from Murrayfield Avenue to the city boundary.
5. A double line from George IV Bridge down to the foot of the Mound.
6. A line, partly single and partly double, from the top of Marchmont Road through Strathearn Road and Strathearn Place which was to be continued through into Greenhill Gardens by the acquisition and demolition of some property. Thus this new line would join into the existing line again in Churchhill.
7. A double line from Lothian Road down Morrison Street into Dalry Road.
8. A double line from Leith Walk along London Road to Abbeyhill.
9. A single line extension from the Colinton Road terminus to the city boundary. It also provided that the old routes from George IV Bridge down the High Street to Tron Church and from the top of Marchmont Road via Hope Terrace and Clinton Road to Churchhill would be abandoned and lifted.

An important part of the 1897 Act was Section 20 which authorised the Corporation to acquire the Edinburgh Northern Tramways Company's existing cable system which is described in the next chapter.

Meanwhile the Edinburgh Street Tramways Company's extension to Joppa had been opened in May 1897. A local group proposed an independent extension to Musselburgh but nothing came of the proposal at that time. The Portobello outpost of the Edinburgh Street Tramways Company was of course now within the City of Edinburgh and the Corporation would have the option to purchase in 1899.

Throughout 1897 the tramway situation was debated at length by Leith Town Council. The Edinburgh Street Tramways Company sought permission to install cable traction between Pilrig and the Foot of Leith Walk in accordance with the terms of their 1892 agreement. For the sake of through running with Edinburgh's future cable system, one section of the council would have agreed to this being done if the cable could have been continued to Bernard Street, but the company pointed out the narrowness of Constitution Street and to their lack of authority for such extension. Most of the council, however, had already come to the conclusion that electric traction was the coming thing, and thought it better to suffer the Pilrig muddle rather than commit Leith to cables. A passenger shelter could be erected at Pilrig. The Edinburgh Street Tramways Company were not now in a good financial position; their system was now too small to be profitable. They were, however, making the most of their opportunities with their buses which now outnumbered their cars. There was some scope for bus activities at this time as the car services in Edinburgh were being subjected to delays on account of the extensive relaying for the cable system.

So in April 1897 the Edinburgh Street Tramways Company offered their system to Leith Corporation at a figure of about £80,000, but Leith considered this too much. Negotiations were continued slowly, however, and the Edinburgh lessees were asked if, and on what terms, they would

Horse cars and country buses at the Waverley Steps, c. 1898. Note the hoarding in St. Andrew Street where the new cable pit is under construction. The bus in the foreground is for Loanhead and the furthest away one is for Roslin, while all three "brakes" in between are plying to the Forth Bridge.

lease the Leith part of the system from Leith Corporation if the latter bought it.

Early in 1898, Edinburgh Corporation agreed to purchase, on 30 June 1898 by voluntary agreement, the remainder of the Portobello line for £40,000, and this induced the Edinburgh Street Tramways Company tentatively to agree to a reduced price for the Leith system. Although this was still a good deal higher than the maximum which Leith Town Council had had in mind in 1895, they now agreed to proceed with the deal, the provost alone objecting. It was intended that the change of ownership and leasing to the "Edinburgh lessees" should take place at the end of June 1898, and with this in view the two companies set out to negotiate a temporary arrangement whereby the horses and men would run through at Pilrig as from 15 March. In the event, a dispute developed at the last minute regarding the apportioning of the receipts and the arrangement fell through. The Edinburgh & District Tramways Company now fully expected a twenty-one-year lease of the Leith system from 30 June 1898, and as will be seen in the next chapter, arranged a new lease with Edinburgh Corporation to run concurrently from that date.

It will be remembered, however, that the Edinburgh & District Tramways Company's present lease from Edinburgh Corporation had never been ratified by the Board of Trade, and when Leith Town Council held a special meeting in April 1898 to confirm their decision, the question was asked: who are the legal lessees of the Edinburgh system? This was sufficient to defer the matter again while enquiries were made regarding the legal standing of the Edinburgh & District Tramways Company. So another special meeting was held on 24 May, at which no answer to the enquiries about the Edinburgh & District Tramways Company was available. It was, moreover, now suggested that there was friction between the company and Edinburgh Corporation. In addition there was now a hitch regarding the taking over of the Edinburgh Street Tramways Company's contract with an advertising concern. So again there was no action. By the next special meeting on 14 June the matter was no further forward, and the same situation pertained on 5 July. The Leith councillors were by now losing interest and on this occasion there was not a quorum for the meeting. For the time being, therefore, the whole matter was dropped, and Edinburgh Corporation advised accordingly.

The latter thereupon asked Leith Corporation to allow them to buy the system from the Edinburgh Street Tramways Company, as they had wanted to do two years earlier. As before, Leith Town Council were not interested in this suggestion, and after allowing the holiday period to pass, replied that they intended to buy the Leith system themselves, and could not agree to its purchase by Edinburgh. After so much vacillation, this gave the local press much ammunition. Why not let Edinburgh buy it and get rid of "The Muddle" at Pilrig?

In view of the foregoing, the Edinburgh Street Tramways Company had, of course, done nothing about their authorised extensions, but as it was now evident that Leith Corporation were not going to take over the

Edinburgh & District Tramways Company horse car No. 88 of latest garden seat type, built at Shrubhill in 1896. It is seen at the Murrayfield terminus on the newly laid cable track. (*A. W. Brotchie*)

system, nor allow cable traction below Pilrig, the company made a start with the connection between Bernard Street and Commercial Street. This was completed early in 1899. The new line from Stanley Road through Newhaven, Annfield, and Lindsay Road to Commercial Street was also put in hand, and this was ready and inspected by Col. Yorke for the Board of Trade on 29 March 1900.

During all this period there had been few material alterations in the pattern of car services. At the beginning of 1896 an hourly service was run from the Post Office to Polwarth Terrace via Dalry, while from 9 February extra cars which had been running between Morningside Drive and the Post Office were extended to Meadowbank. Towards the end of that year a service was tried between Tollcross and Haymarket by extending some of the Tron Church-Tollcross cars, no doubt to meet the bus competition, but by May 1897 it had been taken off again, and the Post Office to Polwarth Terrace via Dalry followed at the end of the year.

The extensions to the Edinburgh system were completed during 1897 and on 18 December the services were pushed out to the new termini at Murrayfield, Gorgie, Braid Hills, and Nether Liberton. The new lines along London Road to Abbeyhill and from Tollcross via Melville Drive to Marchmont were also completed. The Braid Hills to Meadowbank cars now ran via the former new line and from about July 1898 were extended to Portobello, while a service over the latter from the Post Office to Marchmont started in the summer of 1897. At the beginning of 1898 a new afternoon service was put on between Newington Station and Braids, later extended to Nether Liberton and then cut to Morningside Drive. Some cars were also run through between Portobello and Murrayfield.

Edinburgh & District Tramways Company horse car converted to garden seat type with trace horse assisting up the hill past the University to Surgeons' Hall.
(*A. W. Brotchie*)

From about this time the Edinburgh & District Tramways Company ceased painting the cars in the different colours for the various routes, the colour scheme now becoming the maroon and white which has persisted in the city. It was, however, some years before all the cars in their various colours were gradually repainted in the standard livery.

As is related in the next chapter, the Edinburgh & District Tramways Company succeeded in making a trial of the first part of their cable system between Pilrig and St. Andrew Street on 1 June 1899, and so claimed that the cable system should now be introduced below Pilrig also, in accordance with the terms of the 1892 agreement between the Edinburgh Street Tramways Company and Leith Town Council. To this it was retorted that a trial over part of the system could not be accepted as implementing the conditions which would call for such action, and a regular cable service not having been introduced by 1 June 1899 there was no longer any obligation to install the cable in Leith.

On 1 June 1899 also, the Board of Trade inspected the new route along Strathearn Road and Strathearn Place, and the horse car service was transferred to it from the narrow twisting Hope Terrace and Clinton Road route. Strathearn Place was also narrow, but instead of having an orthodox single line, was laid with closely interlaced rails with one common conduit and slot for the future cable. The object of this was to avoid the noise associated with points. There was also a short single line section in Strathearn Road. The old line through Clinton Road was lifted in February 1900. On 31 July 1899 the Post Office-Melville Drive-Marchmont service was extended by Grange Road and the Bridges to form the circular route so well known in more modern days. It was, however, then called the Inner Circle to distinguish it from the old Morningside Circle proceeding via Churchhill. This Inner Circle with a ten minutes service and a fare of threepence was, however, run in the anti-clockwise direction only, the other direction being covered by the diversion of the Commercial Street to Churchhill cars down by Marchmont Road, Tollcross, and Princes Street back to Leith. At the other end of the route, the rails in Bernard Street having been linked to Commercial Street via the new bridge, the cars to Bernard Street and to Commercial Street were making a circle of the two routes back to town.

Then on Monday 23 October 1899 the major change took place due to the introduction of cable haulage from Pilrig to Edinburgh, as will be dealt with in the next chapter. Through services between Edinburgh and Leith then ceased, and the Edinburgh Street Tramways Company were left to provide services between Pilrig and Seafield (every fifteen minutes), Pilrig and Bernard Street (every seven minutes), Pilrig via Commercial Street and Bernard Street (every fifteen minutes), and Pilrig and Stanley Road (every ten minutes). On 2 April 1900 the latter was extended along the new route through Newhaven, Commercial Street and Bernard Street back to Pilrig forming the Outer Circle, though the Inner Circle which had been formed on the connection over Bernard Street bridge then ceased, a fifteen minutes service being provided from

Pilrig to Commercial Street, and additional part-day cars from Pilrig to Bernard Street. On 5 April 1900 the Edinburgh Street Tramways Company announced their intention of turning back the Seafield cars at Pirniefield, but following representations agreed to run every third car to the end of the line. The halfpenny fares were withdrawn at this date also. A threehalfpenny fare now applied between Pilrig and Stanley Road, Pilrig and Annfield via Bernard Street and between Foot of Leith Walk and Pier Place either way. Williamson's punch-type tickets with the stage names in "fareboard" layout were now in use; the 1½d. one was white.

At this time horse cars were still at work on various routes in Edinburgh pending their conversion to cable haulage, and it will be convenient now to leave their dwindling record till we deal with the installation of the cables in the next chapter.

Returning to the political scene, negotiations were reopened between Edinburgh & District Tramways Company — who were now undoubtedly the Edinburgh lessees — Leith Town Council, and the Edinburgh Street Tramways Company. In January 1900 the former company made an offer to lease the system from them if they would purchase it from the Edinburgh Street Tramways Company, as had been proposed in earlier years. Their offer did not satisfy the council however, and in March the Edinburgh & District Tramways Company made a further offer. In this they undertook to extend the cable system to the Foot of Leith Walk, and to electrify the remainder of the Leith system. They offered Leith 7 per cent on the capital expenditure on the cable system and 5 per cent on the remainder. Edinburgh Corporation of course would have received 7 per cent on the additional capital expenditure at the Shrubhill power station where provision had been made for installing power to drive a cable in Leith. By April, figures had been more or less settled in respect of the Edinburgh Street Tramways Company's assets, and the Edinburgh & District Tramways Company had amended their offer to 6 per cent on the whole system, undertaking to carry out the cable part immediately and the remainder within four years. The Leith folk and their council were still divided on the question, one objection still being the change from cable to the future electric car being transferred from Pilrig to the hub of their system at the Foot of Leith Walk. A special ratepayers' meeting was held. However, when the town council discussed the matter on 18 May 1900 they were unable to come to terms with either party, the Edinburgh Street Tramways Company refusing to make a reduction in the price asked for their Morton Place premises, and the Edinburgh & District Tramways Company refusing to agree to the Corporation's proposed charge of 1½d. per unit for electric current from their new electricity station. It all had a familiar ring; and so the matter was dropped once more. Nevertheless the tracks in Leith Walk and Constitution Street were relaid in 1901, the former sufficiently far apart to allow for centre poles in the future.

By 1902 public dissatisfaction with the position in Leith was nevertheless increasing. The cars were said to be dirty and obsolete. Once again, in March 1903, a special committee of Leith Town Council met to consider the matter: something really had to be done now before the statutory opportunity of taking over the company arose again in 1906. A further valuation of the Edinburgh Street Tramways Company's undertaking was made and on 1 June the committee met the Edinburgh Street Tramways Company's chairman James Clark and the directors, and offered £60,000 for their system. The company's financial position was now such that the directors found this acceptable. Consequently a formal resolution was passed by the council on 23 July and confirmed on 1 September. There was still some opposition from a section of the ratepayers and a plebiscite was sought, but this was rejected. Accordingly a Provisional Order was promoted to enable the Corporation to work the system, and Board of Trade approval for its transfer from the company sought. In order to protect itself from possible competition by the old company continuing its bus operations, Section 12 of the Agreement scheduled to the Order required the company to wind up its affairs forthwith and "cease to exist".

With the matter now so far arranged, Leith Town Council this time made an approach to the Edinburgh & District Tramways Company. They suggested the Edinburgh & District Tramways Company might lease their system and electrify it, and also equip the route up Leith Walk and York Place to a proposed siding in the south side of St. Andrew Square for electric traction. If Edinburgh Corporation refused permission for this, they suggested the electric cars could be taken on over the cable system by putting on a cable gripper at Pilrig. Visits were paid to London to see such a scheme in operation there. The company, however, rejected this as impracticable. While they were not anxious to extend the cable system they considered the only way of providing through cars between Edinburgh and Leith was to extend the cable to the Foot of Leith Walk, on which they again offered 7 per cent. But Leith was by now firmly against any cable traction in the burgh, and so negotiations terminated again, this time finally. All that remained to be done now was the transfer of the Edinburgh Street Tramways Company's undertaking, including 29 cars and 200 horses, to Leith Corporation, as provided under their Provisional Order of 1904. This is recorded in the chapter on Leith Corporation Tramways, which also continues the final months of the horse cars in the burgh.

Finally, we have to revert to 1891 to complete the story of the horse bus services. This was a decade of considerable activity by the Edinburgh Street Tramways Company in this field, but it may be noted that one or two of the services to be mentioned were run by other operators.

First, some provisions of the Edinburgh Municipal and Police (Amendment) Act 1891 should now be mentioned. By Section 64 of this Act "It shall be lawful for the Magistrates to license all tramway cars, omnibuses, brakes, or other carriages . . .". Drivers and conductors had similarly to be licensed, and the licence fees were stipulated. Section 65 empowered the magistrates to make by-laws to prevent the running of unlicensed or unsound vehicles and the use of unlicensed drivers and conductors, the prevention of overcrowding, and the regulation of stances and times. Railway companies' vehicles plying from railway stations were exempted from the Act.

The bylaws for tramway cars were duly drawn up and approved by the Sheriff on 3 July 1893. They provided for the licensing and maintaining in good repair of the brakes, steps, handrails, seating, lighting, ventilation etc. of all tramway cars; required the display of licence number, seating capacity, maximum fare and route, all in letters and figures of stipulated size; regulated the behaviour of drivers and conductors; specified stances and places where cars might, or might not, stop; and many other similar matters. The similar bylaws for omnibuses were approved on 16 February 1894. In each case one series of licence number was used. At that time, of course, only horse-buses were thought of, and only horse and cable cars.

The bylaws were of course amended from time to time, up to 1926. Provision had to be made for changing circumstances, the introduction of motor buses and other matters, as well as new routes and stances. Many of the requirements regarding tramcars were later dropped when the tramway system came under direct Corporation control, and were also subject to Board of Trade and, later, Ministry of Transport safeguards, but until 1930 buses continued to be inspected by the Corporation's Hackney Carriage Inspector.

About August 1891 a bus was put on running every fifteen minutes between the Mound and the foot of Easter Road via London Road. About November 1891 another service was started between the Mound

Edinburgh Street Tramways Company three-horse bus No. 66 at Corstorphine, running to the car terminus at Coltbridge. Note the conductor's ticket rolls.

and Warrender Park, via George IV Bridge and Bristo, while the Edinburgh Northern Tramways Company took off their Goldenacre-Trinity Crescent run for the winter. November 1891 saw two more Edinburgh Street Tramways Company services, viz. Cameron Toll to Angle Park Terrace every half-hour, which was a revival of an earlier route; and West End to Ravelston Park every half-hour, which was quite new. In the summer of 1892 the Edinburgh Northern Tramways Company's Newhaven service was increased to fifteen minutes frequency, alternate journeys proceeding via Trinity and the Chain Pier, then popular with bathers. A service from Waverley Steps to Lasswade four times a day was also put on during this summer and the following.

In their submission to the Board of Trade in July 1892 the Edinburgh Street Tramways Company quoted their bus routes as:

Loanhead	1 bus	15 horses
Dalkeith	1 bus	13 horses
Corstorphine	1 bus	13 horses
Cameron Toll	3 buses	18 horses
Ravelston Park	1 bus	6 horses

Early in 1893 the Coltbridge-Corstorphine service was increased in the afternoons, and shortly had a competitor running approximately every two hours from the West End (Hope Street) to Corstorphine, but this did not last out the year. The Goldenacre-Granton, West End-Ravelston Park, and Mound-Warrender Park services were also withdrawn. About the end of 1893 a fifteen minutes service was tried between Post Office and Haymarket, but lasted only some weeks. In the summer of 1894 the Angle Park Terrace-Cameron Toll route was cut to Hope Park Terrace except during rush hours. A new country connection was available between Dalkeith and Pathhead. This was provided by a Mr Cowing using "brakes". On Sundays he started from Eskbank. In October 1894 the Cramond bus ceased to run consequent on the opening of the railway branch to Davidson's Mains and Barnton. The Mound-Easter Road route was also withdrawn.

On 20 May 1895 a bus was again started by the Edinburgh Street Tramways Company between Portobello and Musselburgh, and ran every hour. For the summer the Roslin route was reinstated on 17 June, and the other country routes increased in frequency. It is interesting to note that at this time the Glasgow Tramways and Omnibus Company took up the hiring business in the Edinburgh district, having bought some of Croall's premises, and they put a bus on the Roslin route. From 30 September 1895 the Edinburgh Street Tramways Company put on a bus every hour between Trinity Crescent and Seafield car terminus via Commercial Street and Bernard Street, but on 4 November this was replaced by an hourly Bernard Street-Granton run. There was already an established service on this route of course, and three weeks later Mr Henry Whitelaw took over the operation of the route from the Edinburgh Street Tramways Company. On 28 December 1895 the Edinburgh Street Tramways Company started an hourly service between Junction Street and Dean

A three-horse bus run by the Glasgow Tramways & Omnibus Company on the country route to Roslin from Edinburgh.

Park Street, Stockbridge via Bellevue. This proved popular and was soon increased to a half-hour frequency, and extended via Henderson Street to Bernard Street. In the following spring the Bernard Street-Dean Park Street, and Bernard Street-Granton routes were linked up to form a circular route.

At this time the construction of the cable tramway system was in full swing, and the work inevitably caused delays and inconveniences to the horse car services. The bus operators, including the Edinburgh Street Tramways Company, made the most of the opportunity. In May 1896 the latter advertised their services as follows:

1. Echo Bank to Gorgie every half-hour.
2. Hope Park Terrace to Gorgie every quarter-hour.
3. Bernard Street-Dean Park Street and
4. Bernard Street-Granton, running through to form a circle, every half-hour.
5. Coltbridge to Corstorphine every half-hour.
6. Portobello to Musselburgh every half-hour (hourly in the mornings).
7. Loanhead, four journeys daily.
8. Dalkeith, four journeys daily.
9. Roslin, three journeys daily.

On 4 May the company put on a new service every fifteen minutes from Grange Loan to Haymarket via Marchmont Road and Tollcross. Also that summer a bus was run between Morningside station and Mortonhall. There was one morning journey and then hourly from 11.00 to 4.00. On

Tuesdays and Thursdays the morning and one afternoon trip were extended to Lothianburn. The Portobello-Musselburgh Cross service became half-hourly and the Hope Park Terrace-Gorgie service every fifteen minutes. The Grange to the Mound route was restarted. Then on 10 August 1896 they introduced another fifteen minutes service from Grange Loan to West End running via Oswald Road, Grange Terrace, Causewayside, Bristo, George IV Bridge, Johnston Terrace and Castle Terrace. The Grange to the Mound route was also extended to West End. New fare stages including halfpenny and threehalfpenny fares were introduced, but although the company's bus traffic generally was flourishing, the Grange district was being over served and retrenchment became necessary. The new Grange to West End via Johnston Terrace route was therefore withdrawn from 2 November, while the older route via the Mound was again shortened to the latter point, and the Grange Loan to Haymarket route became Marchmont Road to Haymarket. At the same time some of the company's other services were increased in frequency, and the Cameron Toll to Angle Park Terrace route extended along Slateford Road.

From 14 December 1896 the Corstorphine bus was extended in to Haymarket and combined with the Haymarket-Marchmont route. The Edinburgh & District Tramways Company had itself entered the field earlier in that year with the circular horse bus service running via London Road, Easter Road, Albert Street and Leith Walk, every half-hour. This, however, lasted only till the following summer. About the end of 1896 a fifteen minutes service was put on between the Mound and Blackford Avenue via Causewayside. There was also a short-lived fifteen minutes service in the afternoons from Foot of Leith Walk to Newhaven. In the spring of 1897 another Southside route was started between the Mound and Mayfield Road (Wilton Road) integrating with the Blackford Avenue one.

For the summer of 1897 the Edinburgh Street Tramways Company's Portobello to Musselburgh run became Joppa to Levenhall, as the car service was now extended to Joppa. Later in the year, the Corstorphine to Marchmont route was cut to Corstorphine and Tollcross, and soon afterwards Corstorphine and Haymarket.

During the summer of 1898 a bus was again run to Cramond, four times daily. The Hope Park-Dalry service was increased in frequency, some journeys being extended to Cameron Toll and to Slateford. Later in the year the Corstorphine bus was extended to West End, and, early in 1899, again extended to the Mound. About May 1899 every other bus on the Slateford route was extended to Inglis Green, but this only lasted a few weeks. The Musselburgh-Portobello bus was extended through to Bernard Street, Leith, for the summer on 27 May, fare 5d. In June the Wilton Road terminus was altered to Lygon Road from where the vehicles returned by way of Wilton Road. November 1899 saw further services to the Southside, viz. Mound to Newington and Echo Bank, and Mound to Melville Terrace. These direct Mound to Southside services

Edinburgh & District Tramways Company's horse bus on the short-lived circular route between Leith Walk and Easter Road, 1896.

had become popular and it became the custom for the Edinburgh Street Tramways Company's manager to receive a subscription from the regular travellers for the bus crews at New Year time.

From 2 April 1900 the Leith-Granton bus ran only between Newhaven and Granton by reason of the tramway extensions through Newhaven. In the summer of 1900 some of the Loanhead buses were extended to Lasswade, and an additional service run from Waverley Steps to Liberton via Captain's Road, but the former did not last many weeks. On 29 October 1900 the Edinburgh Street Tramways Company started a new fifteen minutes service from Bonnington Terrace via Bonnington Toll, East Claremont Street, and Broughton Street to the Mound. This lasted until about the following April, when the Captain's Road and Liberton service also disappeared. The Lasswade route was revived in the summer of 1901, but soon after, the Dalkeith route was cut short at Gilmerton. A new fifteen minutes service was started between Angle Park Terrace and Tron Church via Tollcross and Chambers Street. For the summer of 1902 the Dalkeith and Lasswade runs were revived and the Corstorphine bus started from the Waverley Steps along with the other country services.

Improved alternative transport was making itself felt, however, including the cable car service which was now in full swing. Some of the Edinburgh Street Tramways Company's services became uneconomic and a retrenchment was necessary. By the end of 1902 the only remaining horse buses were plying between Leith and Stockbridge half-hourly; Tron Church-Tollcross-Robertson Avenue every ten minutes; Angle Park Terrace-Tollcross every ten minutes and extended to Hope Park Terrace in the afternoons. There was also a half-hourly service from Tron Church to Slateford on Saturday afternoons, and of course the half-hourly services from Goldenacre to Newhaven, and Newhaven to Granton. The Musselburgh-Portobello route still ran, extended to Bernard Street in the summer, while the Corstorphine bus was now only hourly and ran from Haymarket. Then there were still the other country routes to Gilmerton, Loanhead and Roslin, with Dalkeith in the summer also.

Later in 1903 some of the Hope Park Terrace buses were again extended to Echo Bank, while others went to Montague Street. When the Leith Corporation Tramways Order was before Parliament in 1904, the Edinburgh & District Tramways Company lodged a petition to secure their release from their obligation, as successors to the Edinburgh Northern Tramways Company, to run the Goldenacre-Newhaven service. Though this did not materialise, the company interpreted the provisions of the Leith Act as transferring the obligation to Leith Corporation. The latter of course disagreed but the company ceased to run the service after 27 August 1904 in spite of protest.

At the end of 1904, in accordance with the Act, the Edinburgh Street Tramways Company had to be wound up and its operations ceased. The Newhaven-Granton bus was taken over by Leith Corporation who maintained the route till the extension of their tramways to Granton in 1909, after which it was tried briefly from Seafield to Portobello. George

Hall, the Edinburgh Street Tramways Company's contractor for the Corstorphine route, continued this route. The Leith-Stockbridge, Tron Church-Tollcross-Robertson Avenue, and Angle Park Terrace-Hope Park Terrace route were also continued by other contractors. The other routes ceased. A bus painted red and cream, which the North British Railway had run to Levenhall, connecting with the trains at Musselburgh station, also ceased with the opening of the Musselburgh tramways. In January 1905 the Leith-Stockbridge route was extended to Craigleith station and Blackhall but this lasted only a couple of months. In April the Angle Park Terrace-Tollcross-Hope Park route was diverted via Lauriston Place to the Infirmary, and in May George Hall operated from Brougham Street to Angle Park Terrace only, using "brakes".

So at the beginning of 1906 there were only the Leith-Stockbridge, and Tron Church-Robertson Avenue routes left in addition to Leith Corporation's Newhaven-Granton route. The Corstorphine route had succumbed immediately to the newly formed Scottish Motor Traction Company's motor bus. The horses had served the city well and were still trundling the old cars from Tollcross to Colinton Road. As this tramway route was not run on Sundays a horse bus now covered the route on that day. But horses were displaced there too on 24 August 1907, by which time Leith Corporation's horse bus route was the only regular one left. The Leith-Stockbridge route apparently ceased regular operation in the summer of 1906 but continued to be run spasmodically until early in 1907. Two horse buses were still licensed in 1910 but thereafter there were none.

Nevertheless, even though the buses had gone, four-in-hand "brakes" were still to be seen running to Roslin, Carlops, Cramond, Queensferry etc. in the summer. In the summer of 1911 there was basically a twenty-minute service to Queensferry and to Roslin operated by Dan T. Munro, Adam Cramond, James Anthony, with three vehicles each, Croall, Player, James Stewart, W. Fraser & Son, with two vehicles each, and George Hall with one vehicle. Twenty-nine "brakes" were licensed at this time. Dan T. Munro had five named "Lord Roberts", "Waverley", "Defender", "Queen Mary" and "Ivanhoe". George Hall's "Rob Roy" ran to Queensferry at a fare of 1 shilling or 1/6 return. The stance for these routes was changed to Waterloo Place in 1913. The First World War brought a drastic reduction in the number of these, though such machines were occasionally seen in use in the early twenties, four being still licensed in 1923 and two lasting until 1926. Baillie's small horse-drawn wagonette still plied between Barnton station and Cramond until about 1920; he used a closed vehicle in winter. George Hall still advertised his "brakes" to run to Carlops up till the spring holiday in 1922. The return fare was then 4 shillings. Afterwards these firms concentrated on the cab and taxi business.

Some years ago the remains of one of the old horse buses was discovered on a farm near Pencaitland. With a fitting appreciation of its historical value, the dilapidated machine was acquired for preservation

One of the Edinburgh Street Tramways Company's earliest horse cars, carrying licence plate No. 4, on the Bernard Street to Haymarket route at the Post Office about 1875.

by the City Transport Department, who thoroughly rehabilitated it and painted it in dark blue and cream with the Edinburgh & District Tramways Company's name and crest etc.

Some details of the tramway rolling-stock should now be given.

The Edinburgh Street Tramways Company initially ordered twenty cars from the British & Foreign Tramways Co. Limited whose then recently established works were at Greenwich. These cars were rather box-like affairs, 14ft. long with seven windows, above which were ventilators, on each side. There was a longitudinal back-to-back seat, colloquially called a "knifeboard", on the flat roof, to which access was gained from very short end platforms 2ft. 6in. long by a nearly vertical ladder twisted through 180° from the off-side of the platform in what was later called the "reverse stair" direction. The overall length was thus 19ft. The wheelbase was 5ft., the disc wheels being carried in trunnions with only a rubber block for springing. They weighed 47cwt. and seated 18 inside and 18 on top. These cars were immediately found to be too heavy and inconvenient and it seems likely that no more than twelve were delivered.

Sixteen lighter cars were added in 1872, the first of them in February, built in Edinburgh by John Croall & Sons. They weighed 14cwt. less and had much better platforms and stairs of orthodox construction ascending in the ordinary direction. There were six windows and crimson curtains were fitted. They seated 14 inside and 18 outside, and the wheels, which had a series of holes in them, had axleboxes under double elliptical springs. Others of the 1872 cars were built by R. J. Boyall of Grantham and Drew & Burnett of Edinburgh, the latter being Nos. 23 and 24.

These cars were certainly an improvement on the original ones but the company were not yet satisfied, and in 1873 "a new set of extra light cars" was obtained. They are believed to have been built in Scotland but the maker is not known.

In 1874 the company's fleet included four buses for the Trinity and Stockbridge routes, and in 1875 a further six buses, together with seventy horses were bought from John Croall & Sons. At this time there appear to have been 39 cars.

In May 1876 an "open toast-rack" car was introduced on the Portobello route. This had ten rows of seats for six passengers, with reversible backs.

The company's report for the half-year to June 1877 refers to most of the types of car then running being "unsuitable".

They were still trying to find better cars and hence two cars were obtained from John Stephenson & Co. of New York in May 1877. The average life of British-built cars at that period seems to have been about nine or ten years, whereas Stephenson's cars were said to last much longer. These American cars were larger, had eight windows and seated 54. Intended for the Portobello route but proving too cumbersome, they had been transferred to the Morningside circular route. The cars running to Leith had been reduced in size and a larger number of horses used. This latter seems to refer to the original lot of cars, some or all of which were apparently shortened in 1874-5, and then had only five windows and seated 14 inside and 16 outside. In December 1877 two cars were obtained from the Starbuck Company of Birkenhead, which aroused comment on the "glaring colours" in which they were painted. These larger cars, which seated 16 inside and 22 outside, appear to have given satisfaction, and although better horses were needed for them, they were considered to be more profitable. They were placed on the Leith-Haymarket route. Boyall of Grantham, whose cars were considered to be the best of the earlier acquisitions, also supplied three more cars in 1877 for the routes from Leith. In all these new cars polished wood seats were used instead of stuffed squabs as hitherto.

The company appointed a new rolling-stock superintendent, Mr Booth, and in 1879 commenced building new cars at their own works, mainly to replace the older ones which were already worn out and discarded. The first appeared in May. In August of the same year a single-ended car for the circular route was produced. This had eight windows and seated 50. Two or three more of the same type were subsequently built, and it is said that the two Stephenson cars were converted to this type for a time. Others of the old cars were completely rebuilt, some being provided with orthodox stairs ascending in the ordinary direction, but because of the shortness of the platforms the bottom of these stairs protruded outside the dash panels. In 1881 the company decided that no more cars would be ordered from outside builders, all construction to be

The single-ended body of this 1882 car revolved on a centre pin to face the opposite way on reaching the terminus. An arrangement known as Eades. (*A. W. Brotchie*)

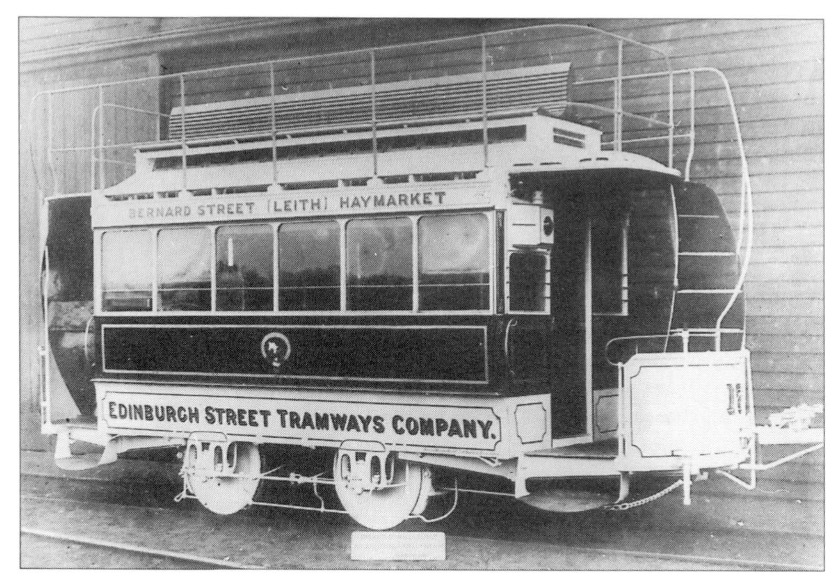

One of the cars built by Brown Marshall & Company of Birmingham in the early eighties. (*A. W. Brotchie*)

undertaken at the company's works, but this did not prove practicable, and about this time, Brown Marshall and Co. Limited of Birmingham also built some cars for the company. These had six windows and their numbers included 14, 15 and 17. At the end of 1881 the fleet consisted of sixty cars and sixteen buses, and at the end of 1882 there were sixty-seven cars, nine of them being open "toast-racks".

Another new type of car appeared on the Leith-Haymarket route in April 1882. These were built on Eades' reversible principle, whereby the whole body revolved on a centre pin on a truck so that on withdrawing a pin, the horse merely walked round with it at the terminus. About seven cars of this type are said to have been built. Like the single-ended cars, they had, of course, a platform and a stair at the rear only, and had seven windows. The design was not perpetuated however: no doubt the orthodox method of unhooking the spreader bar and shaft from the car and walking the horse round with the driver holding up the spreader bar was really simpler. One of these cars was apparently sold to the Stirling & Bridge of Allan Tramway Company, and others are said to have finished their days on the Morningside circular route.

In the first half of 1883 a further open car was added to the stock and also four ordinary cars which were said to be of a lighter and improved type and which were not provided with seats on top, being thus single-deck cars. They had six windows and were built by Hyslop & Co., Edinburgh, for use on the route to Morningside. Two additional ordinary cars were built in the second half of 1883 so that at the end of that year the fleet comprised 64 ordinary cars (which the reports described as close cars) and ten open cars.

Up to this period, the cars carried the licence number issued by the magistrates for the duty in the timetable on which they operated. This number was shown on a plate fixed to the side of the car, so that the number could be changed if the car was removed from that particular service. The livery of most cars is believed to have been red and grey, but commencing on 29 April 1883 cars painted in different colours operated the different routes: at first red, blue and white, followed later by green and yellow, as has been noted on page 36. It seems that soon afterwards the numbers were permanently painted on the dash panels, as this subsequently became the magistrates' requirement, the vehicle and not its duty becoming the subject of the licence number. It is likely that the cars were thus initially numbered according to the duty licence numbers they then carried, spare cars such as the open "toast-racks" having been added at the end of the list. The latter were probably then Nos. 60-9. No. 65 was one of them and had a light wooden roof.

A new car of the company's standard design, seating 16 inside and 18 outside and with six windows, was exhibited at the Edinburgh Exhibition of 1886 and was awarded a gold medal. This was No. 45. A modification to this standard design was introduced in July 1887, in which the knifeboard seat on the top was replaced by transverse rows of garden seats. Suitable older cars thereafter had their knifeboard seat replaced by the transverse garden seats.

One of Edinburgh Street Tramways Company's long "canopy" horse cars of 1890, No. 98, as converted temporarily for use on the demonstration electric line at the Exhibition at Craiglockhart in that year. (*A. W. Brotchie*)

The fleet of buses had increased to eighteen in 1885, but by the end of 1889 this figure had reduced to ten with four coaches in addition. The total number of cars, however, had not changed much in this period, and at the end of 1889 there were 63 ordinary cars and ten open cars. In the following year four of the latter were scrapped, but yet another new type appeared, namely a long single-deck saloon car with eight windows and short end platforms. Ten of these cars were built in 1890-1, and were numbered 90-9. Two, Nos. 98 and 99, were hired by the Electrical Engineering Corporation of London and fitted up to work by electric power on their demonstration electric line at the exhibition at Craiglockhart in 1890. The old single-deck cars, one of which had been No. 82, had now been replaced by standard cars. The remaining open cars were now numbered 85-9 and 100, and some of them were altered to have a passageway down the centre to provide easier access.

In December 1893, when the Edinburgh Street Tramways Company had to relinquish their rights in the city, they had a stock of one hundred cars, including six open ones and the ten single-deck "canopy" cars. They also at that time had fifteen buses and four coaches. Of these the company retained 26 ordinary cars, two open cars and two canopy cars, and of course all the buses and coaches. The other 70 cars became the property of the Edinburgh & District Tramways Company. However, when the actual transfer took place in June 1894, a few cars were apparently unlicensed, some probably being under repair.

A list of the cars as then existing, showing which went to each company and also their colours and routes follows:

No.	*Owning Co.*	*Type*	*Seats*	*Colour*	*Route*
1	E.&D.T.Co.	K	36	White	Morningside Circle
2	''	''	''	''	'' ''
3	''	''	''	''	'' ''
4	''	''	''	''	'' ''
5	''	G	44	''	'' ''
6	''	''	52	''	'' ''
7	''	''	44	''	'' ''
8	''	''	''	''	'' ''
9	''	K	36	''	'' ''
10	''	''	''	''	'' ''
11	''	''	''	''	'' ''
12	''	G	52	''	'' ''
13	''	''	44	Red & White	Bernard St/N Merchiston
14	E.S.T.Co.	''	''	'' ''	'' ''
15	''	''	''	'' ''	'' ''
16	E.&D.T.Co.	''	''	'' ''	'' ''
17	''	''	''	Blue & White	Bernard St/Craigmillar Pk
18	''	''	''	'' ''	'' ''
19	''	''	''	'' ''	'' ''
20	E.S.T.Co.	K	36	'' ''	'' ''
21	''	G	44	'' ''	'' ''
22	E.&D.T.Co.	''	''	'' ''	'' ''
23	E.S.T.Co.	K	36	'' ''	Commercial St/Marchm't
24	E.&D.T.Co.	''	''	'' ''	'' ''
25	''	''	''	'' ''	'' ''
26	E.S.T.Co.	G	44	Buff & Green	Seafield/Gorgie
27	E.&D.T.Co.	''	''	'' ''	'' ''
28	E.S.T.Co.	''	''	'' ''	'' ''
29	''	K	38	Red—White	Bernard St/N Merchiston
30	''	''	''	'' ''	'' ''
31	''	G	44	Green & Buff	Seafield/Gorgie
32	''	''	''	Choc & Buff	Coltbridge/Powburn
33	''	''	''	'' ''	'' ''
34	''	''	''	'' ''	'' ''
35	''	''	''	'' ''	'' ''
36	''	''	''	'' ''	'' ''
37	''	''	''	'' ''	'' ''
38	E.S.T.Co.	''	''	Oak & White	Newhaven/Morn'side Dr
39	''	''	''	'' ''	'' ''
40	E.&D.T.Co.	K	36	'' ''	'' ''
41	''	G	44	'' ''	'' ''
42	''	''	''	'' ''	'' ''
43	''	''	''	'' ''	'' ''
44	E.S.T.Co.	K	36	'' ''	'' ''
45	''	''	''	'' ''	'' ''
46	''	G	44	'' ''	'' ''

No.	Owning Co.	Type	Seats	Colour	Route
47	E.S.T.Co.	G	44	Yellow	Portobello/Colinton Rd
48	E.&D.T.Co.	"	"	"	" "
49	E.S.T.Co.	"	"	"	" "
50	"	"	"	"	" "
51	"	"	"	"	" "
52	"	"	"	"	" "
53	"	K	36	Blue & White	Commercial St/Marchm't
54	"	"	"	Oak & White	Tron/Tollcross
55	E.&D.T.Co.	"	"	" "	" "
56	"	G	44	" "	Newhaven/Morn'side Dr
57	"	K	36	" "	" "
58	"	G	44	Green & Buff	Seafield/Gorgie
59	"	"	"	" "	" "
60	"	?	29	Yellow & Green	Coltbridge/Powburn
61	"	K	36	Choc & Buff	" "
62	"	G	44	" "	" "
63	E.S.T.Co.	K	36	Blue & White	Commercial St/ Marchm't
64	E.&D.T.Co.	"	34	Oak & White	Newhaven/Morn'side Dr
65	"	"	36	Blue & White	Bernard St/Craigmillar Pk
66	"	"	30	Green & Yellow	Post Office/Haymarket
67	"	"	34	Red & White	Bernard St/N Merchiston
68	"	"	"	Oak & White	Newhaven/Morn'side Dr
69	"	"	36	Oak & White	" "
70	"	"	"	Green & Buff	Seafield/Gorgie
71	"	"	"	Yellow	Portobello/Colinton Rd
72	"	"	"	"	" "
73	"	"	32	Red & White	Bernard St/N Merchiston
74	"	"	?	?	?
75	"	"	36	Yellow	Portobello/Colinton Rd
76	"	"	"	"	" "
77	"	G	52	White	Morningside Circle
78	"	K	44	Yellow	Newhaven/Morn'side Dr
79	E.S.T.Co.	G	44	"	Portobello/Colinton Rd
80	"	"	"	"	" "
81	"	"	"	Blue & White	Commercial St/Marchm't
82	"	"	"	" "	" "
83	"	"	"	Oak & White	Newhaven/Morn'side Dr
84	"	"	"	" "	" "
85	"	O	35	Brown	
86	E.&D.T.Co.	"	"	Yellow	
87	E.S.T.Co.	"	"	"	
88	E.&D.T.Co.	"	"	"	
89	"	"	"	"	
90	E.S.T.Co.	C	38	"	
91	E.&D.T.Co.	"	"	"	
92	"	"	"	Oak & White	

No.	Owning Co.	Type	Seats	Colour	Route
93	E.&D.T.Co.	C	38	Ochre-Yellow	
94	"	"	34		
95	E.S.T.Co.	"	38	Oak & White	
96	E.&D.T.Co.	"	"	" "	
97	"	"	"	" "	
98	"	C	28	" "	
99	"	"	34	" "	
100	"	O	35	Yellow	

K = Knifeboard, G = Garden seat, C = Canopy, O = Open toast-rack

Nos. 14, 16, 17 and 32 were six-window cars and Nos. 2, 5, 13, 20, 21, 22, 23, 29, 30, 36, 37, 38, 39, 42, 47, 51, 58, 59, 60 and 83 were seven-window cars, and there were of course still a number of minor differences among the various designs. Nos. 6 and 12 were the Stephenson cars. The canopy cars with 34 seats had them arranged transversely. Subsequently, in 1895-96, Nos. 63 and 78 were cut down to canopy cars, though the former may have been replaced by a new 38-seat canopy car, while Nos. 9, 11, 20, 69 and 70 were rebuilt as garden-seat cars carrying 44 passengers. Nos. 9, 69 and 70 were provided with an additional entrance at the front under the stairs.

Several cars later appeared in different colours, viz. Nos. 2, 4, 9, 46, 64, 70 and 75 became blue and white; nos. 9 and 69 on rebuilding became white cars for the Morningside Circle; nos. 32 and 34 also became white Morningside Circle cars; nos. 38, 68 and 79 became red and white; no. 24 became green and buff; no. 45 became dark brown and buff; nos. 47, 50, 52 and 80 became orange and buff; no. 72 became chocolate and buff; nos. 3, 62 and 93 became oak and white; nos. 78, 95 and 98 became ochre and white, and nos. 11, 23, 33, 36, 37 and 39 became dark brown and white. A few other cars were also changed to other routes without changing their colour.

The reduced fares in the city consequent on the Edinburgh & District Tramways Company taking over operations gave rise to increased traffic and hence that company required additional cars. The Glasgow Tramways & Omnibus Company having just then lost their lease of the Glasgow system, their large fleet of cars was on the market and the Edinburgh & District Tramways Company bought a number of them, all being eight-window knifeboard-seat cars carrying 40 passengers. These cars were numbered 25, 60, 61, 66, 73, 74, 76, 94, 101-105, most of them replacing old cars then scrapped. Nos. 104 and 105 had an additional entrance at the front under the stairs. Four new garden-seat cars with only six windows and a slightly curved roof were also built for the Edinburgh & District Tramways Company by the Metropolitan Railway carriage & Wagon Co. Ltd. of Birmingham in 1895 and were numbered 106-109. These seated 40 and also had double entrances. At the end of 1895 the E. & D.T.Co. built at Shrubhill a knifeboard 36-seat car, No. 110, followed in 1896 by eight garden seat cars with 44 seats and double entrances. They had a neater flat roof and above the seven side windows there were two long panels, the upper one having a perforated design for ventilation. These were Nos. 55, 71, 72, 75, 88, 89, 100 and 111, replacing old cars except for No. 111 which was an addition and may have had only six windows.

The colours and routes of these new cars were as follows:

No.	*Colour*	*Route*
25	Ochre & White	Tron/Tollcross (later Morningside Circle
55	Yellow	Portobello/Colinton Road
60	White	Morningside Circle
61	Yellow	Portobello/Colinton Road
66	Ochre & White	Tron-Tollcross-Haymarket-Gorgie
71	White	Morningside Circle
72	Dark Brown & White	Meadowbank/Morningside Drive
73	Chocolate & Buff	Coltbridge/Powburn
74	" "	" "
75	Red & White	Bernard Street/North Merchiston
76	Yellow	Portobello/Colinton Road
88	Dark Brown & White	Coltbridge/Powburn
89	Yellow	Portobello/Colinton Road
94	White	Morningside Circle
100	Blue & White	Commercial Street/Marchmont
101	Ochre & White	Tron/Tollcross

One of the horse cars bought about 1895 from the Glasgow Tramways & Omnibus Company in use on the route from Tron Church to Tollcross via High Street, George IV Bridge and Lauriston. It appears to be No. 101. (*A. W. Brotchie*)

No.	*Colour*	*Route*
102	Dark Brown & White	Coltbridge/Powburn
103	White	Morningside Circle
104	"	" "
105	Yellow	Portobello/Colinton Road
106	Dark Brown & White	Meadowbank/Morningside Drive
106	" " "	" "
107	" " "	" "
108	" " "	" "
109	" " "	" "
110	Green & Buff	Seafield/Gorgie
111	White	Morningside Circle

When the Edinburgh Street Tramways Company relinquished their line between Waterloo Place and Meadowbank on 31 January 1896, six of their cars were transferred to the Edinburgh & District Tramways Company's stock. These were Nos. 23, 44, 49, 52, 53 and 85; and so the total number of E. & D.T.Co. cars now became 87, while the E.S.T.Co. now had only 24.

With the extension of the city's routes outwards the Edinburgh & District Tramways Company required more horse cars to operate them pending the commencement of cable traction, so in 1897 two more cars, probably with six windows, were added, Nos. 113 and 114. (No. 112 was a cable car built that year.) Then in 1898 when the remainder of the Portobello route passed to the city, another four horse cars were transferred from the Edinburgh Street Tramways and these seem to have been Nos. 47, 50, 51 and 80. The Edinburgh & District Tramways Company's total therefore rose to 93 and the Edinburgh Street Tramways Company's horse car fleet was now down to twenty, but their number of buses at the end of 1898 had increased to 44, with 13 coaches in addition.

At this time all the cars of both companies were of course still using the one sequence of licence numbers and no renumbering would be necessary for these inter-company transfers, but in October 1899 through running between Edinburgh and Leith ceased and the licences of the E.S.T.Co. cars therefore lapsed, so that their old licence numbers could now be used for E. & D.T.Co. cars in the city, including some of the new cable cars, which new cable cars also extended the licence numbers up to 169.

The numbering now became complicated however, as a horse car when submitted for licence renewal was often issued with a different licence number instead of its former number. For example, in 1900, former E.S.T.Co. car numbers 15, 84, 90, 95 and 100 were now ex-Glasgow Tramways & Omnibus Co. cars and 14 was a refurbished garden-seat car; 16, 22, 54, 58, 86, 87 were old knifeboard-seat cars, though these numbers had previously been carried by garden-seat cars, while Nos. 170 and 171 were also used for a knifeboard-seat and a garden-seat car respectively, but it is not possible to disentangle any of these cars' former numbers.

Towards the end of 1899 however, it was the Edinburgh Street Tram-

Edinburgh & District Tramways Company horse car No. 72, built Shrubhill 1896, but with six windows, at Colinton Road terminus just prior to closure of this last horse car route. The horses are being led around to the other end for the return journey to town. (*L.R.T.*)

ways Company who required additional cars for working their Newhaven extension, which was about to be opened, whereas with the advent of cable traction in the city, the Edinburgh & District Tramways Company were shortly to reduce rapidly their horse car fleet. The E.S.T.Co. therefore bought six cars from the E. & D.T.Co. early in 1900 and these appear to have been Nos. 2, 17, 22, 100, 110 and one other, increasing their fleet to 26.

Four Edinburgh & District Tramways Company horse cars were broken up in 1900 and another 23 were sold, six of them to the Stirling & Bridge of Allan Tramways Company. The E. & D.T.Co.'s stock is recorded as including 57 horse cars at the end of 1900, though only 55 seem to have been licensed. Another 14 horse cars were sold by the Edinburgh & District Tramways Company in 1901, and three of these were bought by the Edinburgh Street Tramways Company whose total thereby increased to 29. These seem to have been Nos. 7, 75 and 170. Another two of the newer horse cars, Nos. 53 and 113, were rebuilt and converted to cable cars in 1901. The Edinburgh & District Tramways Company recorded a total of 41 horse cars at the end of 1901 but only 30 seem to have been licensed. Further reductions brought the number down to 20 in 1903, which seem to have been Nos. 5, 13, 17, 19, 25, 27, 35, 47, 49, 51, 52, 66, 72, 76, 87, 90, 92, 97, 102 and 108. By 1905 only seven horse cars remained in the Edinburgh & District Tramways Company's stock and these included Nos. 5, 17, 35, 47 and 72, all garden-seat type.

Of the 29 cars handed over by the Edinburgh Street Tramways Company to Leith Corporation in October 1904, seven, including No. 63, were immediately withdrawn, leaving 22 which included those which were still carrying numbers 7, 14, 15, 17, 22, 26, 28, 38, 39, 54, 75, 79, 82, 83, 84, 87, 90, 95, 100, 110 and 170. Nos. 38, 54, 87, 90 and 95 were sold within a month or two, and in October 1905 Nos. 39 and 83 were bought by the Stirling & Bridge of Allan Tramways Company for £12.10s.0d. each. The Edinburgh & District Tramways Company surprisingly also bought back three cars in 1905-6, paying £6 each for Nos. 110 and 170 in 1906 and £4.10s.0d. for No. 26 "less wheels and axles" in 1905. Nos. 110 and 170, knifeboard-seat cars, appear to have become E. & D.T.Co. Nos. 5 and 47 while No. 26, a garden-seat car, may have become E. & D.T.Co. No. 35, replacing the existing cars with those numbers. The last three E. & D.T.Co. horse cars remaining in use in 1907 were Nos. 5, 47 and 72.

A further three E. & D.T.Co. horse cars were rebuilt and converted to cable cars, becoming Nos. 15 and 19 in 1905 and No. 17 in 1908, but it is unlikely that these were their numbers as horse cars. It is possible that No. 17 had been horse car No. 72, which latterly had been a six-window car, and which may have originally been No. 111. It is also possible that No. 19 had been horse car No. 5 (not the later ex-E.S.T.Co. No. 110) earlier renumbered from 114. The bodies of all the horse cars converted to cable cars were repillared to make three windows of greater height and they were mounted on a shallow steel frame for the conversion.

3

Cable Tramways, the Mechanical Marvel

We have seen how the Edinburgh Street Tramways Company abandoned the idea of laying tramways down the steep hills on the north side of the city, making do with the little horse buses. This was quite clearly not satisfactory; five horses were often required to one bus and they just could not be run in snow or icy weather. The steam engines which had been tried on the Portobello line had not been well received, and in any case they would have been impracticable on such steep grades as these. Some other mechanical system would have to be devised.

In San Francisco, also abounding in steep hills, a new idea, namely cable haulage, had recently been developed by A. S. Hallidie, a Scot born Andrew Smith who added Hallidie in honour of his illustrious physician godfather. It was first introduced this side of the Atlantic by E. S. Eppelsheimer on the Highgate Hill line in North London opened in May 1884, but others had already seen in it the answer to the Edinburgh problem. Eppelsheimer had been with Hallidie's firm in America.

A Bill was therefore introduced in 1883 for tramways from Hanover Street via Canonmills, Inverleith Row, through Royston Terrace and Monmouth Terrace into Trinity Road, East Trinity Road, Main Street Newhaven, and Annfield to the Custom House, Leith. A double line was proposed as far as Canonmills, thereafter single with passing loops near Eildon Street, in Royston Terrace, in Trinity Road, in Annfield, in Portland Place, and near the terminus. At the foot of Craighall Road there was to be a double line triangular junction with another terminus in Maitland Place, Newhaven. Another double line branch was to go off along George Street and down Frederick Street, through Stockbridge to Comely Bank. Any form of power could be used, including ropes or electricity. From a contemporary article it seems that flat rails were at first envisaged for a cable system, the centre slot serving for guidance. A meeting was held in Newhaven to explain the system, tramways in the narrow streets being regarded unfavourably by the residents. To secure Leith Town Council's support the promoters agreed to divert their line from the narrow Main Street to Pier Place and to continue behind the back of the Peacock Hotel. They also agreed to charge penny fares and to run a bus at a penny fare between Newhaven and Granton. However, there was other opposition and the Bill failed.

Dick Kerr & Co. were behind the scheme and they came back next

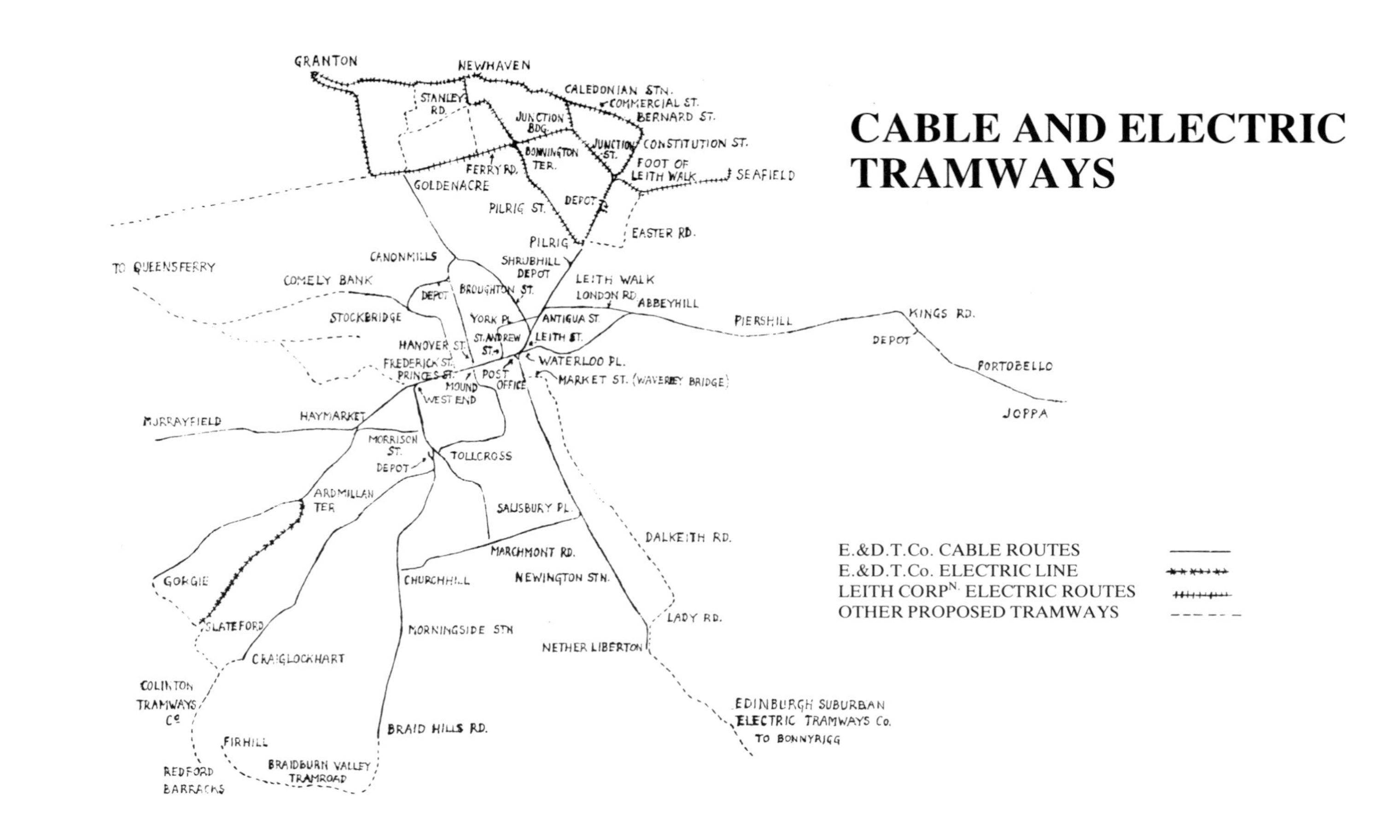

CABLE AND ELECTRIC TRAMWAYS
E.&D.T.Co. CABLE ROUTES
E.&D.T.Co. ELECTRIC LINE
LEITH CORP$^{N.}$ ELECTRIC ROUTES
OTHER PROPOSED TRAMWAYS
GRANTON
NEWHAVEN
CALEDONIAN STN.
COMMERCIAL ST.
BERNARD ST.
STANLEY RD.
JUNCTION BDG.
JUNCTION ST.
CONSTITUTION ST.
BONNINGTON TER.
FOOT OF LEITH WALK
SEAFIELD
FERRY RD.
GOLDENACRE
DEPOT
PILRIG ST.
PILRIG
EASTER RD.
CANONMILLS
SHRUBHILL DEPOT
TO QUEENSFERRY
COMELY BANK
DEPOT
BROUGHTON ST.
LEITH WALK
LONDON RD.
ABBEYHILL
STOCKBRIDGE
YORK PL.
ANTIGUA ST.
PIERSHILL
KINGS RD.
HANOVER ST.
ST. ANDREW ST.
LEITH ST.
DEPOT
FREDERICK ST.
PRINCES ST.
WATERLOO PL.
POST OFFICE
MOUND
MARKET ST. (WAVERLEY BRIDGE)
PORTOBELLO
WEST END
JOPPA
MURRAYFIELD
HAYMARKET
MORRISON ST.
DEPOT
TOLLCROSS
ARDMILLAN TER
SALISBURY PL.
DALKEITH RD.
MARCHMONT RD.
GORGIE
CHURCHHILL
NEWINGTON STN.
LADY RD.
SLATEFORD
MORNINGSIDE STN
NETHER LIBERTON
CRAIGLOCKHART
COLINTON TRAMWAYS Co
EDINBURGH SUBURBAN ELECTRIC TRAMWAYS Co.
TO BONNYRIGG
BRAID HILLS RD.
FIRHILL
BRAIDBURN VALLEY TRAMROAD
REDFORD BARRACKS

session with a similar Bill. This time it was proposed to take the line round Goldenacre to Trinity Road instead of by Royston Terrace and Monmouth Terrace, and to reach Newhaven via Primrose Bank, Trinity Bridge and Trinity Crescent. There was to be a double line throughout, except through Main Street. The Comely Bank route was to be separate, starting in Frederick Street. The gauge proposed was 3ft. 6in. Again there were discussions with Leith Town Council who now raised many objections, especially about the use of Main Street. Edinburgh Town Council, however, supported the Bill, and as they were responsible for two-thirds of the whole route, Leith's case was not strong. Nevertheless the promoters agreed to amend their Bill, making Newhaven their terminus, and adopting the 4ft. 8½in. gauge. Cable operation was specified, and sufficient inside accommodation at a penny per mile fare, though a first class compartment at a higher rate was allowed. Single-deck cars were originally envisaged.

This time the Bill was passed and the Edinburgh Northern Tramways Company was thus formed on 7 August 1884. John Waddell was chairman and W. Hamilton Beattie, engineer. Three years were allowed for completion of the works.

Construction was of course an entirely different proposition to that of horse tramways, and though preparatory work by the contractors, the Patent Cable Tramways Corporation, was in hand in 1885, it was October 1886 before track laying started on the route between Hanover Street and Goldenacre, along with the erection of an engine house in Henderson Row. The contractor's engineer was a young man called William Newby Colam who had been Eppelsheimer's chief assistant. He was to play an important part in the development of cable traction.

Both the Trinity and Stockbridge routes included a long hill at the town end, as steep as 1 in 11 near the top. The company decided to finish the 1½ miles of route to Goldenacre first, and as they had also decided to locate the engine house and car depot in Henderson Row, a hundred yards or so off this route near the bottom of the hill, and to make it serve the Stockbridge route as well in due course, a new Act was required to authorise the connecting lines to the depot. As the time for completion had nearly expired and the Stockbridge route was not yet started, the Edinburgh Northern Tramways Act 1887 (5 July 1887) allowed a further two years for the construction of this route as well as the two connecting lines to the depot, for which three years were allowed. The powers to proceed with the continuation from Goldenacre to Newhaven were allowed to lapse and it was never constructed, a bus being run instead as required by Section 74 of their original Act as already mentioned.

At last the Hanover Street to Goldenacre line was ready at the end of 1887 and its opening was planned for 2 January 1888. Some hitch, however, arose concerning an agreement with the Patent Cable Tramways Corporation, and the Board of Trade inspector also called for some modification to the cars. The steps had to be arranged to fold up when not in use as the maximum width was otherwise exceeded. The

Edinburgh Northern Tramways Company: small horse bus run between Goldenacre and Newhaven. There are no outside seats though two boys have climbed up beside the driver. (*L.R.T.*)

opening of this route took place on 28 January 1888 without ceremony, though there was considerable public interest. A five minute service of cars was run with connecting buses to Granton, Trinity and Leith, as already recorded. The old Edinburgh Street Tramways Company's buses on the route of course ceased. Major John Boulton, one of the promoters, was appointed manager.

About a week later, on a Saturday, the first breakage of the cable occurred, but repairs were completed ready for the Monday morning service again. The system worked well after this, and in May 1889 work was started on the $1\frac{1}{4}$ mile Stockbridge route. This route was inspected by Major-General Hutchison for the Board of Trade on 5 August, the inspection car being hauled by horses as the cable was not yet installed. There was a further Board of Trade inspection on 29 January 1890 and on 17 February the line was opened with a five minute service of cars, again replacing the Edinburgh Street Tramways Company buses.

The gauge of these lines was, of course, 4ft. $8\frac{1}{2}$in.; 75lb. rails were used. The conduit was formed of concrete with cast-iron frames embedded to carry old rails which formed a centre slot $\frac{5}{8}$in. wide. The cable, of $3\frac{1}{2}$in. circumference $^{6}/_{13}$ steel wire rope, was carried over 14in. diameter cast-iron pulleys placed in recesses at 50ft. intervals. Horizontally mounted pulleys with one deep flange on the bottom were used on curves. At the town end terminus of each line the cars ran into the stub end by gravity while at the other end the cars ran out of the stub end by gravity on to the double line where the returning cable was picked up. At Comely Bank the grade was so slight that a little persuasion was sometimes needed to get the car to run out. The cable was returned round a large horizontal pulley in each case.

As already mentioned the power house and car shed were situated in Henderson Row, a hundred yards or so from the Goldenacre route near the bottom of the hill. The cable was diverted from the down line into the power house where it was driven by a 10ft. 6in. diameter driving pulley. After passing round a tension pulley loaded to 7 cwts. it returned to the down line. Cars on the down line passed Henderson Row by gravity. There was both a facing and a trailing connection on the down line connecting with the single line in Henderson Row which led into the car shed. The car shed had nine stalls, each accommodating two cars, access to and from which was gained by a traverser. There was originally no slot in this part of Henderson Row and the car grippers had to be lifted out through a small hatch before leaving the main line and running by gravity through the facing connection into Henderson Row, from where a horse pulled them along to the shed. Similarly, the horse took them out to the trailing connection where the cars gained the down line and the gripper was inserted through another hatch. At a later date the slot was provided in Henderson Row as in the case of the Comely Bank route and the grippers remained on the cars, the services of the horse being normally dispensed with.

To reach the Comely Bank route the cars came off the opposite end of the traverser, which lay parallel to Henderson Row. They had to travel on the single line to the other end of Henderson Row where there was a passing place and continue along Hamilton Place on single line and over a trailing connection onto the up line of the Comely Bank route, again near the bottom of the hill. Again the cable was diverted from the down line to reach its driving pulley in the Henderson Row power house. This was about 550 yards and too far for the cars to be effectively dealt with by horses however, so that the cable was used in both directions. The outgoing and incoming cable being under the same slot in the single line, care was necessary to see that the car gripper got the correct cable. Cars going to the car shed were run back by gravity round the trailing connection from the up line into Hamilton Place, but to proceed onto the up line round the curve from Hamilton Place, a separate short auxiliary cable was provided. This was driven from the shaft of one of the main cable diverting pulleys there and was just put into operation when required by means of a clutch operated by a key. Latterly this was removed and in the mornings the cars were pushed and pulled round the curve onto the main line in groups of three, the last one using the Hamilton Place cable and pushing the two in front till the first one was on the main line. It then took the main line cable and pulled the other two round behind it. As at Henderson Row on the Trinity route, two crossovers were provided, the facing one on the town side and the trailing one on the Comely Bank side. It had been originally intended to provide two connections at Hamilton Place but experience at Henderson Row indicated that one would be sufficient.

An innovation was tried at the Hamilton Place junction. It will be appreciated that if the driver of a car coming down the hill towards Comely Bank did not, through forgetfulness or some other reason, release the gripper at the corner of Hamilton Place where the cable was diverted to the power house, the cable would be pulled from its pulley and considerable damage and dislocation of traffic would ensue. Approaching the critical point, therefore, the cable was led a few inches out of line with the slot, and if it were pulled into line under the slot by a car gripper, it bore against a cast steel lever in the form of an inverted "L" pivoted at the bottom. When this lever was moved by the cable bearing against it, the top leg moved across the underside of the slot and therefore arrested the progress of the gripper, and of course the car. This device, which was known as a pawl, had to be of great strength, since it had to absorb the energy of a car running into an immovable object. Such an occurrence was naturally fraught with considerable danger to the passengers, and so at a point just before the pawl would come into action, another striker was arranged which made contact for a large electric bell. It was hoped that this would warn the driver in time for him to release the gripper before bringing the pawl into action, but it seems to have been found that the bell was ineffective and it was subsequently removed. The pawl device remained, however, and was provided also on the later lines in the city at appropriate places.

The power house was provided with two non-condensing horizontal steam engines of 300 h.p. by Dick Kerr & Co., Kilmarnock. Each engine was capable of working either or both of the cables. Messrs Babcock & Wilcox provided the boilers.

Hanover Street route cable car at Goldenacre in early Edinburgh & District Tramways Company livery.

The other type of cable car used by the Edinburgh Northern Tramways Company on the Comely Bank route (Nos. 129-136) at Comely Bank terminus during World War I. (*A. W. Brotchie*)

The company's first eight cars were built by the Metropolitan Carriage Company and were numbered 1 to 8. The saloon, seating 20, had six windows each side and was divided into two sections forming first and second class. The platforms were rather longer than normal and the dash panel was continued part of the way along the step side leaving a comparatively narrow access adjacent to the saloon on both sides, passengers entering and leaving the forward saloon by the front platform. This arrangement was subsequently abandoned and the partition in the saloon removed. The steps were mounted on the bogies and as previously mentioned had to be arranged to fold up. A full-length square-ended canopy was provided and the 32 "outside" seats reached by a "reversed" stair. These cars, weighing six tons, were kept on the Goldenacre route and carried the legend "Trinity Route" on the canopies. The square-ended tops earned them the nickname of "coffins". The second batch of eight cars, presumably Nos. 9 to 16, worked the Comely Bank route carrying the inscription "Stockbridge Route". These were built by the Falcon Engine & Car Works Ltd. and were somewhat shorter, having that firm's peculiar corner entrance platforms, ordinary stairs and very short canopies. There was no division in the saloon and the seating capacity was 18 inside and 22 outside. They were 23ft. 3in. overall and weighed about four tons.

Both types of car ran on bogies with outside plate frames. The gripper at each end of the car was a single-jaw arrangement, the subject of a patent by Mr Colam, mounted in a frame behind the leading axle and operated by a horizontal wheel on a pillar which protruded through a hole in the floor of the platform. The hole was slotted to allow for movement on curves. A small horizontal ratchet lever by which the gripper could be kept tight protruded underneath the handwheel. Brake blocks were provided to all wheels. On the Metropolitan cars these were applied by a foot pedal on the platform which operated the brakes of the bogie underneath. If the driver required the wheel brake at the back of the car he had to give three beats on the bell, which was the signal for the conductor to press the pedal on the rear platform. The Falcon cars had orthodox inter-connected brake gear applied by one of two large levers to the left of the driver. The other lever similarly worked track brakes. The track brakes on the Metropolitan cars appear to have been worked by a separate horizontal handwheel. An oil lamp was provided at each end of the saloon, and the driver gave warning of approach by striking a brass bell suspended from the canopy. Following the new licensing arrangements applied from 1894 these sixteen cars became Nos. 121-136.

There were two other cars of which little is known. They were long single-deck vehicles seating 26 and said to have been of American construction, though this seems doubtful. No. 137 appeared in August 1894 and No. 138 in August 1895. They were apparently found unsuitable and little used, being delicensed in 1900. However, No. 137 was relicensed again as No. 7 in August 1904 and finally withdrawn in May 1913, though it was still in existence in Henderson Row car shed in 1916. No. 138 also reappeared as No. 13 in April 1905 but remained so only until May 1908. The Northern Company's cars were painted blue with cream panels and adorned with a hand-painted crest depicting a car encircled by a rope.

The Board of Trade regulations, repeated in the company's rule books, limited the speed to six miles per hour, and were very emphatic in prohibiting gravity running except at the special places, mentioned earlier, where this was necessary. Cars were not allowed to pass one another on the Canonmills curve. At the end of August 1890 the company sought an increase in speed to 8 m.p.h. but this was not sanctioned.

The fare from Hanover Street to Goldenacre was 3d. first class and 2d. second class or "outside", and the tickets were available for the bus journey to Trinity or Granton without extra charge. Intermediate fares were also available. The first class was discontinued in August 1888 and the fares were later reduced, halfpenny stages being introduced in January 1895, together with special fares for letter carriers, 1d. return for a 1d. stage and 1d. single for a 2d. stage.

In September 1890 the company suggested an extension by way of the Mound and George IV Bridge to the Grange district but Edinburgh Corporation refused to support the scheme and it was dropped. The following year the company's chairman, now John Paterson, proposed an extension at the other end, from Goldenacre down Ferry Road and over the Edinburgh Street Tramways Company's tracks to Junction Bridge, with possibly a branch down Craighall Road. Nothing was done at the time but in 1896 the company prepared a Bill on these lines for the 1897 Parliamentary Session. In this they proposed the following extensions:

1. From Goldenacre down Ferry Road as far as Craighall Road;
2. A continuation of this along Ferry Road to Newhaven Road;
3. A branch from these down Craighall Road as far as Stanley Road;
4. A continuation of this down the hill to Newhaven;
5. From the Comely Bank terminus to Crewe Road. All were to be double line and worked by cable.

However, proposals for unification with the new system being planned for the city were in the air, and the company's activities ceased on 31 December 1896, the foregoing project being apparently withdrawn. It had been arranged for the Edinburgh & District Tramways Company to run the system meantime until formalities could be completed for the acquisition of the line by Edinburgh Corporation. This was accomplished by Section 20 of the Edinburgh Corporation Act of 1897 (3 June 1897) and the whole undertaking passed to Edinburgh Corporation on 1 July 1897 for the sum of £110,000. The rolling-stock etc. was immediately resold to the Edinburgh & District Tramways Company and the vesting was backdated to midnight of 31 December 1896. It then became part of the Corporation's system leased to the Edinburgh & District Tramways Company, and the Edinburgh Northern Tramways Company's affairs were wound up as provided for in the 1897 Act. Meantime, in 1896, with traffic increasing, the Edinburgh Northern Tramways Company had

One of the six cars ordered by the Edinburgh Northern Tramways Company in 1896, Nos. 139-144, seen at Comely Bank during World War I.

ordered six more cars and built an extension at the back of the car shed adding two more stalls to accommodate them.

In the half-year to 30 June 1894 the Northern Company ran 173,791 miles and carried 1,697,639 passengers, with receipts at 10.89d. p.c.m. and expenses of 5.33d. p.c.m. of which 0.73d. represented motive power. The figures include the horse bus service on which there was a small loss.

Now, to revert to the Edinburgh & District Tramways Company's horse car system in 1896, we saw in the last chapter how plans for the cable installation were in hand. As mentioned, the construction of the two new power houses at Shrubhill and Tollcross had been started, and also the relaying of the tracks with the heavier rails and conduits. A formal start was made at Newington by Lord Provost McDonald on 9 September 1896. Reconstruction was generally commenced at the outer termini and progressed inwards to Princes Street where work was not commenced till 5 April 1897. 83 lb. rails in 32ft. lengths were used, and 200 to 300 yards were usually done at a time, the horse car service being carried on over the other single line by means of temporary crossovers and transferring to the new lines on completion. The junction work was left to the last as this was quite complicated, involving the construction of extensive pits under the roadway. A good deal of delay arose through alterations and extensions which from time to time, right up to 1897 as we have seen, were proposed and incorporated, often entailing considerable changes in the equipment which had already been designed.

All the extensions authorised in the 1897 Act were not fully carried out, but most of the 1896 ones were. The Newington line was extended as far as Nether Liberton, at Gilmerton Road end. The Morningside line was extended as far as Braid Hills Road. The line along Gorgie Road was laid as far as Saughton Park, and the old piece of line up to Polwarth Terrace abandoned. The Murrayfield line was extended to the boundary at Saughtonhall Drive, the railway arch at the old terminus having to be replaced by a girder bridge to allow for this. The Gilmore Place to Craiglockhart route was not included in the conversion scheme at all, the traffic being considered insufficient at that time, and it remained a horse car line until a much later date. Nor were the triangular junctions at St. Andrew Street and West End perpetuated. For the time being also, plans for the Portobello route power house were deferred, as Dick Kerr & Company suggested that it might be suitable for an experiment with electric traction.

Provision was made in the Shrubhill power station for driving a cable to Leith, and in February 1898 Mr Colam produced a scheme whereby a cable system could be continued right round the circular route by Bernard Street, Commercial Street, and Junction Street, including the new swing bridge over the harbour! In this scheme the cable would have been led via Junction Street to the Commercial Street side of the bridge and back via Foot of Leith Walk to the Bernard Street side of the bridge, and then back to Shrubhill. Constitution Street would have been single line. The swing bridge itself was to be provided with an auxiliary cable driven from the Bernard Street side. Unfortunately precise details of this ingenious scheme are lacking, but the difficulties will perhaps be better appreciated when we come shortly to describe the method of operating the cable system generally. Leith, however, was still not interested in cables.

With all these delays, it is perhaps not surprising that contracts for the construction of the various junction pits were not signed until April 1898, and since so much time had already been spent on the still far from complete construction work, the two companies approached the Corporation for an extension of their lease, which as things stood, seemed likely to allow them only about eighteen years operation. Further, negotiations for leasing the Leith system from 30 June 1898 then seemed likely to materialise, so this would be a suitable date for a fresh start. The current lease had never received the Board of Trade's approval, and as Sections 22 and 23 of the Edinburgh Corporation Act of 1897 had empowered the Corporation to work the tramways themselves or to lease them without seeking Board of Trade approval, it was a good time to regularise the position. Thus the three parties entered into a new lease in July 1898, by which "the Corporation let to the Tramways Company the whole tramways belonging to or that might hereafter be constructed or acquired by the Corporation, and relative lands, premises, and works, for a period of twenty-one years from and after 30 June 1898". The company undertook to pay the Corporation 7 per cent on the capital expenditure, as from the date of commencing the public service. As each section was opened the 7 per cent became payable on the corresponding proportion of the capital expenditure incurred, the sums involved being the subject of negotiation over which little difficulty seems to have arisen until the final stages were reached.

With the first part of the new system nearly ready the company abandoned the idea of electric traction to Portobello, and the Corporation thereupon authorised a start on the power house for that route too. At first it had been intended that this be situated in the vicinity of Meadowbank, but later a site in Portobello High Street was decided upon. The Edinburgh Corporation Act 1899 (13 July 1899) authorised:

1. Doubling the Portobello line between Fishwives' Causeway and Hope Lane.
2. Doubling the junction leading to the depot at Livingstone Place.
3. A slight shortening of the single line in Strathearn Place at Whitehouse Loan.

The present schemes were then completed by the Edinburgh Corporation Act 1900 (30 July 1900) which provided for access to a new Portobello depot and power house near Pipe Street, a trailing junction into Thornybauk leading to Tollcross depot, doubling the curves at Salisbury Place junction and at Churchhill junction, and doubling the line between Tollcross and the Infirmary.

Returning to 1899, the council, and the public, were getting impatient for the cable cars. The Tramways Committee met regularly and heard Mr Colam's progress report. Fourteen cars had been delivered, and over a hundred more were ready at the maker's works awaiting completion of the depot accommodation. Then, on 23 May, the Shrubhill engines were put in motion for the first time, though the cables were not as yet laid.

Two pairs of horizontal compound non-condensing engines each of 500 h.p. were provided, one being kept as a reserve. The high pressure

Shrubhill cable power station. This part of the building became the "Heavy Repair Shop" in electric car days and dealt with truck repairs. (*E. O. Catford*)

The trial run from Shrubhill to St. Andrew Street on 1 June 1899. It is evident much work remains to be done.

cylinders were 23in. diameter and the low pressure 40in. diameter, the stroke being 5 feet. They were supplied with steam at 160 lbs. per sq. in. and ran at 45 r.p.m., governors keeping the speed within 10 per cent with 100 per cent overload. Three boilers were installed. The engines drove a counter-shaft by means of a series of driving ropes, and the grooved cable-driving pulleys of 10 feet diameter were driven on this counter-shaft by means of Lindsay coil clutches. Provision was made for driving three cables, though the third one, for Leith, never materialised. The balance weights of the tensioning carriage were arranged on the wall of the engine room. There were now two tracks in the entrance to the depot, one facing from the down line in Leith Walk, the other trailing onto it. They led to a traverser which ran down the middle of the shed. The Shrubhill to St. Andrew Street cable was put in on 29 May and a car tried on the line late the following night. The new cables were of 3⅞in. circumference, and were drawn in as follows: lengths of light cable were dropped through the slot, spliced together below and led round the cable driving pulley; the engine and light cable then pulled the main cable into place over the route.

1 June 1899 was a red-letter day. The Tramway Committee, the Lord Provost, Mr Pitcairn the manager, Mr Colam, Mr John Kerr and Mr Moir of Messrs Dick Kerr & Company, and several other notables, assembled at Shrubhill at 12.30 where they boarded one of the former Northern Company's new cars, No. 142. Promptly on the sound of Edinburgh's well-known one o'clock gun, the car moved off and made the inaugural

Tollcross cable car depot showing the traverser from which the cars reached their lyes. (*Gavin Booth*)

trip to St. Andrew Street and back without any hitch. Thereafter from 3.00 p.m. till 6.00 p.m. that day the car plied the line giving free rides to all and sundry, and naturally it was well filled.

The line was not yet available for public service however. Much pit work remained to be done also at the Post Office, the West End, Tollcross, and most of the other junctions. The horse cars were running past these obstructions on temporary single lines at the side of the street. The work was considerably held up by delays in deliveries of the steel troughing which was required for the roofing of the pits. However, the West End pit was completed on 3 July, and as from 23 August the horse cars from Craiglockhart were turned back at Gilmore Place to ease matters at Tollcross. There were hopes of starting the Pilrig to Braid Hills Road service at the beginning of October. Leith asked the Board of Trade not to sanction the opening until arrangements had been made for through running to Leith, but this was of course still impossible.

The public grew more impatient. The company was criticised for not employing a night shift, but replied that they had not enough suitable labour. However, the Tollcross engines were now ready and the Tollcross-Braid Hills Road cable was drawn in on 18 and 19 September. To expedite the Salisbury Place pit the horse cars on the Grange Road route were turned back either side of the junction as from 25 September, and now the Post Office, Morrison Street and Haymarket pits were the only ones still to finish. The Princes Street cable from Tollcross was ready on 27 September and on Sunday morning 1 October a trial car was run from Tollcross to Shrubhill, and from there right to Braid Hills Road and back to Tollcross. This ran well, and accordingly the Board of Trade was asked to inspect the line on 11 October. Meanwhile another successful trial run at full speed, i.e. 8 m.p.h., was made over the same route on the morning of 8 October. The trip was repeated in the afternoon with the directors, officials and press on board, but this was not so auspicious, as on proceeding from Shrubhill to Braid Hills Road and approaching Tollcross, the car "hit the pawl"! Although the party was considerably shaken no one was really hurt. However, the car was taken into the depot and the rest of the trip abandoned. This mishap was ascribed to the mistaken action of a workman in the Tollcross pit, the company explaining that such a thing would not happen normally!

Sir Francis Marindin, the Board of Trade inspector, came on 12 October. The inspection party included the Lord Provost and the Tramways Committee and, of course, Mr Pitcairn, Mr Colam and several others. The Tollcross power house was visited first and there Mr Colam described and showed the inspector the intricacies of the system in the extensive pit running out to the main line, full of whirring cables and pulleys etc. The Lord Provost and his colleagues seem to have been particularly impressed by the magnitude and complexity of the undertaking. The engines, boilers and driving gear here were similar to those at Shrubhill, but there were four boilers and three pairs of engines arranged for driving five cables.

The party then boarded one of the cars in the depot, and at 11.15 a.m. set off for Pilrig. A slight hitch at the St. Andrew Street junction is recorded, but Pilrig was reached safely and the return trip to Braid Hills Road also passed off without untoward incident. Returning from Braid Hills Road a brake test was satisfactorily carried out, the cable being released coming down the hill and a speed of 15 m.p.h. gained before applying the brakes. The inspector had not forgotten the St. Andrew Street incident so the journey was continued thence and this time there was no hitch, and the party adjourned to a luncheon provided by the Tramways Company at the Royal Hotel.

A few days later, on 19 October, the town council held their official inspection of the system, and made a trip from Tollcross to Pilrig. Again there was a hitch at St. Andrew Street, the auxiliary cable for the curve being too oily for the car to grip, but Mr Colam jumped into the pit and by the application of some sawdust soon had the trouble overcome. After this trip it was stated that if the Board of Trade certificate was received in time, public service would commence on Monday 23 October, and it was intimated that the through service of horse cars to Leith would cease on that date. The certificate did not arrive in time, but meantime the company were running a few trial cars empty every day to accustom the drivers to their somewhat complicated duties.

One of these trial cars came to grief on 23 October, again at St. Andrew Street junction, where the points were lying for the public horse car service towards the Post Office. The cable was pulled out of the car gripper and "stranded". It continued to run all right until the stranded portion reached the Tollcross pit where it caught in another car's gripper. Warning of the impending danger arrived just in time and the cable was stopped, but the entangled gripper had to be removed from the car at Tollcross and of course with the cable stopped, all the other trial cars between Tollcross and St. Andrew Street were halted; consequently the public service of horse cars was also held up. That was the end of cable running for that day and the cable cars had to be brought in by horses. Such mishaps had already occurred once or twice on the Northern lines.

The Tollcross depot was reached by a short line through the lane known as Thornybauk. There were facing and trailing connections on the incoming track at the foot of Home Street which came together with their inner rails against one another in Thornybauk. They then spread to provide a passing place from where a single line ran straight into the depot. The entrance was opposite Thornybauk, further west than in electric car days, and the floor was higher so that there was a slope up inside onto the traverser, from which cars could be run out by gravity. An auxiliary cable was provided to take cars through Thornybauk to and from the main line, and crossovers were laid in Home Street and Earl Grey Street. The former would be worked by gravity. The latter being level, cars had to be pushed over by manpower. As the cars were relatively light this was fairly easily done once they were started, by means of a pinch bar under the wheel. The main cables were taken out to

Earl Grey Street direct, under the street called West Tollcross and not round Thornybauk. Other crossovers were provided at the Waverley Steps — worked by the returning cable — at the foot of Lothian Road and at Morningside Station, which operated by gravity, and at West End of Princes Street, relying on "push".

At last the Board of Trade certificate arrived and the company gave notice on 26 October that commencing that day a number of cable cars would be introduced into service between Pilrig and Braid Hills Road between 8.10 a.m. and 8.30 p.m. Eight cable cars carried passengers that day and there is no record of any mishaps. Two days later, however, a Pilrig-bound car failed to release the cable in time at Tollcross and the cable was knocked off its pulley. A few hours' delay ensued during which the horse cars did their best to provide a service. The number of cable cars on the line was increased gradually and the horse car service correspondingly reduced. Thus without great ceremony was the cable car introduced to public service in Princes Street.

Meantime work was proceeding as fast as possible on the remaining junction pits, and the other new routes.

It is now necessary to attempt to describe the method of operating the system at junctions etc. The bylaws stipulated that gravity or impetus was not to be used, and to meet these conditions Colam designed for the new cars an improved gripper with jaws on either side. This was mounted ahead of the first axle and its operating rod provided with a knuckle-joint and sliding coupling so that its top part was carried in a fixed pedestal on the platform and operated by a vertical spoked wheel. By this means the objectionable hole in the floor was avoided. It was arranged that the driver could disengage the front gripper operating rod and work the rear gripper instead. This was effected by means of a small lever on the pedestal which transferred the motion of the car driver's hand-wheel to the gripper rod at the other end of the car by means of a shaft running underneath.

The method of working at junctions can be illustrated by considering a left-hand junction. It would be arranged for cars to approach with the cable in the right-hand jaw of the gripper, and on reaching a predetermined mark in the roadway just before the junction, the car was stopped. At this point the centre slot was diverted to the left for about two inches, and when the gripper which followed the diverted slot was fully opened, the main cable jumped out of the right-hand jaw to take up its normal straight position. At the same time the auxiliary cable for the curve which was close to the left-hand side of the gripper slipped into the left-hand jaw as it opened. After rounding the curve with the auxiliary cable, the car was again stopped and the other main cable similarly picked up. A car going straight across the junction instead of round the curve also stopped before the junction and took the main cable in its rear gripper. It moved forward again thus until the front gripper had passed clear over the auxiliary cable of the curve onto the main line. It then stopped again and dropped the cable from the rear gripper picking it up in the front one and proceeding once more, the rear gripper then passing clear over the said auxiliary cable. The main cable passed underneath the auxiliary cable on the curve, and so cars proceeding from the curve into the main line did not let go of the auxiliary cable until they were on the main line and ready to pick up the main cable. In the case of the St. Andrew Street junction the auxiliary cable was pulled into position in the gripper of a car for St. Andrew Street by means of a pulley actuated by the pointsman pulling up a chain. In Earl Grey Street the Princes Street cable and the Braids cable similarly overlapped so that cars stopped to drop the one and pick up the other. At Shrubhill depot entrance the main cable was diverted from both lines into the power house and the auxiliary cable used for taking cars out from the depot was used for the short distance down to the terminus at Pilrig where the cars ran into the stub end by gravity. There was an overlap with the main cable at the depot entrance on the up line. It should be mentioned that when the Shrubhill cable reached St. Andrew Street it was returned round a large vertical pulley and after doubling back a short distance served a crossover, and so enabled cars to be turned back towards Pilrig. An extension on the shaft of the vertical returning pulley drove the auxiliary cable which worked the junction curves at half speed, and this cable had its own tensioning device in the pit. The auxiliary cables were 3½in. circumference. Pawls were provided at all points where it was essential for the main cable to be released.

There were no other complications on the Pilrig to Braid Hills Road route when first opened but with the coming into operation of other routes shortly afterwards, involving numerous such complicated manoeuvres at the many junctions, the whole system became very cumbersome to operate. For various reasons many simplifications became imperative, one of the earliest and most obvious being the securing of authority to run cars by gravity at certain places. But meantime the initial cabling arrangements and opening of the various routes has to be dealt with.

The winter of 1899-1900 was severe and it was not until 7 March that a trial car could be run on the next section to be cabled, viz. Tollcross to Salisbury Place, from where the cable returned up to Churchhill, and back to Marchmont Road and Tollcross again. Crossovers were provided in Salisbury Place, Churchhill, and the top of Marchmont Road, and equipped with the returning cable as at St. Andrew Street. This cable also drove auxiliary cables for the curves at the junctions at these three places. That at Churchhill was probably led underneath the main Braids outgoing cable, as the Churchhill auxiliary did not see normal service. In the other two the auxiliary was uppermost round the curve as was normal. The Grange route horse cars were replaced on 4 April by a cable car service between Post Office via Tollcross and Marchmont Road to Salisbury Place on a temporary permit prior to Board of Trade inspection. It would appear that the section between Marchmont Road and Churchhill was covered by a shuttle service from Salisbury Place.

The next step was the pulling in of the Nether Liberton cable from Shrubhill. This was 33,500 feet long, the longest on the system, and was installed on 18 April. It was arranged meantime to run "blind" (i.e. the cable was not located under the slot and could not be picked up by a car gripper) from Shrubhill to Picardy Place junction, and it also ran blind from Leith Street to North Bridge using a separate and straighter pipe for part of the distance. The outgoing cable came up to the incoming line in North Bridge and was used to work a crossover in gaining the outgoing line there. An auxiliary cable was provided between Leith Street and Princes Street and another one from in front of the Post Office round into North Bridge, which on its way back passed over the top of the former one going to Princes Street. Other crossovers which could be used by gravity were laid in Leith Street, South Bridge and Newington Road, the latter facing.

On 22 May Col. Yorke carried out his inspection, starting from Picardy Place junction and proceeding to Nether Liberton, thence back to the Post Office. He continued back again as far as Salisbury Place and along Grange Road to Churchhill and down to Tollcross. From here the party returned by Churchhill and Salisbury Place again to the Post Office. Everything proved satisfactory and cable car service was provided between the Post Office and Nether Liberton the following day. Two days later the cable cars commenced working the complete route from Pilrig to Nether Liberton. The Churchhill to Salisbury Place service was also extended to Pilrig.

Horse cars were still operating on Princes Street to Murrayfield, to Gorgie and to Craiglockhart, but a siding was laid from Home Street to the south side of Tollcross and the company gave notice that as from 4 June the Craiglockhart cars would operate into Tollcross only. The service was arranged to run in connection with the cars on the Marchmont route and a penny transfer ticket made·available between West End and Merchiston Avenue. This was valid on any incoming car from Tollcross, but outwards from the West End it was at first issued on Marchmont Road cars only.

The Princes Street cable was extended on 5 August. Reaching the West End from Tollcross it was turned left to Haymarket, to a crossover on the Murrayfield side of the Haymarket junction, and returned through this crossover back to the West End before proceeding along Princes Street to the Post Office and back to Tollcross. An auxiliary cable was provided for the curves to and from Lothian Road. It was arranged for cars proceeding towards Haymarket to use the rear gripper in Princes Street, and stopping on the Lothian Road curve crossing they picked up the cable for Haymarket in the front gripper.

The extension to Haymarket was inspected by Col. Yorke on 9 August and cable cars were running between Post Office and Haymarket the following day. It was announced that horse cars would cease to operate on Princes Street from 13 August, Haymarket becoming an interchange point, but there is some doubt as to whether this was achieved so promptly. The auxiliary cable for the curve between Princes Street and North Bridge was also inspected by Col. Yorke on 9 August, so that the

Marchmont circular route was completed again. This was carried under the auxiliary cable from North Bridge towards Leith Street, so cars from Princes Street to North Bridge used the rear gripper and stopped on the crossing to change to the front gripper.

The Murrayfield route was completed next and the cable car service inaugurated on 10 September, prior to the Board of Trade inspection. The Gorgie route, much of which was new, and the new Morrison Street line were completed soon afterwards, but in this case the change-over was withheld until, at last, after much prodding, Col. von Donop arrived on 14 December. He inspected all these lines, travelling from Haymarket to Gorgie, thence to the east end of Morrison Street and back to Haymarket. Boarding another car he then went to Murrayfield and back. The public service of cable cars between Pilrig and Gorgie via York Place, and also between the east end of Morrison Street and Gorgie was put on right away. The latter was very short lived. There being very little traffic it lasted two weeks.

Both the Gorgie and Murrayfield cables were driven at Tollcross power station, and the Morrison Street route was built mainly to take them to Haymarket. From Tollcross they ran in a blind tube to Morrison Street. The Murrayfield cable then continued blind to Haymarket where it took up its position under the Murrayfield track, and returning from Murrayfield as far as the Haymarket crossover it entered the blind tube up Morrison Street for Tollcross. The Gorgie cable operated the Morrison Street tracks starting with a crossover at the Lothian Road end. An auxiliary cable was provided for the Lothian Road junction and appears to have been led under the main north-going cable in Lothian Road since it was not intended for normal service. Another auxiliary cable was provided between the Haymarket junction and the junction between the Morrison Street and Gorgie lines, and was led over the outgoing cable between West Maitland Street and the Murrayfield direction, and under the cable from Gorgie into Morrison Street. Both termini stub-ends were worked by the cable in both directions. Crossovers were provided at Shandwick Place, the east end of Dalry Road, west of Ardmillan Terrace, and at Westfield Road. Some were "facing" to suit gravity operation in the desired direction. From 17 September 1900 the cars stopped for passengers only at places indicated by signs fixed to lamp-posts.

With the end of 1900 we have reached the stage where most of the system had been converted, only the Mound route and the Portobello route with its new London Road branch to Leith Walk being uncompleted, though these new tracks had been finished for some time. Since 1897 a horse car service had been running between Meadowbank and Post Office on the new London Road line, but in order to advance the cabling this was withdrawn on 20 February 1901 and replaced by a shuttle service of horse cars between Abbeyhill and Leith Walk only. Henderson Row power station was being enlarged and an additional pair of engines of 500 h.p. provided to drive the Mound route cable.

About this period, however, there were a number of serious breakdowns, mostly due to mishaps with auxiliary cables at junctions, which put sections of the system out of action for several hours. On these occasions the stranded cable cars were drawn away by horses to adjacent sections which were still functioning and temporary shuttle services of horse cars provided. It is interesting to note that at this period early morning workmen's services continued to be provided by horse cars. There was some complaint in the town council regarding these mishaps and the company seems to have been apprehensive too, for in April 1901 they quietly reverted to the service from Post Office via Tollcross and Marchmont Road to Salisbury Place instead of the circular route. The Churchhill to Pilrig service also reverted to its former Churchhill-Salisbury Place run. The Salisbury Place auxiliary cable thus dropped out of normal use and was altered to lie under the main cable coming in from Nether Liberton instead of over it. The pawl on the incoming cable was removed, as cars gripping it did not require to let go.

At first the public were led to believe this was a temporary measure, but after a week or two it became known that the company had no intention of restoring the circular service. The matter was raised in the town council and the town clerk was instructed to write to the company demanding the restoration not only of the so-called inner circular service but also an outer circle via Churchhill as well. The company declined and announced that as from the following Monday, 22 April, the Murrayfield-Nether Liberton service would also be cut, cars working between Murrayfield and Waverley Steps, and between Nether Liberton and Post Office only. Transfer tickets were made available but the inconvenience of changing cars at this important point raised a further storm of protest. The company said delays were avoided by the new scheme which was therefore in the best interests of the public. The latter were not slow to allege the failure of the cable system. The town council for their part would accept no excuses and insisted on the restoration of the former services, but without effect. They had a meeting with the company who then alleged insufficient traffic to warrant the circular services. In July the town clerk issued a comprehensive report on the situation. It was disclosed that of the £32,210 2s. 11d. rental due at Whitsun, the company had defaulted to the extent of £20,500. The company had alleged that the auxiliary cables were unworkable and that under present conditions they were unable to earn sufficient revenue to enable them to pay the sum due. They had suggested that at certain places the main cables should be used instead of the auxiliaries, and that the rental should be reduced to 5 per cent rising to 5½ per cent in 1902 and by ½ per cent each year until 7 per cent was reached in 1905, the abatement to be made up in later years. If these proposals were accepted they would agree to work the system, but they were not prepared to relinquish their lease unless upon adequate terms. The town clerk had replied to the company pointing out that the company knew all about the estimated capital costs and about the auxiliary cables when they undertook their lease, and it was suggested that the difficulties with the auxiliary cables were exaggerated.

It must be admitted that the method of working the junctions was very cumbersome. For example, the average time taken to proceed from St. Andrew Street junction to North Bridge is said to have been nearly four minutes. The company therefore had already started working cars by gravity at certain places, though of course without official sanction. Cars from St. Andrew Street were being run by gravity into Princes Street, and shortly afterwards the auxiliary cable was altered similarly to that at Salisbury Place. Also, at Haymarket, outgoing cars were running by gravity from West Maitland Street to the point at which the main Murrayfield or Gorgie cables were picked up. At Tollcross, cars proceeding towards Braid Hills were run by gravity across the junction, and at Marchmont Road cars from the Churchhill direction crossed the junction by gravity. Yet another example was between Picardy Place and London Road where cars from Post Office were run by gravity, picking up the York Place cable for Pilrig after passing London Road.

While this was going on, the Mound route was completed. On Sunday 25 August 1901 the Goldenacre cable was altered to run between Goldenacre and Henderson Row, and a new cable put in between Henderson Row and Hanover Street and continued in a blind tube under Princes Street to the Mound, and up to Tollcross and back. An auxiliary cable was provided for the junction into Brougham Street, and crossovers were provided in George IV Bridge and in Lauriston Place at Tollcross. Col. von Donop inspected the new line on 10 September and the public services between Mound and Marchmont Road commenced the following day, the horse car line in the High Street being abandoned.

The dispute between the company and the Corporation lingered on. In November the company again paid over only about half of the sum due in rent, and offered to sell their assets to the Corporation so that they could take over the working of the system themselves. The Corporation then initiated legal action for recovery of the sums due, and a novel turn followed. On Saturday 30 November the company announced that as from the following day they would run their cars on Sundays between 10.00 a.m. and 10.00 p.m. This upset the Corporation further, who claimed the company had to obtain their permission for Sunday services. All day on the Saturday they tried to stop the scheme, but on the Sunday the cars ran as announced, and indeed proved very popular with the public. Eighty-two cable cars were operated, but the horses had their day of rest as usual, and only the Salisbury Place-Churchhill section suffered poor patronage. Another innovation on that day was the introduction of "Bell-Punch" tickets with the stage names printed on them. It is believed that hitherto thin paper tickets torn off a roll had been used.

The Corporation again invoked the law and sought to interdict the Sunday service, but the court refused to intervene. The drivers and conductors were not entirely satisfied however. They had been paid at time-and-a-half rate, but sought a limitation of their weekly hours and also a two shillings per week increase. The company for their part would not immediately agree, and wished to await the outcome of the legal question. So on the fourth Sunday, namely 29 December, the car crews did not turn out though the engineering staff did. By the afternoon, however, Mr Pitcairn had gathered together some inspectors and others, and a skeleton service with eighteen cars was provided between Pilrig and St. Andrew Street, and between Post Office and Haymarket, Morningside and Newington; also between Hanover Street and Goldenacre. The following week the company conceded the two shillings increase for cable car crews, the Colinton Road horse car crews to receive a shilling a week as from the date of cable car operation to Portobello, and this was accepted by the men.

Meantime at their meeting on 4 December the Corporation reiterated their intention of recovering the sums due in rent, opposing the Sunday service, and declining the company's offer to sell. This time, however, they decided to leave the question of the restoration of the through services until these more important issues were settled. The company's answer to the court was to the effect that the sums claimed were not justified since the tramways capital account had been wrongly debited with the cost of street widenings and acquisition of properties necessitated by this; also that the allegedly experimental auxiliary cables should not have been so charged. They pointed out that many of these were disused and they made the system unworkable. They claimed the right to run the cars on Sundays if necessary and pointed to the need to obtain all the revenue they could get. Shortly afterwards the company offered to pay in £20,000 if the Corporation would drop the legal proceedings and take the matter to arbitration, but still the Corporation declined.

On 20 December the Mound to Marchmont Road service was altered to work only between the Mound and Tollcross due to insufficient through traffic, but on 8 March following it reverted to the former arrangement and was divided into three halfpenny stages with a penny fare for the full journey.

In February 1902 the financial dispute was considered by the court and the company ordered to pay £20,000, the balance to await settlement of the matters raised by the company. A more amenable spirit on both sides was arising however, and the company actually paid over £30,000, while the Corporation conceded that there might be a case for amending the tramways' capital account in respect of street widenings, etc.

While these affairs were being negotiated, pressure was applied for the completion of the Portobello route, by the April holiday if possible. To enable the pit work outside the depot to be expedited the horse cars were temporarily withdrawn between the depot and Joppa from 10 February.

On 24 February the company made a further gesture and reintroduced working round the Salisbury Place junction, cars proceeding round the curve into Salisbury Place by gravity. The Pilrig-Churchhill service was thereby restored, though the circular route was still cut at the Post Office — cars working from Waverley via Tollcross, Marchmont, and Salisbury Place to Post Office and back. From 9 March this route ceased to operate on Sundays.

Meantime a great effort was being made with the Portobello route. The power station, with two 500 h.p. engines driving the cable drums through gears instead of ropes as in the earlier power stations, and supplied by three boilers with automatic stokers, was complete; as was also the depot, with accommodation for 22 cars. Then on 16 April the cable between the Portobello power station and Waterloo Place was installed, followed by the shorter one between the power station and Joppa on 19 April. The two cables overlapped outside the depot and an auxiliary cable was put into operation when required to take cars into the shed. Cars ran out of the shed by gravity. At the Joppa terminus the cars were worked both in and out of the stub-end by the cable and two stopping places provided, with means to ensure the right cable was picked up. At Waterloo Place the double tracks made connection with the Princes Street tracks, though the Portobello cable was turned back just short of the junction. This connection was not then normally used, and could only be worked by means of a "fly-shunt". A facing crossover was provided in Waterloo Place through which cars gravitated before returning to Portobello and Joppa. Other crossovers were provided at Montrose Terrace, Cadzow Place, Meadowbank, Piershill, King's Road, at either side of the depot, and at Pitt Street in Portobello. On the following day, Sunday, two trial trips were made successfully, but the Board of Trade inspector had not yet visited the line and on the holiday Monday the public had to be content with the horse cars. Col. von Donop made his inspection on 1 May. It was over by 9.30 a.m. and the public service of cable cars commenced immediately with thirteen cars. Outgoing cars were arranged to run by gravity over the junction with the new London Road line at Abbeyhill, but it does not appear as though the London Road cable was then installed.

This London Road cable was an extension of the Pilrig to St. Andrew Street cable which, on its run back down Leith Walk, was diverted under the up main line cable at London Road junction, and taken to Abbeyhill where, after passing the junction, it was returned; and passing over the outgoing Portobello cable, ran back along London Road and round the curve onto the up line in Leith Walk, from where it was again returned and took up its place on the down line beyond the London Road junction. No auxiliary cables were therefore provided at the London Road and Abbeyhill junctions. All cars were run down Leith Walk between Picardy Place and a point beyond London Road junction, or round into London Road, by gravity. Crossovers were provided at each end of the London Road line. There was also one in Leith Walk above the London Road junction.

The cable was extended along London Road in July 1902 and a service provided between Meadowbank and the Leith Walk end of London Road. The public desired a through service to Princes Street, however, so on 20 October 1902 this was replaced by a service between Abbeyhill and Morningside Station via London Road and York Place.

The system now extended for 21¼ miles and was considered complete.

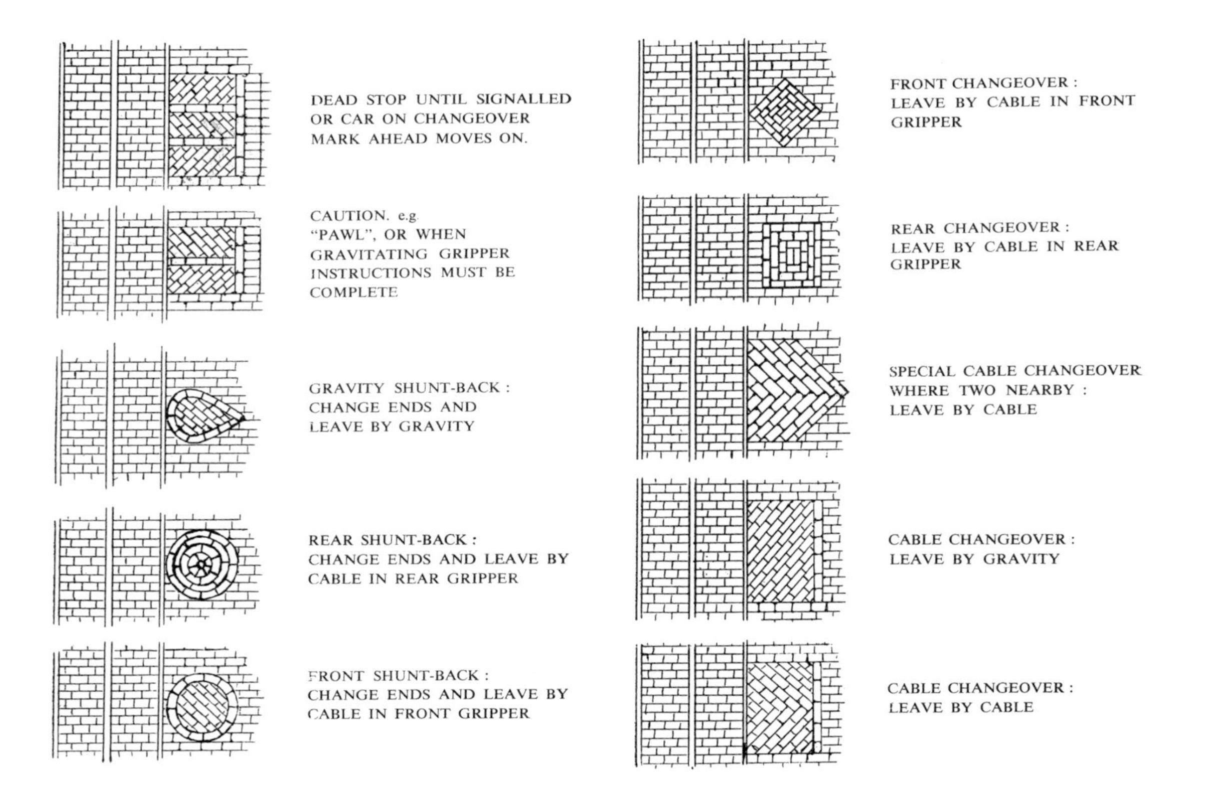

The Road Marks Edinburgh cable tramways.

Meanwhile the negotiations between the company and the Corporation had been proceeding, and on 29 July 1902 a new agreement between them was signed. This resolved all the matters which had been in dispute, including reduction of the capital account and the sums due by the company, the future rates of rental, through working and Sunday services.

On 21 December 1902, the Marchmont circular route and the Murrayfield-Nether Liberton service were restored, the auxiliary cable from Princes Street to North Bridge having been altered to lie above the other auxiliary from North Bridge towards Leith Street. Cars for the latter direction were then run by gravity.

The system was now operating quite successfully. In January 1901 the company had placed the drivers under the control of the engineering department, and later in the year an instruction book was issued to them, containing an appendix wherein was laid down the correct procedure in regard to left or right-hand jaw and front or rear gripper for each section of every route. The precise spots at which cars had to stop to change cables or carry out other manoeuvres were afterwards marked by squares, circles, or other special shapes, each with its own meaning, laid in setts between the two pairs of rails; and pointsmen were provided to ensure, by examination, that all was correct before cars were allowed to proceed at the various junctions. See diagrams on page 101.

Nevertheless minor mishaps continued to occur from time to time, and there were also instances of cars hitting pawls. Some of these latter occurrences were accompanied by injuries to passengers and gave rise to discussions with the Board of Trade regarding the use of pawls. The company believed the prevention of serious damage, and hence dislocation of the service, justified their use where really necessary, but the introduction of gravity running at various places, as already mentioned, had enabled several of them to be eliminated. Further improvements of this nature were effected from time to time. On 17 January 1904 the main cable was extended from Shrubhill to Pilrig and its diversion to and from the power house arranged on the down line. Cars proceeding towards Pilrig passed Shrubhill by gravity, and had a clear run with the cable coming up from Pilrig. At Tollcross junction the declivity was too slight for effective gravity operation, and the cable heights were adjusted, also early in 1904, to allow for safely fly-shunting cars proceeding towards Braid Hills. The same scheme was put into operation at the West End for cars proceeding towards Haymarket, in October 1905. Where fly-shunting was used cars were first brought to a stop at the "Dead stop" Road Mark until signalled forward by the pointsman.

These and other minor alterations considerably lessened the risk of accidents as well as simplifying the operation of the system, and enabled driving by the rear gripper to be dispensed with except in one or two special places. The pawls were still retained at certain necessary locations, however, and were again under discussion later as we shall see.

In 1903 there was a strike by the car crews over the introduction of a new pay system, and there were unfortunately instances of assault and sabotage. Mr Colam retired in December 1904 and was succeeded by Mr E. F. Harris.

In 1904 the question of the company's payments to the Corporation came up again. The capital expenditure on constructing the system was said to amount to approximately £1,000,000, but the company had been paying the 7 per cent on an estimated total of £1,250,000, which included the cost of purchasing the Northern Company's system. The Corporation now said their total was higher — nearly £1,300,000 — while the company wanted a reduction. Some reduction appears to have been made and in 1905 the position appears to have been more amicable, as a further revision was agreed upon. The company's "Deferred" shareholders did not receive their first dividend till 1908.

An increase in speed was considered desirable and feasible, and as the maximum speeds had been fixed in the local Acts, the Corporation secured an Order in 1905 to permit the Board of Trade to fix the speeds notwithstanding the Acts. The cable speeds then became as follows:

Mound	7¾ m.p.h.	Braids and Princes St.	10¼ m.p.h.
Stockbridge	8 m.p.h.	Joppa	10½ m.p.h.
Goldenacre	8¾ m.p.h.	Portobello	11¾ m.p.h.
Liberton, York Place, Grange, Gorgie, Murrayfield			9½ m.p.h.

It is opportune now to review the services and fares in operation. The "Tickets and Fares" book dated 1903 quotes the following services, the identifying letters being used for ticket purposes only:

A. Murrayfield & Nether Liberton
B. Pilrig & Gorgie
C. Pilrig & Braid Hills
D. Abbeyhill & Morningside
E. Marchmont Road Circle (not on Sundays)
F. Mound & Marchmont Road
G. Pilrig & Churchhill
H. Pilrig & Nether Liberton
J. Post Office & Joppa
L. Tollcross & Colinton Road (horse cars)
M. Princes Street & Goldenacre
N. Princes Street & Comely Bank
BX. Post Office & Gorgie
CX. Post Office & Morningside or Braid Hills

The "Bell-punch" type tickets now used showed the stage names in "Fareboard"* layout and did not carry any printer's name. The centre column carried the fare, route letter and the wording: "Edin. & Dist. Tram.Co.Ltd. Valid to stage opposite punch hole by car on which issued.

* "Fareboard" layout refers to a ticket on which the boarding stages were shown in one column with corresponding alighting stages opposite in the other column, the two columns usually being separated by a centre column in which was shown the fare, the company's name and other information on validity.

To be punched in presence of passenger"; and, printed across the foot of the ticket: "Issued subject to the Bye-laws." A variety of advertisements appeared on the back. The colours were 1d. white; 2d. pink; 3d. mauve, the fares conforming fairly closely to those in force prior to the Second World War. Separate issues of tickets were provided for routes A, B, C/D, E/F, G/H, J, L, M/N. Children under ten years paid 1d. for any one journey. There were certain ½d. stages on E and F routes, also from Pilrig, Joppa, and Goldenacre, and certain special children's and workmen's ½d. stages also, and a blue ticket was available for these. A pale brown 1½d. ticket was provided for four 1½d. stages on E, J and M routes, while there was quite a selection of 1d. transfers for which a green ticket was used, the wording on the centre column being slightly different. The bottom half of some of these tickets was also used for children's, workmen's and messengers' 1d. fares. The transfer fares however were soon withdrawn with only four exceptions, and to compensate for this an additional service was introduced on 1 August 1903 from Haymarket to Piershill via Leith Street but returning via York Place, running every five minutes and extended to Portobello on Saturdays and Sundays in summer. Special 1d. tickets were sold at the company's office for use of scholars up to 16 years of age, messengers, e.g. Post Office telegraph boys, and were accepted as cash by conductors who issued the appropriate ordinary ticket in exchange. These special tickets had no columns or stage names and most of them were printed sideways. From January 1903 season tickets could be obtained for the Joppa route at 70/- per annum, available between Waterloo Place and Joppa and between Abbeyhill and St. Andrew Street via London Road. Much of the face of the J tickets was then used to advertise the advantage of buying a season ticket. A parcels delivery service was started on 3 October 1904.

The frequencies of the various services were altered from time to time but each service generally had cars every three, four, or five minutes, which compares well with frequencies today. some changes were made in the services later. Commencing about September 1904 a service was put on between Ardmillan Terrace and Salisbury Place, but on 1 October 1906 this was altered to Ardmillan Terrace and Abbeyhill via York Place and London Road, the Morningside Station and Abbeyhill service being changed to Morningside Station and Pilrig. Also on 1 October 1906 the Mound to Marchmont Road route was again terminated at Tollcross, and the Pilrig to Churchhill service shortened to Pilrig and Salisbury Place. The Marchmont circular service was cut once more, this time at the top of Marchmont Road, and the cars run on an increased frequency from there via Tollcross, Princes Street and Salisbury Place to Churchhill, and back again. This alteration was not popular and after considerable discussion the Corporation referred the matter to an arbiter, the Dean of the Faculty, who, in February 1908, decided that the company must operate the circular service if required to do so by the Corporation. Pressure being brought to bear this was restored later in the year and the Pilrig-Salisbury Place service extended to Churchhill. The public were still

The Pilrig "Muddle", c. 1905-6. The cable car driver is waiting with his hand on the gripper wheel ready to tighten it and put the car in motion. The pointsman has already checked that the cable is in place in the half-open gripper, and the brakes are off. The car has come out from Shrubhill depot to proceed to Murrayfield and take up service on the Murrayfield-Nether Liberton route. Leith electric car No. 32 emerging from Pilrig Street on the left, and Leith No. 19 on the right. (*F. C. Inglis*)

dissatisfied with the service provided however, and in February 1909 the council agreed to the Marchmont-Tollcross-Post Office-Salisbury Place-Churchhill scheme, the Pilrig-Churchhill service again being cut back at Salisbury Place. The junction at the top of Marchmont Road was then taken out, as had already been done some time previously at Churchhill and at the east end of Morrison Street. Meanwhile a new fare table was introduced on 1 April 1906 giving longer stages of about half a mile, three for 1d., four for 1½d., six for 2d. and eight for 2½d. Transfer fares were offered at interchange points where there was no through service. Transfer tickets to Leith had been introduced on 26 November 1905.

Mr Pitcairn retired on 30 August 1906. He had been appointed manager of the Edinburgh Street Tramways Company in 1884 and had come to be very highly regarded by his staff and directors alike. He had introduced a new disciplinary system by which staff were graded into three classes with a small differential in pay, and instead of a man being fined or suspended for an offence he would normally be reduced in grade for a spell. A man's class was at first clearly stated on his cap badge, but this was changed to a less public indication in the form of a diamond, crescent or other sign above the word driver or conductor. Mr Pitcairn was succeeded by Mr C. W. Shepherd, who had been Traffic Superintendent.

In January 1907 most of the routes were given numbers, and these were displayed on a coloured oval board mounted on the upper deck rail. The numbers and colours were as follows:

1	Murrayfield & Nether Liberton	Red board
2	Pilrig & Gorgie	Blue board
3	Abbeyhill & Ardmillan Terrace	Blue board
4	Pilrig & Braid Hills	Green board
5	Pilrig & Morningside Station	Green board
6	Marchmont & Churchhill	White board
7	Pilrig & Nether Liberton	Red board
8	Pilrig & Salisbury Place	Red board

The Hanover Street route, Comely Bank route, Mound route, and Joppa route never carried numbers. The bullseye light in the saloon bulkhead was then arranged to show the corresponding colour at night. Later the long destination board carried above the saloon windows was discarded in favour of a more conventional small board carried at the bottom of the centre window. About 1911 the bullseye light in the saloon bulkheads was removed and a slide arranged with opaque glass behind took its place. Into this slide a metal stencil was inserted after dark, being illuminated by the saloon interior lighting. These stencils showed only the termini and the name was often abbreviated; hence a long-standing designation "Toll-X". The old Northern section cars were not provided with these amenities. At the end of 1907 the company agreed to fit higher guardrails on the top deck and stairs, but the work proceeded slowly and in 1911 some forty cars had still not been dealt with. In October 1907 the Board of Trade sanctioned an increase of speed for the Henderson Row cables to 9 m.p.h.

Reverting to 1905, the question of extensions and future policy was under discussion in the town council. The Musselburgh company were already inside the city boundary with their line to the cable terminus at Joppa, though the city had powers to acquire it upon six months' notice if they wished. Other electric tramway promoters were seeking routes into the city. The town clerk was asked to report and he recommended the Corporation to ensure ownership of all lines constructed within the boundary, and to consult the present lessees in regard to any extensions. It was considered that the conversion of the Gilmore Place-Craiglockhart horse-car line to either cable or electric traction was now necessary.

The Corporation's Provisional Order for 1905 therefore sought authority for the reconstruction of the Craiglockhart line, which it was proposed to extend to the city boundary, and beyond it to Craiglockhart Avenue. The line was then to go down Craiglockhart Avenue to Slateford and back to town by Slateford Road and Fountainbridge. In May 1906, however, the Corporation decided to withdraw from their application all but the reconstruction of the existing line and its extenson as far as the top of Craiglockhart Avenue. Even so, the portion outside the city boundary was not included in the resulting Edinburgh Corporation Act 1906 (passed 4 August 1906). Authority for another new route was included in this Act however, namely down Broughton Street from the foot of Leith Street to Canonmills, with a branch down East Claremont Street to

John E. Pitcairn, Manager E.S.T.Co. and E. & D.T.CO. 1884-1906.

Bonnington Toll: also connections from York Place and from Picardy Place. Cable traction was to be used for the Craiglockhart line unless the company agreed to some other system; while if cable traction was not provided for Broughton Street, that line was not to be included in the company's existing lease. The Corporation might then work it themselves.

The Corporation were now thinking hard about the high capital cost of the cable system, which many already regarded as obsolete, and a considerable controversy arose. Sir Alexander Kennedy was consulted and favoured a surface-contact electric line. A full size demonstration of the "Kingsland" surface-contact system had been given in the North Bridge Arcade in June 1906. A council deputation therefore set off to inspect the various systems to be seen at work in the country. Their tour took them to London where the conduit system was seen. They saw the "Dolter" surface-contact system at Hastings, and also at Rotherham and Mexborough; the "Lorain" surface-contact at Wolverhampton, and the "G.B." surface-contact at Lincoln. The "Kingsland" surface-contact system was also further explained to them at the Traction Corporation Ltd.'s London office, as they had as yet no line in operation in this country. This company was anxious to provide a six months' trial on the Morrison Street route, or from the Mound to the High Street, and while the Corporation were willing, the Edinburgh & District Tramways Company were not. The Dolter concern offered to equip the Craiglockhart line on a sort of "not satisfied no payment" basis. The Edinburgh Suburban Electric Tramways Company, to be mentioned in a later chapter, and who were then in course of negotiating an agreement with the Corporation, offered to extend their proposed system along Melville Drive to Tollcross and connect up with the Craiglockhart line on the overhead system. this however was rather ruled out as the Corporation did not want to evict their present lessees, who for their part preferred to continue a uniform system, which meant cable. They were however prepared to agree to an electric system if the Craiglockhart route was continued from Tollcross down to the Mound, and with certain safeguards on costs. On the other hand they refused to agree to electric traction for Broughton Street.

The council deputation duly reported. They felt the "G.B." surface-contact system most suited Edinburgh, but the difficulties of installing this on a cable line, as would be necessary between Tollcross and Gilmore Place, did not appear capable of solution. Only the overhead electric system could be used there, and to bring that system down the Mound in view of Princes Street just would not do. So on 5 February 1907 the council decided to reconstruct the Craiglockhart line for cable traction. As before, Mr Colam was offered the joint appointment as engineer for the new works, but this time refused, so Sir Alexander Kennedy was appointed. On 26 February 1907 the town council decided to construct the Broughton Street line to Canonmills, likewise for cable traction.

The contracts were let, to Dick Kerr & Co. Ltd., in July, and the three

Cable cars in Princes Street at a standstill. The cable has been damaged and stopped. (*A. W. Brotchie*)

The cable repair gang at work. (*A. W. Brotchie*)

horse cars withdrawn from the Craiglockhart line on 24 August 1907, to allow work to proceed. So ended horse traction in Edinburgh.

The residents beyond the Craiglockhart horse car terminus had been pressing for the extension of the line to be carried out at the same time, as they claimed it would be less costly than adding it later. The Corporation agreed on 11 June 1907, and the construction of the extension out to the city boundary was put in hand also. The first half-mile or so of this route had interlaced tracks with a single slot, and there were two passing places. The extension was nearly all interlaced track, but on this section separate slots were provided. Where a single slot was used great care was necessary, and the rule book pointed out that the gripper could not be opened more than two turns with safety. If opened further the cable was liable to slip out altogether. Opening the gripper one turn to let the cable slide though while holding the car with the brake was normal traffic stop procedure. Seven turns ensured the cable was dropped for change-over purposes.

The new cable was driven from Tollcross power station, provision having been made in the original design for additional power output. During the alterations in the power station there was a serious mishap in the early hours of 3 November 1907, resulting in the Grange and Murrayfield cables being out of action that day, though by great effort full service was restored for the following day.

An auxiliary cable was provided at the Gilmore Place junction, and manual signal lamps were installed on the sections which were in effect single line, for use in fog.

After a trial run on 7 April 1908 with No. 27, Major Pringle inspected the whole line for the Board of Trade on 14 April, starting from Princes Street in one of the new top-covered cars. Everything proved satisfactory and a five minute service between Post Office and Craiglockhart was inaugurated immediately after the inspection was completed. This service was numbered 9, displayed on a yellow board.

Meanwhile construction of the Broughton Street line was proceeding. This was to be ready for service on 1 June 1908 under a penalty of £20 per week. The work was not so straightforward however and necessitated some rearrangement of the cables. The Henderson Row-Goldenacre cable was led blind as far as Canonmills where it then took up the line to the foot of Leith Street, returned to Goldenacre, back to Canonmills, and then blind to Henderson Row. An auxiliary cable driven from it served the short distance between Henderson Row and Canonmills where, in returning, it worked a crossover. The facing crossover below Henderson Row was relaid in the trailing direction and apparently worked by one of the cables. Another trailing crossover was provided above the junction also. The junction to the Broughton Street line and its pit were not constructed, however, there being a gravity crossover at the end of the new line. No auxiliary cable was provided at the junction at the foot of Leith Street, the main Broughton Street cable being taken through the junction into Leith Street, and cars for Pilrig gravitating across it. Some difficulties arose with the pulleys in the dip in the line near the Canonmills terminus, which further delayed the opening, and in the event, it was not until 20 October 1908 that Col. von Donop inspected the line for the Board of Trade. A top-covered car was again used for the inspection, and the Craiglockhart-Post Office service was extended to Canonmills the same afternoon. Some modifications to the cables at the Post Office had also been required for this service, probably involving a lowering of the two auxiliaries for the two North Bridge curves so that the cars from Leith Street to Princes Street could safely make the two "flying-shunts" over them. At the town council meeting on the same day that the line was opened, the Corporation called upon the company to complete the junction at Canonmills so as to enable the Broughton Street route cars to run through to Goldenacre. The company demurred, but in face of public clamour for the through service, started to build the junction, pointing out at the same time that through running would still not be possible owing to the difference in the old Northern system pulleys etc. A transfer ticket was made available from 9 November. The Corporation insisted that through running was necessary, and in June 1909 authorised expenditure on the necessary modifications between Henderson Row and Goldenacre. The company objected to this further addition to the capital account, but when the Corporation then sought payment of £880 now due under the penalty clause for late completion of the Broughton Street line, the company agreed to carry out the work and provide a through service, with the Corporation forgoing their £880. The work then proceeded slowly, but in December 1909 the Broughton Street cars were running through to Goldenacre showing "Leith Street & Goldenacre" on their destination board. When the junction was made the Canonmills-Henderson Row auxiliary cable was led under the main Broughton Street-Goldenacre cable, and cars from Goldenacre to Hanover Street took the junction by gravity. This new link provided an orthodox route by which the Northern section cars could be hauled to the Shrubhill workshops when necessary. Hitherto such transfer had been effected by means of a single trailing connection from Hanover Street eastwards to Princes Street laid in 1906. This connection had no conduit and was removed on the opening of the Broughton Street route.

After clearing the junction at the foot of Leith Street, the Broughton Street tracks were interlaced with a single slot for a short distance, and just before the end of this section the York Place route was crossed at right angles. Both routes were on gradients, but the new line being the steeper, the York Place cables were led underneath and cars proceeding up York Place had to take a good flying-shunt. This raised the question of pawls again. It was intended to provide pawls here but on account of objection to pawls raised by the Tramways Company's insurers they were not put in. Much thought was given to the provision of an audible warning or lamp but such an arrangement was found to be impracticable. The first accident due to a York Place car not releasing its cable occurred only five days after the opening of the Broughton Street line. Several passengers were injured and the Broughton Street line put out of action for the rest of the day.

Early in 1909 Sir Alexander Kennedy, who had now been appointed permanent consultant to the Corporation Tramways Committee, was asked to report on the subject of pawls in general, of which there were four slightly different designs in use at 22 locations viz.:

Portobello Depot, outgoing line	Type A
Portobello Depot, incoming line	" A
Shrubhill Depot gate, down line	" A
Waterloo Place, incoming line	" A
North Bridge, down line	" A
West Register Street, east-going line	" A
Haymarket, Clifton Terrace, east-going line	" A
Earl Grey Street, incoming line	" A
Earl Grey Street, outgoing line	" A
Brougham Street, incoming line	" B
Top of Marchmont Road, outgoing line	" B
Strathearn Road, Marchmont, incoming line	" B
Haymarket, West Maitland Street, outgoing line	" B
Foot of Lothian Road, incoming line	" B
West End, Princes Street, outgoing line	" B
Top of Leith Street, up line	" B
Antigua Street, up line	" B
Pitt Street, up line	" B
Stockbridge, at Hamilton Place, down line	" C
Abbeyhill, Montrose Terrace, down line	" C
South St. Andrew Street, down line	" D
Foot of the Mound, down line	" D

He considered that passengers were just as much at risk from an accident where no pawl was provided as they were from a car hitting a pawl, and as a pawl prevented serious damage to the machinery, he felt unjustified in recommending their removal. The number of pawl accidents and the number of passengers injured was given for the years to 30 April as:

1904	18	accidents	54	passengers	injured
1905	13	"	21	"	"
1906	13	"	21	"	"
1907	30	"	60	"	"
1908	25	"	38	"	"
1909	8	"	15	"	"

The 1909 figures covered only the nine months to 31 January. St. Andrew Street and North Bridge were the two locations with the highest number of accients, 19 at each over the period. Very few accidents arose from a jammed gripper, but he pointed out that accidents due to forgetfulness of a driver "are inherent to the cable system which requires the enforcement of regulations both numerous and more stringent for its efficient and safe working, than any other system of traction". In the case of the Broughton Street-York Place crossing he thought the presence of a pointsman at all times the cars were running, as he had already recommended, would almost entirely obviate the question of forgetfulness. The Board of Trade concurred with Sir Alexander Kennedy's report and the provision and duty of the pointsman at the Broughton Street-York Place crossing was incorporated in the bylaws on 4 May 1909. The pointsman had to ensure that York Place up line drivers had fully opened their grippers before passing the "Caution" Road Mark. On the down line there was a compulsory stop before the crossing and cars then proceeded across by gravity.

The branch to Bonnington Toll and the connections to York Place and to Picardy Place were not constructed.

Towards the end of 1907 a Mr N. Thomson had proposed a sixty-year lease of the whole system with a view to electrification, but this found no favour with the council.

An improvement was effected at the London Road junction in 1908 when a new pit was built and an auxiliary cable provided, apparently for the benefit of upgoing cars. Another alteration was made at the Lauriston Place-Brougham Street junction where the original auxiliary cable had earlier been removed and the main cable extended in its place for taking the Mound route cars to and from the depot. A new pit was built in Lauriston Place in 1909 and an auxiliary cable provided for the junction curve again.

One other extension to the cable system remains to be considered. This was to the Gorgie route which it was intended to extend for about half a mile from Saughton Park to the then new road called Chesser Avenue, and then to continue along Chesser Avenue to the new cattle markets. The Corporation sought powers for this line in their 1908 Provisional Order, and also for a new link from the Murrayfield terminus to the Gorgie line along what is now Saughtonhall drive, then being constructed. This latter was however withdrawn. In March 1908, when the Cope Collis Syndicate Ltd. sought permission for a conduit electric line along Saughtonhall Drive, it was refused. Preparations were in hand for the Scottish National Exhibition to be held at Saughton Park in that year, however, and it was urged that if part of this extension could be laid in time for the exhibition opening on 1 May it would be very useful for storing cars to meet the expected heavy traffic. In October 1907 the Board of Trade agreed to work being put in hand for this purpose forthwith, notwithstanding that Parliamentary sanction could not be obtained for some time. The company agreed to compensate any affected parties. The work was pushed ahead as far as Chesser Avenue and finished in time for Major Pringle to inspect it on the same day as the Craiglockhart line, namely 14 April 1908. The extension was then available for storing cars for the exhibition traffic; the normal service not being extended to the new terminus until after the Board of Trade's certificate arrived in September, the Provisional Order by that time having passed through parliament. A service from Lothian Road via Morrison Street to the exhibition was proposed but did not materialise. Traffic was very heavy leaving the exhibition and queue barriers had to be installed. The Tramways Company issued an illustrated guide.

On the excuse that a threehalfpenny fare was inconvenient for the exhibition crowds, the company raised the Gorgie and Murrayfield fares to twopence. After the exhibition closed a deputation to the company sought a restoration of the old fare, but the company then revised their scale to give three stages for a penny and six for twopence throughout the system, dropping the threehalfpenny fares. This took effect from 27 November 1908.

The remainder of the proposed Chesser Avenue extension was never built. Dick Kerr & Co. were ready to start work on it in February 1910 when it was pointed out that there would be difficulties with the cable on account of the rise over the bridge at the cattle market. So the matter was reconsidered, and instead, the Corporation decided on a new line from Ardmillan Terrace along Slateford Road to the cattle market. It has to be mentioned, however, that another concern, the Colinton Tramways Company, proposed to build a tramway on private ground from Slateford to Colinton, and also a line from East Fountainbridge to Ardmillan Terrace, as related in Chapter 7. With all this in view it was decided that the Slateford Road line should be electrically operated, and that it should be excluded from the subjects of the 1898 lease to the Edinburgh & District Tramways Company. Accordingly a Minute of Agreement was drawn up on 14 June 1910, by which the Slateford electric line was to be worked by the Edinburgh & District Tramways Company "as a line distinct and separate from the Tramways let under the Lease of 1898" to the thirtieth day of June 1919. Provision was made for through running over the Colinton Tramways. The line made a single line trailing connection with the outgoing Gorgie line at Ardmillan Terrace, and was single with passing places. The overhead system was adopted, current being supplied from the Corporation's Dewar Place electricity station to a feeder pillar at the foot of Ardmillan Terrace. The work was put in hand very quickly and the line was opened on 8 June 1910, prior to the date of the agreement. The company converted four cars for this service, the two normally in use being hauled to and from Shrubhill depot night and morning by cable cars.

On Saturday and Sunday afternoons in the summer of 1908 a service had been run between Ardmillan Terrace and Joppa, proceeding via Waterloo Place on the outward journey, but using the London Road and York Place route on the return. This return route avoided the additional complications that the Post Office junctions entailed for west-going cars. There were several requests for such a through service to be provided regularly in both directions between Regent Road and Princes Street, but these were turned down on account of the aforementioned complications for west-going cars.

Further changes were made in the services. In the summer of 1909 the number 3 service was altered to run from Ardmillan Terrace to Pilrig, and number 5 became Abbeyhill to Morningside Station again, but near the end of the year the previous arrangement was reverted to, though the aforementioned alteration was tried once more in the following summer. A penny transfer ticket between Abbeyhill and Surgeons' Hall was made available from 24 September 1909, while in July 1909 a penny fare for dogs or luggage, using a brown ticket, was introduced. The opening of the new amusement park at the Marine Gardens* brought additional traffic to the Portobello route for the summer, and through services were sometimes run.

Long-service stripes for a ten years' unblemished record and a merit medal for conspicuous action by staff were introduced about the end of 1908, and in 1909 a comprehensive rule book was issued. A glance at some of its contents is interesting. There was a page of instructions on "How to deal with offenders against the bye-laws"; another on "How to report street accidents"; several on "General Instructions", and several more on "Special Instructions to Drivers and Conductors". The first of these is perhaps of particular interest in showing the exacting nature of the driver's duties. "No one shall be appointed a driver unless he is under thirty-six years of age and can produce a written character for carefulness and sobriety and is in possession of the necessary technical certificate. He must then qualify to drive on all routes." For the necessary technical certificate the man had to know:

1. The construction of grippers, bogies, and brakes, with the names of their parts.
2. How to use the grippers and gearing, brakes and sand.
3. How to drive a car.
4. How to deal with a faulty gripper, slot-roller, sleeve, die, guide-pin, cradle and slide-bar.
5. How to deal with a faulty friction-plate, gripper-centre, gripper leg and screw-fork.
6. How to attach and detach a gripper.
7. Names and positions of changeover marks.
8. Examinations of grippers and cables at changeover marks.
9. Names and positions of cables on all routes.
10. Position and displacement of cables on curves, crossings and supporting pulleys.
11. Names of all junctions.
12. Use of slot and track points, and how to rerail bogies.
13. Use and position of slot-stops (i.e. pawls).
14. Management of gas generators and car lighting.

Another of the Special Instructions may be quoted: "When making the

* The amusement park with its "figure-eight" scenic railway was an enterprise in which the Tramways Company had a financial interest, and in April 1910 the Marine Gardens Figure-Eight Co. Ltd. was formed to run it. Activities lapsed during the war and the company was wound up in Jaunuary 1917.

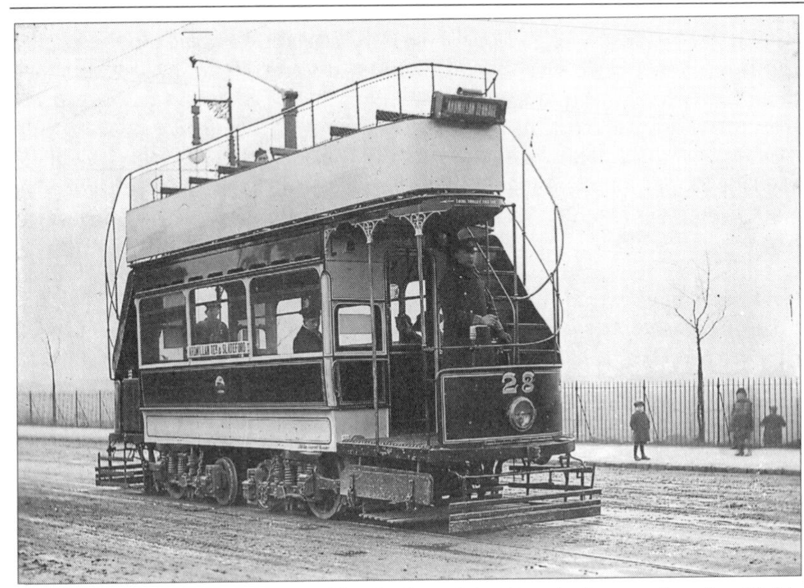

The Slateford route electric car near Slateford terminus. Note the "country" road and fields. (*E. O. Catford*)

usual traffic stop the driving-wheel of the gripper must be operated from the top spoke, and given one complete turn with the right hand, the left hand pulling on the brake lever. When restarting, the driving-wheel is to be brought back the full turn, and gripper closed by the same spoke, the right hand remaining in touch with the wheel throughout the operation, the left hand easing off the brake lever. The driving-wheel to be left at rest when travelling at full speed, and in position to ease off the gripper immediately if required. When making an unusually long traffic stop, the driving wheel of the gripper must be opened two full turns, and when stopped for a delay the gripper must be opened full out on the straight road. When leaving the platform of car for any purpose, both wheel and slipper brakes must be put on."

There were seventeen pages explaining the various road marks and special detailed instructions for working cars at certain junctions, single-lines, curves etc. A page on "How to Act in Case of Accident to the Company's Running Plant" is also of significance: "1. Accidents require you to take time to think. Obtain assistance if you cannot answer the following questions: What is wrong? What has to be done? Is everything in position to commence work? 2. Accidents are either important or unimportant, and much loss of time and expense may be saved by men who quickly realise this. 3. Important accidents are generally such as Drivers cannot deal with themselves, and require immediate written information sent to the nearest Road Official or Depot by telephone, cab, or car for assistance. 4. Unimportant accidents are generally such as Drivers can deal with themselves, and require reporting to the first Road

Official when seen. 5. Displacement of the cables or pulleys at any part of the lines or stopping marks must be carefully noted and reported on at once. 6. Cables leaving a gripper should always return to their usual position, failure to do this must be looked for, the cause discovered, noted and reported on at once. 7. Should the cable stop, slip, or jerk while the gripper is closed on it, ease off the gripper at once, and do not again close it on the cable until it has gathered speed, and report the occurrence. 8. Should the cable be known to be damaged, grippers must be opened and cleared from the cable and closed up. The Road Officials will then instruct when cars are to be restarted. 9. After losing a cable, and before attempting to retake it, remember which jaw of the gripper is the correct one to use, and that the cable cannot be taken otherwise than on the straight track."

The book was completed with the inclusion of the Board of Trade and Corporation bylaws. "Road Officials" included staff inspectors, traffic inspectors, pointsmen, and ticket inspectors, but there were also fitters at the most important points. Telephones were provided at the junction pits.

Attempts were being made to devise a better form of lifeguard for the cars. Electric cars normally had the gate and automatic tray device under the platforms, but there was no room for this on the cable cars which were provided only with a fender. It was a problem which proved intractable. However, another safety measure applied in 1909 was fitting of wire mesh between the top deck rails of the cars. The Princes Street tracks were relaid in the summer of 1910. Passenger "islands" were introduced at Antigua Street and at Easter Road in 1911, also a passenger shelter — Edinburgh's first — at Ardmillan Terrace in February 1911. At this time the only transfer fare in operation seems to have been that to Slateford. A decorated car ran during the Royal visit to the city in the summer of 1911.

There was labour trouble again on 18 July 1913 when the men ran their cars into the depot and came out on strike for an additional halfpenny per hour, having refused the company's offer of a farthing. New men were gathered from around the country and lodged at Shrubhill while undergoing intensive training in the strange technique of driving a cable car. A row developed over these men not having licences, and when application was made for these on 29 July the magistrates refused them. Thirty-five cars were by then in service, and one or two hostile acts occurred. However, a settlement was effected on 30 July through the mediation of the Lord Provost, and normal service resumed the following day.

The question of the further development of the city's transport was again to the fore at this period, though it was realised that extension of the cable system could not now be profitable. There had recently been proposals for a line from Fountainbridge through the Grassmarket, Bristo, Preston Street, and Duddingston to Portobello, and also via Palmerston Place to the Queensferry Road. In July 1911 the burgh engineer inspected the petrol-electric tramcar running at Morecambe, and suggested a trial with such a machine in Edinburgh. Three months later a report on Motor Bus Traction and the "Rail-less Trolley Car" was submitted. Three routes were suggested. However, in September 1912 a review of the various systems of street traction was called for, and the burgh engineer's resulting document was a comprehensive survey of the possibilities of all kinds of tramways, trolley-buses and motorbuses.

On the basis that 25¾ route miles of cable tramway were operating in the city, the cost of construction, track work only, was given as £29,000 per mile of double track. Working expenditure was shown as 5¼d. per car-mile, and rent and rates worked out at 4d. per car-mile. Since the revenue averaged 10½d. per car-mile, the company apparently made a small profit of 1¼d. per car-mile. It may be remarked that the horse-power per car employed worked out at the very low figure of about 15. The capital costs were of course very heavy, and although up to that time the operating costs at 5¼d. per car-mile were the lowest in the country, Leith Corporation's electric tramways had succeeded in reducing their operating costs to a new low record figure of 4½d. per car-mile. So, to quote the review, "It is not likely, in face of these facts, that any extension of the cable system will be contemplated". This of course proved to be the case.

For the future, the burgh engineer ruled out the conduit electric system on account of cost, and the surface-contact electric system mainly on the grounds of potential danger. The overhead electric system he considered suitable except for Princes Street, and it was shown to be economical. For lighter traffic routes, petrol-electric cars, trolley-buses or motor-buses were considered again. The three proposed new routes were considered further. These were: the northern route, from Blackhall via Stockbridge and Broughton Road to Pilrig; the central route, from Ardmillan Terrace via Fountainbridge, Bread Street, and Johnston Terrace to the Tron Church; the southern route, a circular run via Preston Street, Dalkeith Road, Lady Road, West Mains Road, Blackford Avenue, Marchmont Road, and Melville Drive. It will be noticed that these mostly covered roads which had earlier been served by horse buses.

For the first two, trolley-buses were suggested, though were it not for the narrowness of Fountainbridge and the old canal bridge, a tramway would have been preferred here. For the southern route, only the motor bus was considered likely to pay, though a trolley-bus route from the foot of Marchmont Road via Preston Street and Dalkeith Road to Cameron Toll was put forward as an alternative. The town council deliberated on these proposals. In any event Parliamentary powers would be required, and the lessees of the existing tramway system would have to be considered too.

However, in the Edinburgh Corporation Act 1913 (passed 15 August 1913), it was secured that the Corporation "may provide, maintain, repair, work and use (but shall not manufacture) motor omnibuses, or may lease or otherwise arrange for maintenance, repair, working and running of such motor omnibuses". The Corporation could impose such reasonable charges as may be approved by the Board of Trade. Arrangements made had to have the consent of the Edinburgh & District Tramways Company and if the buses were driven by electricity there was the usual clause for the protection of the Post Office telephones.

The Corporation then entered into an agreement with the Edinburgh & District Tramways Company to work motor buses for them at bare cost, the Corporation to purchase the vehicles. At the end of 1913 it was decided that the southern circular route should be tried, and tenders were invited for three single-deck and three double-deck petrol-electric buses. In the event six single-deckers were bought, three Leyland S8s and three Tilling-Stevens TS3s, the latter only being petrol-electric. All had 29-seat rear entrance saloon bodies with clerestory roofs. There was a narrow door at the front for use in emergency and for which the driver held a key. The Leylands were Nos. 1-3 with registration numbers S4440-2, and the Tilling-Stevens were Nos. 4-6 with registration numbers S4443-5. All were lettered "Edinburgh Corporation".

The Tramways Company housed the buses at Tollcross depot and the service commenced on 3 August 1914. However, on 19 October 1914, the War Department commandeered the three Leyland chassis. A reduced service was then maintained by two of the Tilling-Stevens — the third being under repair — but this was not effective and the service operated for the last time on 31 October 1914. Thus ended, for the time being, supplementary forms of transport under Corporation auspices. The three Tilling-Stevens were sold to the Scottish Motor Traction Company for £2,400, and later the bodies of the three Leylands were sold to Munro of Auchendinny. The proposed northern and central routes were of course dropped until after the war.

The Corporation had already decided, on 31 October 1912, to take over the tramway system and operate it themselves on the expiry of the company's lease; and towards the end of 1914 a Minute of Agreement was drawn up with the company regarding this. In the agreement the Corporation were to be allowed to experiment with petrol-electric tramcars as long as they did not hinder the company's traffic and the company agreed to work them on certain proposed extensions, which were included in the Corporation's Provisional Order in 1915. In this Order authority for the following tramways was sought: an exension from Craiglockhart to Colinton; a tramroad from the Braid Hills terminus through the Braid Burn valley to join up with the proposed Colinton extension at Firhill, most of which would be on its own private right-of-way; an extension from Murrayfield terminus to Corstorphine, the proposed new terminus being just beyond Templeland Road; a siding into the old stable premises near the Corstorphine terminus; a short line from Shandwick Place into Hope Street; connecting lines between Morrison Street and Haymarket Terrace, and between Lauriston Place and Home Street. The extensions were of course outwith the then city boundary. It was envisaged that the overhead electric system or petrol-electric tramcars would be adopted. The Colinton proposal was, however, complicated by the existence of the already mentioned

The original Corporation Leyland motor bus of 1914, No. 1, operated for them by the Edinburgh & District Tramwas Company. (*Gavin Booth*)

Colinton Tramways Company, and the Commissioners enquiring into the Corporation's Order would agree to the Corporation's proposal only if the latter bought up the Colinton company for £9,000. Although the company were willing to sell and the War Office offered to relieve the Corporation of the company's agreements with them, provided a through car service to the barracks was given, the Corporation would not accede. There was thus a year's delay, and the Edinburgh Corporation Order Confirmation Act 1916 (passed 17 May 1916) did not include the Craiglockhart to Colinton line, though the other routes sought were authorised.

The war, however, was putting a stop to any such schemes and nothing could be done till afterwards. Indeed its impact was making itself felt on the cable system — dependent as it was on coal, steel and skilled labour. While electric cars could be handled quite well by women, the arduous duty made this hardly feasible with the cable cars. Women conductors were not employed until June 1915, as the men had been very averse to them.

There were proposals that the Corporation should buy up the operating company at a negotiated figure without waiting for the expiry of the lease, but no agreement could be reached. There was, however, an increase in fares to 1d., 1½d. and 2½d., and the through fares to Leith were withdrawn on 11 November 1915.

By the end of 1915 the condition of the system was engaging public attention. The position certainly was bad, though the difficulties of the period have to be appreciated. 5,000 of the 13,000 pulleys were defective — or missing! Stoppages occurred daily. Even the company's chairman at its annual meeting on 4 February 1916 admitted it was "not in the condition it ought to be". He indeed ascribed the unfortunate situation to "inefficient inspection", and the many inexperienced drivers. Mr Wilson had replaced Mr Harris as the company's engineer on 1 January 1916. Mr Shepherd resigned a week afterwards, but continued to act as secretary to the company. He was succeeded by Mr J. D. R. Cox. The council were considering what redress they had for "the collapse of the tram services". Many of the cars too were in bad condition, and as the magistrates were the licensing authority for the cars, the company were allowed to continue operations on a month to month basis while they got the system into order, as they promised to do.

Inspection of the running gear of the cars was felt to be beyond the Corporation Hackney Carriage Inspector's resources, so Hurst Nelson & Co. Ltd. of Motherwell were called in to inspect and report on the whole fleet which they did in April and May 1916. In general they considered maintenance had been inadequate, with excessive wear on gripper and brake gear almost universal. Only two cars were reported "in order". But a good effort was being made and a list of cars on which the required repairs had been effected was submitted to the magistrates every three months. Much was done in other directions too. In April 1916 stoppages of the cable had averaged three per day. By October it was reported there had been only 33 stoppages over the preceding 41 days. The longest one, however, had been for nearly seven hours. Still, the Lothian Road and Shandwick Place tracks were relaid, and a new cable installed on the Portobello route.

At this dark period the public were, naturally, exasperated. Passengers who had no sooner paid their fare when the system broke down demanded their money back. On this being refused one enterprising gentleman walked off with the spare driving wheel from the car! He was handed over to the police, but was not charged. Another threatened the company with a charge of obstruction of the streets under the 1879 Act. Yet another, having twice taken a penny transfer ticket from the West End to the Infirmary and found the Mound route at a standstill, took a cab on both occasions and sued the company for his 2/- cab fares. The court ruled he had a case, but as the company had now offered to repay his two penny fares, he was advised it would not be worth pursuing. A mishap which could have been serious but which, in retrospect, has its humorous aspect, was reported on 28 April 1916. The Liberton cable got stranded and entwined in the gripper of an outgoing car near Hope Park. As the poor driver could not release it, his car was carried forward willy-nilly at cable speed, he tolling his bell and doubtless shouting of his predicament. First one car and then another were overtaken and pushed relentlessly onwards. At Preston Street a refuse cart failed to get out of the way of the cavalcade and was pushed into a motor lorry which thereby had a wheel knocked off. By the time the cars had got well down the hill towards Newington Station someone had telephoned to Shrubhill and the cable

A cable car used as a recruiting office in World War I, at Nether Liberton. (*L.R.T.*)

was stopped. It was fortunate no more damage was done. Another mishap on 14 December is of interest. Car 60 was derailed on the curve descending the Mound but did not get far off the track. Cars on this route were by then provided with only one gripper, at the "uphill" end, so that their leading bogie was not restrained by a gripper in the slot when it encountered some obstruction, thought in this case to have been a displaced hatch cover.

Economy measures became necessary, and the number 3 Abbeyhill-Ardmillan Terrace service disappeared entirely in the summer of 1916, the number 5 service being again and finally diverted to Abbeyhill.

In October 1916 the Corporation obtained a further report on the future transport possibilities, prepared jointly by the city engineer, Mr J. B. Hamilton the Leeds Tramways manager, and Mr Brodie the Liverpool city engineer. Soon afterwards negotiations commenced between the Corporation and the company regarding the terms of the Corporation's take-over. In this the Corporation had the advice of Mr Hamilton, who suggested an offer of £25,000 for the rolling-stock. The company wanted £75,000. Eventually £50,000 was agreed upon for not less than 200 cable cars, four electric cars, and 14 spare bogies, all in good condition. The track was to be handed over fit for six years work, except in respect of curves and junctions. On 30 July 1918 the Corporation appointed Mr R. Stuart Pilcher, of Aberdeen, as their tramways manager, so that he had a year to lay his plans for taking over the system on expiry of the company's lease, and for its future.

On 19 August 1917 the company had again increased the fares to 1d., 2d. and 3d., the alternative of a reduced rental having been refused by the Corporation. Another increase took place on 15 April 1919 when 1½d. became the minimum. The Corporation, however, announced their intention of reintroducing the penny fare immediately they took over the system. By this time a short "universal" ticket in fareboard layout, with all the stage names crammed on in very small print, was in use. The 1½d. ticket was now blue. Earlier the 3d. ticket had become a dull brown and a bright brown 1d. ticket for dogs, with all terminal points shown, had been introduced.

The company's lease duly expired on 30 June 1919 and the system passed into the city hands. The story of its last few years will be continued in Volume 2. Meanwhile the rolling-stock has still to be described.

The type of car running on the northern lines was not considered appropriate for the main part of the system, a larger and more orthodox design being desired. Accordingly the Edinburgh & District Tramways Company designed and built at the Shrubhill works a prototype car, the main features of which were orthodox platforms, entrances and stairs, though the full-length canopy did not enclose the latter. The saloon had three large windows to each side. The car ran on inside-framed bogies, with the gripper mounted ahead of the first axle and its operating rod provided with knuckle-joints and a sliding coupling, operated by a spoked wheel vertically mounted on a fixed pedestal, as described earlier.

This car was turned out in October 1897, numbered 112 and originally painted red, instead of the company's usual chocolate and cream. It normally ran on the Comely Bank route, and the braking arrangements were similar to the other cars on that route, but latterly it ran on the Portobello route.

The six cars ordered by the Edinburgh Northern Tramways Company in 1896 also arrived from G. F. Milnes & Co. Ltd. later in 1897. They were 17in. shorter but otherwise there were only minor differences from No. 112. These six cars were numbered 139 to 144, one of them, as already noted, being used for the inaugural trip on 1 June 1899.

From No. 112 the standard design was evolved. The standard cars were a little longer and roomier, the saloon accommodating 20 passengers as against 18 in the earlier cars. Both types seated 28 on top. The overall length was 26ft. 6in. and the weight about 4¾ tons. They cost £445 each complete. The destination was indicated on a small board hooked onto the edge of the canopy and generally it named an intermediate point and the terminus. The other side was lettered for the return journey, the board being reversed at the terminus. A long board carried on the panel above the saloon windows gave the termini and principal points passed. The conductor's bell was operated by a short lever rotating a rod running through the saloon above the windows. Orders were placed with Brown, Marshall & Co., Birmingham, totalling 120 cars. G. F. Milnes & Co. supplied 25. The saloon ceilings of the Brown-Marshall cars were finished in decorative white panels, and those of the Milnes cars were polished brown panels. When the service started 24 cars had been received and delivery continued through 1900 and 1901. The cars were numbered in scattered fashion, the highest number being 208. (See list in Chapter 8, Volume 2.)

Twenty additional cars were obtained from the Preston works of Dick Kerr & Co. Ltd. in 1903. These were of the standard pattern but of a more solid appearance, the windows having square corners and small lights above as was usual practice at the period. They seem to have had the seats covered with cloth when built. Their numbers were 209 to 228. A neater style of painting was adopted, the company's name, previously emblazoned on the sides in large letters, was omitted, and much smaller numerals were used for the car number on the dash. This style then became standard for all cars.

The saloons were lighted by oil lamps, but in 1905 acetylene lighting was introduced, though this improvement was not extended to the old northern section cars. Later, some of the latter were provided with a shallow form of headlamp mounted in front of the dash.

At this time it was evident that additional rolling-stock would soon be required and the company turned to building cars at the Shrubhill works themselves. In 1906 Nos. 25 and 27 appeared, being almost identical to the Dick Kerr cars of 1903. A new development was afoot however, and people were asking why top-covered cars should not be provided. After all, Leith Corporation, who had by now bought up the old Edinburgh

Street Tramways Company lines and electrified them, were running top-covered cars. The matter was considered at intervals. It was calculated that the Murrayfield and Dalry Road railway bridges could be negotiated by top-covered cars at a squeeze, but the Gorgie Road bridge beyond Ardmillan Terrace would be too low. The chief difficulty was that all the depot roofs would have to be raised. However, the town council pursued the matter, with the result that Tollcross depot roof was modified; and two further cars were built early in 1907. These were Nos. 37 and 48. The former had an all-enclosed top saloon with two windows in its rounded ends, while the latter had ordinary open balconies. In each case the stair was outside, just as on the standard open-top cars. There was a ceremonial trial trip to Braid Hills on 24 May and No. 48 was decided upon as the more acceptable pattern. Similar top-covers were thereupon fitted to Nos. 25 and 27 and to all the Dick Kerr cars of 1903, the weight of which with top-covers became 9 tons 8 cwts. The Shrubhill and Portobello depot roofs were then raised also.

In view of the forthcoming extensions to the system a further twelve top-covered cars were built by the company at Shrubhill between 1908 and 1911, while all the standard Milnes cars (except Nos. 28, 38, 64 and 74, which were converted in 1910 to electric cars for the Ardmillan Terrace to Slateford line) were provided with top-covers also. The programme was completed with seven more top-covers which were fitted to Brown-Marshall cars in 1912. These were Nos. 12, 24, 111, 137, 151, 152 and 206.

Summer crowds changing between Edinburgh cable cars and Musselburgh electric cars at Joppa, c. 1919. (*E. O. Catford*)

Interior of cable car of Brown-Marshall build when new. Note the curtains, later discarded.

About 1915 estimates were considered for fitting top-covers to further Brown-Marshall cars but nothing came of this.

In 1916 a new body was built for one of the old northern section cars, No. 125. This now had three windows a side instead of six but was otherwise the same. Nos. 123 and 126(?) were then similarly dealt with.

It remains to be mentioned that between 1901 and 1908 five of the newer horse cars were reconstructed as standard pattern open-top cars. They were, however, rather shorter, similar to No. 112, though differing in minor details. These cars were Nos. 15, 17, 19, 53 and 113. It may also be mentioned that there were no cable cars with the following numbers: 75, 76, 84, 86, 87, 90, 92, 93, 95 to 99, 102, 108, 110, 170 and 171.

The Cable Car Depot Allocation, 1916, was as follows:

Shrubhill:	1, 3, 5, 6, 9, 12-4, 16, 18, 22, 24-7, 29, 31-5, 37, 39, 42-3, 45-52, 54-7, 59, 62-3, 65-70, 72-3, 77-9, 82-3, 94, 103-4, 106-7, 111, 115, 117-9, 137-8, 145, 147-9, 151-4, 156, 159-60, 162, 164, 167-9, 173-7, 179-80, 182-5, 187, 190-201, 205-9, 211-3, 220, 222, 225-7.
Tollcross:	2, 4, 8, 10-1, 20-1, 23, 30, 40-1, 44, 58, 60-1, 71, 80-1, 85, 88-9, 91, 105, 116, 120.
Henderson Row:	7, 121-36, 139-44.
Portobello:	15, 17, 19, 36, 53, 100, 109, 112-4, 210, 214-9, 221, 223-4, 228.
Unknown:	101, 158, 163, 172, 178, 202, 204.

To conclude this chapter a few general notes on this marvel of mechanical ingenuity may not be out of place. It is rather sobering to think today of the miles of conduit under the streets and the vast pits under the main junctions — the locations of the pulleys and cables etc. being precise to fractions of an inch. These pits were provided with electric lighting, and there were telephones too. Throughout the streets there was the continuous faint rumble of the cable over its pulleys — a sound to which residents were so accustomed they would wake up when it stopped for the night after the last car was in. There were the complexities of operation, with pointsmen to inspect that all was well with each car at the main junctions so that no accident to the cable occurred. Snow caused little difficulty: the cars kept running and acted as snowploughs. On the other hand there was the necessity of regularly cleaning out mud and sludge from the conduit, a job undertaken by the City Cleansing Department. Severe frost could give rise to trouble by causing swelling and closing in of the slot, and the slot was subject also to malicious mischief by the insertion of pieces of wood, horseshoes etc. A good deal of trouble of this sort seems to have been experienced around 1900. At this time it was a favourite prank of the youngsters to tie a tin-can on a piece of string which was then lowered into the slot and onto the cable till it got caught on it. Authority, however, was not amused by the sight of the can rattling along the street at cable speed. Many an apocryphal story has been told involving the system, such as that of the drunk who was wont to guide himself home by hooking his walking stick through the slot on the cable, who found himself one night at Murrayfield instead of Gorgie.

Although Edinburgh's cable cars were a music-hall joke, it must be

Cable car No. 37, "The Crystal Palace", was the only one of its type. The photograph was taken at Craiglockhart on its last day of use, 18/3/23. (*A. W. Brotchie*)

Cable car with top cover at Craiglockhart terminus. No. 50 was built at Shrubhill in 1908. (*E. O. Catford*)

acknowledged that the system worked remarkably well on the whole, and economically too in its earlier days; besides sparing the city the overhead wires to which there was such strong objection at that period.

The Edinburgh cable tramway system at $25\frac{3}{4}$ route miles was by far the largest in Europe, where there were only a few other minor lines, though there had been larger installations in America at San Francisco, Chicago and Kansas City, and also in Melbourne, Australia. The last named was not finally closed down until 1940, and a short cable tramway line survived at Dunedin, New Zealand, until 1957.

4

The Early Motor Buses

Edinburgh was the scene of some of the earliest motor services. The first public motor service in the city commenced on 19 May 1898, running between the Post Office and Haymarket. John Love was the enterprising pioneer who, a year later, together with Norman Doran Macdonald and Rowland Outhwaite, formed the Edinburgh Autocar Company Ltd. with a capital of £50,000, Mr Outhwaite acting as manager.

The company ran a fleet of thirty-one "public motor cars" which were mostly Daimlers fitted with wagonette type bodies, i.e. with a seat for four along either side facing inwards, with another one or two beside the driver, who took the fares. Entry was at the back. The narrow wooden wheels had solid rubber tyres. A second service between the Post Office and Newington was also run, and the fare on each route was one penny.

Other owners using one or two generally similar vehicles set up competition, but information on these activities is scanty. Some were run possibly to other districts wherever or whenever there was traffic offering. If there was a breakdown on a section of the cable tramway system, the "motor car" service was intensified and did a roaring trade. At the end of 1899 the Edinburgh Autocar Company put on a service to a nearby village, probably Corstorphine, operating to a timetable and a fare of ½d. more than that charged by the horse buses. The journey time was 20 minutes against 40 minutes by horse bus. This service, however, lasted only for three months. Nevertheless, although the Autocar Company sometimes carried as many as 5,000 passengers per day in their various journeys, the "penny stinkers", as these cars were dubbed, had more enemies than friends, and the company was in difficulties after about eighteen months. H. P. G. Brackenbridge then took over the management for a time, but the fleet was sold in July 1901, and at that time also included an 18-seat Lifu steam-driven bus.

John Love himself then seems to have acquired some of the vehicles, and continued to run the services to Haymarket and to Salisbury Place, operating from a small garage in Abbeyhill. About 1902 he also retired from the scene and Rossleigh & Company of Annandale Street, one of the pioneer motor firms in the city, and also the Scottish Automobile Company, with H. P. G. Brackenbridge as manager, took over the routes with eight of the vehicles, and the service continued thus until 1904. The Edinburgh Autocar Company Ltd. was wound up in December 1903,

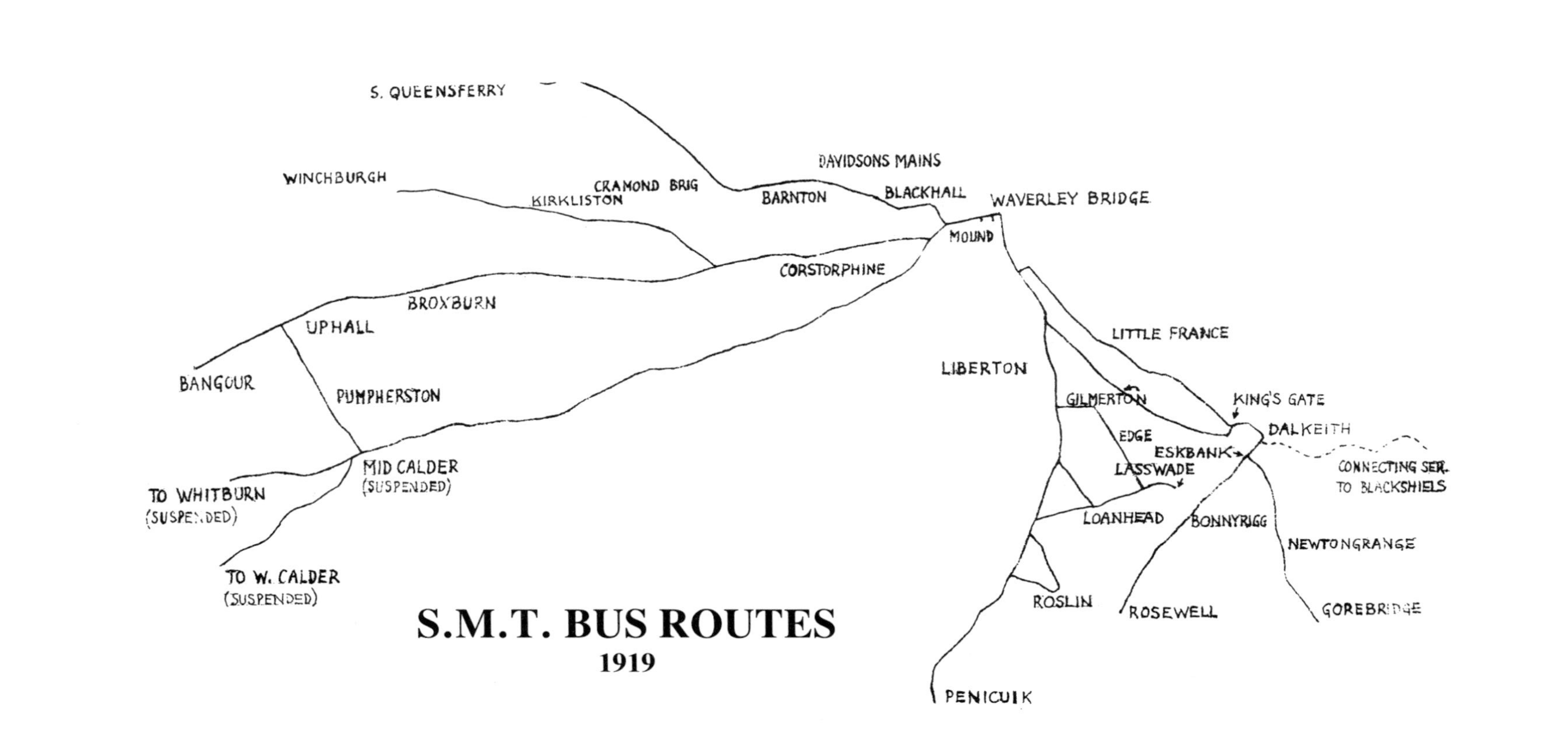

S.M.T. BUS ROUTES
1919

but operations commenced again under the Edinburgh Autocar Company name, and in 1906 they were running some of their small vehicles on the Portobello road and apparently to Musselburgh. At that time the maximum speed of the vehicles permitted by the magistrates was increased from 10 m.p.h. to 12 m.p.h. There seems little doubt that the machines were effective, for earlier the Autocar Company had successfully used them on private trips as far as Inverness and London. Indeed several of them served other owners for many years, including one said to have been registered S56. Others numbers known are S73 and S130.

Soon, however, more up-to-date machines with wagonette bodies fitted with an awning and running on pneumatic tyres appeared. During and after the first war one or two of these were still being run between the Murrayfield tramway terminus and the zoo on busy days, and they could bustle along at a smart pace with a full load. One of them, No. 290, was run by W. H. Herd, who will be mentioned later as a touring operator. Another was run by the Zoological Society itself: it was a 16 h.p. Albion dating from about 1907 which had been obtained second-hand. Four were still licensed in the city at that time and up till 1923, when the number came down to two, but one remained as late as 1928.

An early manufacturer of motor vehicles was William Peck, whose Madelvic Motor Carriage Company started producing electrically- driven cars in a fine new building at Granton in 1898. One is said to have run for a time in public service between Granton and Leith. The firm changed hands in 1900 and became the Kingsburgh Motor Construction Company, turning out a 12-seat petrol-driven machine with the driver seated over the bonnet. New owners took over the concern in 1902 and developed a small business in motor buses and petrol-driven tramcars under the name of Stirling's Motor Carriage Company, later Stirling Motor Construction Company (1903) Ltd. Companies subsequently occupying the premises for motor vehicle construction were the Scottish Motor Engineering Company Ltd., Caledonia Motor Engineering Company Ltd. and Caledonia Motor Construction Company Ltd. The works were finally closed down about 1907. The Stirling Motor Construction Company (1903) Ltd. produced double-deck buses of the then orthodox pattern which were known variously as the "Granton" and "Stirling" models. An effort was made to interest Leith Corporation in the firm's products as alternatives to the proposed electric tramways, but none were put to work there. Some of their "Kingsburgh" buses were ordered by a London firm, and the manufacturers are said to have run a demonstration service for a while between Post Office and Haymarket. John Stirling and his associates formed the subsidiary, Edinburgh Motor Omnibus Syndicate Ltd., on 21 May 1903, but no further operations materialised, and the company was dissolved in September 1905. John Stirling, who came from Hamilton where he had been running motor services from 1897, had built the Edinburgh Autocar Company's vehicles and was one of the earliest men in the business in Scotland. He died in Vancouver in 1945.

One of the "penny stinkers" running between the Post Office and Haymarket from 1898. Photograph taken after the introduction of number plates in 1903. (*Gavin Booth*)

The press took little notice of the "public motor cars" so the activities of most of the operators are difficult to trace. One of the earliest country services noted was from West Linton to Edinburgh via Penicuik, started on 1 July 1904, but soon this ran only from West Linton to Penicuik. One Henry C. Baillie, of Stenhouse, Liberton, ran a service, eight trips a day, from Nether Liberton to Gilmerton, commencing about April 1906.

A Stirling wagonette with a small platform at the back and an awning was being run between Dalkeith and Gorebridge in 1905; ownership is not known but its registration number was S284. Motor services also replaced the Eskbank to Pathhead coaches. This route was extended to Blackshiels and run by W. Cessford who used four Dennis "toast-rack" charabancs. He had competitors, and these rivals found themselves in court, having come to blows in July 1906. He is believed to have ceased operations during the First World War. A competitive service between Dalkeith and Pathhead appears also in the timetables for March 1909. This would doubtless be run by Adam Young whose route from June 1909 became Eskbank-Blackshiels and was connected with the S.M.T. Company's services, appearing — though as a separate section — in their timetables. Adam Young also ran his vehicles to Nether Liberton on occasion.

The Irish Motor Service Company Ltd., of which J. G. W. Butler was managing director, saw scope for expansion in the Edinburgh area, and sent over a 12-seat Albion to start an "Edinburgh and Loanhead Motor Service" about November 1905, on which Edmondson card tickets like railway tickets were used. In 1907 the company transferred its office from Dalkey to Edinburgh and its title later became the Scottish & Irish Motor Service Company Ltd. The company owned a few charabancs, and another which came over from Ireland, a Halley, G1350, was used in 1908 between Princes Street and the exhibition at Saughton Park. It was operated by the Edinburgh Exhibition Motor Service Company, presumably a subsidiary company. G1350 was back in Ireland in 1912.

At the end of 1904 the old Edinburgh Street Tramways Company had statutorily to be wound up, though consideration had been given to reconstituting the company to provide country motor services. Clearly there was scope for development of this traffic. On the other hand the motor bus was still in its teething stages, so the question was, could a really reliable vehicle be obtained and a dependable regular service be established? A group of local men determined to try, and formed the Scottish Motor Traction Company which weathered all the difficulties of those days and the war years to develop into the national network of today; but before recounting that company's activities the other smaller operators of the period should be mentioned.

The most remarkable project at this time was the Edinburgh & District Motor Omnibus Company Ltd., registered in London on 8 February 1906 with authorised capital of £200,000. The promoters all gave London

A number of wagonettes ran between Murrayfield car terminus and the zoo prior to 1920. This one was an Albion owned by the Royal Scottish Zoological Society.

addresses, but Norman D. Macdonald had been pursuing his motor bus interest, along with John Wilson of the *Edinburgh Evening News*, in running the London Power Omnibus Company, and these two were appointed directors of the new Edinburgh company, together with Sir Robert Dashwood of West Wycombe; the chairman was William Roberts of Birmingham who was also director of another London bus company. The proprietors stated the object was "to establish motor bus services in Edinburgh, Leith and surrounding districts", it being explained that J. Morris, recently returned from managing the Barcelona tramways, had recommended that Edinburgh would offer the best field for a motor bus enterprise. He suggested a start with 20 buses, but envisaged up to 175! The company had already made an agreement with the Motor Car Emporium, of London, for the provision of 150 buses, and Morris reckoned that on such a fleet a dividend of 18 per cent would be earned! J. Liversedge & Son Ltd., London, were to build the bodies. The idea of Edinburgh being swamped with 150 buses gave rise to some concern in the city, but the council claimed they could control the situation.

At a company meeting on 24 May it was reported that less than £29,000 of the authorised capital had been subscribed by 700 shareholders, mostly in the south, and that the company were able to order only 30 vehicles, of which 15 were buses, 10 charabancs and five chassis. Even these were not readily forthcoming, but eventually when five open-top 34-seat double-deckers of Dorkupp and Vulcan make had arrived, a service was commenced on 27 October 1906 between Post Office and Murrayfield. Halfpenny fares were offered. J. Morris was now managing director.

What was described as an "experimental" service was also run between Craiglockhart station and Tollcross and sometimes to the Post Office. A circular route to the south side was started shortly afterwards: this ran via Princes Street, Tollcross, Melville Drive, Marchmont Crescent, Sciennes Road, St. Catherine's Place, Salisbury Road and the Bridges. In January 1907, after some difficulty, a licence was obtained for a service from the Post Office to the Foot of Leith Walk, though there is doubt as to whether this actually started. The vehicles were brightly painted in blue and white picked out in gold, and with scarlet frames and wheels: acetylene lighting was provided. One of the Dorkupp double-deckers was registered S712. There were two Dorkupp toast-rack charabancs, one of them being S704. The company also used a Granton double-decker of 40 to 50 h.p. which was registered S702.

In contrast to the policy adopted by the S.M.T. Company, which was not competitive with the tramway company, Morris seems to have thought he could fill his buses with passengers from the tramways. But very soon, although more money had been raised from some new Scottish shareholders, the company was in difficulty. At a meeting on 20 March 1907 it was resolved that the company could not continue in business and that it should be wound up voluntarily. It was claimed the charabancs were profitable but there was no room in Edinburgh for the company's buses. An action had been raised against the Motor Car Emporium which was not fulfilling its contract to provide the vehicles, it being also in financial difficulty. (The Motor Car Emporium was compulsorily wound up in August 1907.) At this time the Edinburgh & District Motor Omnibus Company had eight vehicles in running order and seven chassis; two Vulcan charabancs were expected the following month. It appears the Dorkupps were ineffective.

So the bus services ceased forthwith. An extraordinary general meeting with Mr C. E. Hogg in the chair was held in London on 3 April and broke up in disorder. A proposal to sell out to another company was rejected, but an investigating committee was formed. Norman Macdonald, in a letter to *The Scotsman,* supported this but refuted the complaints of those who criticised the company's management, though he offered no reasons for the failure. Only four employees were retained. From other sources it appears the crews were not effectively supervised. On 2 May there was a petition for compulsory liquidation, but this was later withdrawn and voluntary winding up proceeded, the assets being sold off at the end of May. Norman Macdonald was well known in legal circles and he also took much interest in railway matters. Both he and Rowland Outhwaite lived to a good old age to see the eventual triumph of their *protégé.*

Motor services were run between Levenhall and Port Seton and Tranent by the Musselburgh tramway company, in connection with their tramcars, from 1906, and are referred to in the chapter dealing with that company. From October 1909 a motor service was provided at weekends from Aberlady to the terminus of the Musselburgh cars at Cockenzie and, subsequently, Port Seton. This was run by Guy Bros. of

A Dorkupp double-deck bus of the ill-fated Edinburgh & District Omnibus Company.

Aberlady with a Republic lorry, registered SS999, on which a charabanc-style body was mounted.

The only motor buses licensed in the city at 28 May 1910 were twenty belonging to the Scottish Motor Traction Company and a 28-seat Maudslay charabanc which Dan T. Munro had just bought. This was painted red and had a wood roof, and he ran it on the Queensferry route in the summer, his journeys being integrated with the S.M.T. Company's timetable. However, the War Department commandeered this vehicle on the outbreak of war in 1914, and he was left with only his horses and the "four-in-hand brakes".

In May 1912 John Jordan of Broxburn acquired from Alexander Sym, also Broxburn, a small 20 h.p. Halley charabanc, SX134, and in November he started a service into Edinburgh, Waverley Bridge, using this vehicle together with a 34 h.p. Halley 30-seat single-deck bus, with a platform entrance at the rear of the body, by Steele of Wishaw, which Sym had registered in September as SX275. Ownership of this bus was transferred to Jordan in December and it bore the legend "The Seat of Comfort" though those who remember it had other ideas. The old charabanc was unofficially known as "the wee tub". There were four trips a day with an extra late one on Wednesdays and Saturdays, and three trips were run on Sundays. In April 1913 this service was extended to Uphall, and about 1914 was increased in frequency, though some of the journeys ran as far as Broxburn only. For this increased service a third Halley, this time of 40 h.p., was bought: it does not seem to have been registered in West Lothian.

In 1912 James Bowen of Musselburgh was running the Levenhall-Tranent service, but this now started from Musselburgh station and provided seven trips (eight on Wednesdays and Saturdays), with "extra cars Levenhall-Tranent on Saturdays and Sundays". Later he ran also to Wallyford and Smeaton.

The Scottish & Irish Motor Service Company Ltd. do not seem to have been active in the Edinburgh area at this period, but in March 1913 they returned, advertising a new service to Gilmerton, Dalkeith and Newtongrange by "cars . . . comfortably upholstered and fully protected from the weather and lighted by electricity", which they called "The Green Busses". This enterprise does not seem to have lasted long and nothing further is heard of the company.

White's Motor Hiring Company Ltd. was formed in February 1914 and bought a 30-seat Halley charabanc, S4011. It does not appear that the company operated any public service at this period, but with premises in Russell Road they were the first in the field after the war.

Edinburgh Corporation's brief venture with motor buses in 1914 has been dealt with in Chapter 3.

November 1914 brought another operator onto the scene with Munro's Motor Bus Service from Waverley Bridge to Penicuik, some journeys proceeding via Liberton village and others via Liberton Brae and Roslin. This lasted until the following June when the two Straker-Squire saloon buses with clerestory roofs appear to have been commandeered by the War Department. One of them was registered S4614. Munro's garage was at Auchendinny.

Another small concern, the Edinburgh & District Motor Company Ltd., had come into being on 30 March 1914, and in the summer bought

Jordan's "Seat of Comfort" 1912; a Halley running between Broxburn and Edinburgh. (*R. L. Grieves*)

three Commer charabancs; but these also were commandeered by the War Department and in 1915 six Caledon chassis were acquired for passenger service, though no indication of any public operation at that time has been found. However, on 3 July 1916, a "Circular tour" via Barnton, Forth Bridge and Kirkliston was advertised at a fare of 2/-, with thirteen departures from the Mound daily, but this lasted only until 21 July. The West Lothian County Council complained of damage to their roads by the Queensferry bus traffic and refused to sanction the Edinburgh & District Motor Company's route. From 22 July the Scottish Motor Traction Company provided this circular service for a few days, and the Edinburgh & District Motor Company's activities thereafter seem to have been confined to contract work. The Scottish Motor Traction Company considered buying up the Edinburgh & District Motor Company, but with new wartime restrictions and the increasingly difficult petrol situation, the deal was deferred until September 1918, when a few Albion and Commer charabancs then owned by the Edinburgh & District Motor Company passed to the Scottish Motor Traction Company.

The Scottish Motor Traction Company had also bought up Jordan's service and vehicles in February 1917, so at May 1919 the company was the only bus operator in the city, though five horse brakes and four motor wagonettes were still licensed to other owners, and outside the city Bowen's Musselburgh-Tranent service still ran. But for the smaller operators a new post-war era was about to begin, which will be dealt with in Volume 2. Meantime the Scottish Motor Traction Company must be dealt with in more detail up to 1919.*

The Scottish Motor Traction Company Ltd. was registered on 13 June 1905 and incorporated on 14 June with an authorised capital of £50,000, though only £15,000 was raised at first. The chairman was the Master of Polwarth, George Oliver acted as secretary from an office in Queen Street, and the other directors were R. C. Cowan, J. A. Hood, F. B. Lea, A. B. Patterson, and F. McDougal Wallis. F. B. Lea was appointed managing director. The routes originally proposed were to Queensferry, Eskbank, Loanhead, Lasswade, Penicuik via Morningside, Juniper Green via Fountainbridge, and Kirkliston. Premises in Lauriston Street were leased for a garage to hold twenty vehicles.

The directors wisely decided not to start public services from Edinburgh until they were satisfied they had vehicles and experience enough to carry them through. A specification for a vehicle to meet the requirements which they thought necessary was drawn up, which included a speed of 12 m.p.h. on level and 3 m.p.h. on a 1 in 6 gradient when loaded.

In July 1905 two Lifu steam-propelled vehicles were ordered from Morton of Wishaw, five double-deck Durkopp buses from the Motor Car Emporium, London, at £885 each, and also five double-deckers from the Maudslay Motor Co., Coventry. The two steamers, registered

* For a full history see *From S. M. T. to Eastern Scottish,* as mentioned in the Introduction.

A Halley owned by the Scottish & Irish Motor Service Co. Ltd. running in Edinburgh in 1908.

Straker-Squire bus used on Munro's Edinburgh-Penicuik service, 1914.

SX32-3, arrived in September, but were kept from Edinburgh eyes, being tried out around Bathgate until November when they were rejected as unsatisfactory. When the first Durkopp arrived on 7 October it failed in its hill-climbing performance, so the company repudiated the contract and awaited the Maudslays. The suppliers of the Durkopp raised an action which resulted in the company agreeing to retain one Durkopp only at a reduced price of £810. It was not used and was eventually sold.

About the end of 1905 William J. Thomson was engaged as engineer. In May 1906 his duties were reviewed and he gradually took over the management from Mr Lea. He was elected to the board of directors on 31 December 1920 and subsequently became Lord Provost of Edinburgh.

On 24 December the first Maudslay arrived and fortunately it was satisfactory, so the first public service between the Mound and Corstorphine was started on 1 January 1906 with this one bus. An hourly service was provided, taking half an hour each way. The fare was 3d. The driver's name was said to be Rollinson and the conductor was Benjamin Thomson, well known in later years as Inspector "Wee Ben". Ben had come from the horse buses of the now dissolved Edinburgh Street Tramways Company. He has related how the Master of Polwarth insisted on getting the first ticket from him although he had been instructed not to take his fare.

The second Maudslay was not received until early March, but the others soon followed. The company used the Edinburgh licence number as their fleet number, and these first five Maudslays were thus Nos. 52-6 with registration numbers S543-7. They were of orthodox pattern for the period, seating 16 inside on longitudinal cane seats and 18 on garden seats upstairs. A curved hinged door was provided to the saloon. The engine was rated at 30 to 40 h.p. with chain drive to the artillery type wheels. A "sprag" brake could be dropped on the ground under the middle of the bus to prevent a run-back downhill should the vehicle stall. The colour scheme was green with cream panels and the company's title was shown in full on the sides. The destination was shown on a small board hung from the driver's canopy, and on a route board below the side windows. Acetylene lighting was fitted. With these vehicles the company was now able to expand.

On 21 April 1906 a bus was put on between the Mound and South Queensferry at 10.00 a.m., 12.00, 2.00, 4.00 and 6.00 p.m., at a fare of one shilling, and another at 45 minutes intervals which turned off this route at Barnton to run to Cramond, at a fare of 6d. On 23 April the Corstorphine service was changed to start from Waverley Steps, and in June became half-hourly for the summer, while there was a late trip to South Queensferry at 10.30 p.m., for which a shilling and 3d. was charged. There were also extra morning journeys to Davidson's Mains only. A timetable and fares leaflet was now issued regularly.

Further Maudslay double-deckers arrived in the autumn and, except for the first one, these had rather wider bodies, being fitted with transverse seats in the lower saloon and a sliding door. They seated 18

(Sir) W. J. Thomson, manager and later chairman of the Scottish Motor Traction Company, 1906-1949. (*Modern Transport*)

inside and 19 on top. There were eventually sixteen Maudslays, four of them with 32-seat "toast-rack" charabanc bodies with a wood roof and a windscreen behind the driver.

The additional vehicles were used on new services from Waverley Steps to Loanhead starting on 29 September 1906, with a few journeys terminating at Liberton; and on 21 October to Dalkeith via Gilmerton and Eskbank with additional journeys to Gilmerton only. Advertising of the new services was erratic and apparently not always reliable. The fare to Corstorphine was reduced to 2½d. and in December this route was extended right out to Uphall, though of course the bus could now do only four trips per day. The Queensferry and Cramond routes were suspended for the winter in November, but a short-lived service at twelve-minute intervals was then started between Waverley Steps and Colinton Road.

This ceased on 5 January 1907; the road was said to be too rough. Further new services were started to Penicuik on 22 December 1906, to Bonnyrigg and to Gorebridge on 27 December and to Pathhead on 29 December. The Penicuik route originally ran via Kirk Brae and Captain's Road, but from December 1907 it ran via Liberton Brae. A service to Kirkliston started on 2 February 1907 and on 1 March it was extended to Winchburgh, but the West Lothian County Council objected and the route was dropped altogether after a few more weeks. Apart from this the other services were immediately popular and were soon augmented. On 30 March 1907 the Forth Bridge and Queensferry route was restarted, but the Pathhead route was dropped. The Cramond route was also restarted for the summer on 4 May, while from 3 August until the end of September a charabanc circular tour via Roslin and Penicuik to Carlops, returning via Flotterstane, was run twice daily. A Sundays-only service to West Calder commenced on 6 October 1907, with three trips, while the Cramond service ceased again, and the Forth Bridge service was run on Sundays only for a further month before suspension for the winter. The first tickets were of unorthodox pattern, printed by Pillans & Wilson, Edinburgh. They carried no stage names or numbers. The 3d. one was pink.

One of the earliest accidents occurred on Saturday afternoon, 5 October 1907. The bus from Loanhead shed a wheel nearing the foot of Liberton Brae and toppled over, scattering its top-deck passengers. Five were detained in the Infirmary.

In March 1908 the timetable appeared in a railway-like tabular form,

Two of the S.M.T. Co.'s original Maudslay double-deckers, S546 and S547, at the Mound for Cramond and Forth Bridge respectively, in 1906-7.

One of the second lot of Maudslays with wider bodies and transverse seats, seen at the Penicuik terminus.

A Maudslay charabanc of 1907, No. 66, at the Mound.

the fares being given on the back. On Sundays slightly higher fares were charged and short distance fares were not offered. From 1 March the Bonnyrigg route was extended to Rosewell, and an additional service run to Gorebridge via the Old Dalkeith Road (described as via Little France), Dalkeith and Eskbank. This replaced the service to Dalkeith via Gilmerton and Eskbank. The Forth Bridge service restarted on 9 April, and the Carlops tour on 8 June. The service to Cramond was not revived.

By now the company had established its position on these routes to the surrounding country, mainly where the railway services were less convenient or more circuitous. The service frequencies were being gradually augmented. Passengers carried in one week in July 1908 were as follows: Queensferry 2,400, Loanhead 3,500, Penicuik 2,700, Rosewell 3,180, Gorebridge 5,250, Uphall 3,500, West Calder 350, Carlops 250. Ordinarily two vehicles were used for the Queensferry route, two for Loanhead and Penicuik, four for Gorebridge and Rosewell, and two or three for Uphall. With one more on the Carlops tour or West Calder, this left one or two out of the then total of thirteen to cover maintenance, breakdown, or the occasional accident. Although there were mishaps from time to time, which were liable to be exaggerated in some quarters, no very serious accident has been recorded.

The Forth Bridge and Carlops routes were again operated for the summer season in 1909, and in June 1909 a connecting service from Eskbank to Pathhead and Blackshiels was shown in the timetables. The West Calder Sunday service ceased after September, but from 5 February 1910 the route was partly covered by a new daily service to Midcalder and Pumpherston, and the Sunday journeys to West Calder were restarted too on 6 March. In May 1910, and until October, two of the Blackshiels connections continued over Soutra hill (1,200 ft.) to Lauder on Saturdays, Sundays and Mondays, and this was repeated during subsequent summers till about 1914, though latterly on Sundays only. The seasonal Forth Bridge and Carlops routes were again run in 1910. For the November 1910 timetable a reassessment of running times was made and nearly all were adjusted by a few minutes, some lengthened and some cut.

A parcels service had been set up early in 1908 with agents in the various towns and villages and with the Edinburgh & District Tramways Co.'s parcel service co-operating in the city. One of the minor problems was that some of the surrounding towns, being Royal Burghs, continued to exercise their ancient rights to levy petty customs. These were, however, generally resolved by payment of a small annual sum, and after about 1930 such payments were dropped altogether. Private hire work was of course undertaken from the beginning. Another arrangement that should be mentioned was a contract to carry the Post Office mails to and from various places. In some cases the service buses were used, and from June 1911 the following interesting note appears against the 5.45 a.m. buses to Penicuik and to Rosewell: "Passengers are only carried on the top of the 5.45 a.m. bus to . . ., the inside being reserved for mails". It must have been a cold journey in winter if the rule was enforced. From October these two journeys are shown as starting from the G.P.O. The Forth Bridge and Carlops routes ran for the 1911 summer season as usual. Larger premises were built in East Fountainbridge for the buses.

In November 1911 a Saturday and Sunday service was offered via Gilmerton and King's Gate to Dalkeith, Eskbank and Rosewell, and by 1918 all buses via Gilmerton made this diversion through Dalkeith before reaching Eskbank. Four Rykneild chassis were bought in 1910, two becoming charabancs and two receiving double-deck bus bodies, three more such bodies having been bought at that time.

On 1 May 1912 the Pumpherston route was extended to join the Uphall route, making a circular service, both ways, at a round fare of two shillings from any point (two shillings 3d. on Sundays). Late services outwards from the city up to 11.00 p.m. were being given on most routes, and at this time it was arranged for the returning buses to run direct to the garage via Nicolson Street and Lauriston Place from the south, or via Lothian Road from the west, instead of going right in to the Waverley Steps. A change was made on 1 July 1912 when the starting point was moved from the Steps to the top of the Waverley Bridge. A glazed frame remained fixed to the railings at the top of the Waverley Steps, however, until the mid-twenties, in which the company displayed their timetable sheet, later expanded to two sheets. The Forth Bridge and Carlops routes were again run for the season, and their starting point remained at the Mound. Two new circular tours were run in August and September 1912. The first was an all-day trip on Mondays, Wednesdays and Fridays via Portobello, Haddington, Dunbar, North Berwick, Aberlady, Haddington and back to town via Newcraighall, with halts at Haddington, Dunbar and North Berwick. The town council was invited to an inaugural trip. The other ran twice a day on Tuesdays, Thursdays and Saturdays via Queensferry and Hopetoun to Linlithgow, returning via Winchburgh and Kirkliston. On both these tours, however, intermediate point to point fares were available. In November 1912 some return fares were offered on the Pumpherston and West Calder routes, and also to the Forth Bridge in the 1913 season. Earlier, in 1912, tickets to the value of 10 shillings were offered at 12¼ per cent discount. It may be noted that children under 12 were allowed half fare but were required to give up their seat to a full fare passenger. Dogs were charged at one-third of the full fare.

On 11 December 1912 there was a strike of the bus crews over some dismissals. There was an attempt to run a few buses by some of the maintenance men, but then they came "out" too, and all services came virtually to a standstill. Earlier in the year the men had joined a trade union and they claimed the dismissed men, as active participants, were being victimised. There was much industrial unrest at the time. As Christmas approached the Post Office had to make alternative arrangements for the mails, but on Christmas Eve the men went back to work on undisclosed terms. It may be mentioned that the company ran a bonus scheme, and that many employees were shareholders.

From February 1913 to about 1916 some of the Blackshiels connections were extended to Humbie, and from 2 March the Sunday service to West Calder was diverted to Whitburn instead. The 1913 summer services followed the same pattern as previous years, the tours starting in June, and "Special Evening Drives" to various destinations were run. A few Penicuik journeys were diverted through Loanhead. On 1 November 1913 some of the Uphall buses were extended to Bangour.

Perhaps the most important event in 1913, however, was the appearance of a new bus designed and built by Thomson and his staff. A great deal of thought had been given to this vehicle which was undoubtedly far ahead of its time. A novelty, which did not become general practice elsewhere until many years later, was the location of the driver alongside the engine, thus enabling a 32-seat saloon body to be accommodated on a vehicle only 23ft. long, the maximum then allowed in Edinburgh. There was a seat facing backwards against the front bulkhead and the saloon was partitioned into two parts, the rear for smokers, the front for non-smokers. The off-side rear corner was curved and the rear seat curved round inside it. There was a "cut-away" rear entrance, with a short screen, to the saloon, in the little corner outside of which the conductor could stand on the top step. The body was built with a full width front, only the plain radiator projecting through, though on the first example built the radiator was replaced by a slightly sloping cowl and the roof of the driver's cab was lower than that of the saloon, while on the next three buses the driver's cab was extended and the cowling altered, the saloon partition being also moved further back. All these were subsequently altered to the standard pattern in which the roof of the driver's cab was raised to the same height as the rest of the body with a gentle sweep down over the driver's portion, though this curve down at the front did not apply to the first few standard bodies. All windows had top-lights of ground glass on which were painted the names of the places on the route to which the bus was allocated, the termini being also shown on the two above the windscreen and on the back. After the war the ground glass and painted names were abandoned and paper bills stuck on inside, enabling buses to be changed about as necessary. The earlier bodies had sliding windows in the saloon, but these tended to rattle and were later made fixed and an additional pillar introduced. Green leather cushion seats with spring backs were provided and the conductor's bell was a straightforward pull-cord. The buses were, of course, fitted with electric lighting. After the war a clock was provided on the saloon bulkhead. No use was made of the near-side of the driver's cab except sometimes to carry parcels.

A 38 h.p. Minerva Silent Knight engine was fitted driving a four-speed chain-driven gearbox and worm-driven rear axle. During the war the Tyler engine was used. Solid tyres were of course fitted but the vehicle was well sprung. The company aptly called their protégé the "Lothian", but this name did not appear on the machines. The first bus appeared in April 1913 and was licensed in June for the Uphall route. It proved very successful, being decidedly faster, smoother and quieter than any of its contemporaries. The first body had been built by G. Hall & Co. of Pitt Street, but the company then acquired another workshop in Valleyfield Street and commenced bodybuilding themselves. The company's full title was now dropped from the sides of the vehicles and only the initials were used, though it was not till the early twenties that use of the initials came to be used in everyday speech. Previously the Traction Company was the usual abbreviation. As more Lothians appeared the old Maudslays and Rykneilds were withdrawn, having served the company well.

The full range of services applied again in the summer of 1914. In September the Loanhead route was extended to Lasswade, and an interesting variation was the running of the 1.10 p.m. outward journey via Captain's Road and thence direct via Edge though this diversion ceased after 1917. A new longer all-day tour to the Borders country was run, and called for new charabancs, so a 31-seat charabanc body for the Lothian was produced. In the first one the radiator was sunk in flush with the front of the bodywork, but subsequently this was altered to a projecting radiator in the same style as the buses. The first one was also painted green, but afterwards pale yellow was adopted for the charabancs. In June 1914 two 29-seat Albion charabancs were bought, but these were commandeered by the War Department. When the war broke out there had been little immediate effect and the summer tours continued until September 1916. As has been mentioned in another chapter Edinburgh Corporation sold their three Tilling-Stevens buses to the S.MT. Co. in December 1914. Two of these were later fitted with charabanc bodies, but as they did not prove suitable for the S.M.T. routes they and the third chassis were resold to the Birmingham & Midland Motor Omnibus Co., who used that make. The bus bodies seem to have been retained meantime.

For a short time early in 1915 the Bangour service was apparently given on Saturdays and Sundays only, and from April some of the Penicuik buses were diverted through Roslin. From 22 to 24 July 1916 the Queensferry route was run as a circular service via Barnton, Queensferry, Kirkliston and Turnhouse and vice versa, to compete with the Edinburgh & District Motor Company, who then gave up. With so many naval personnel accumulating at Queensferry this route became heavily loaded and the service was substantially increased to a half-hourly one and continued through the winter too. As the vicinity of the Forth Bridge was under guard, the road between the top of the Hawes Brae and the east end of the town of Queensferry was closed and the buses proceeded via Dalmeny station and Hopetoun crossroads to enter the town from the west end. The Mid Calder half of the Pumpherston circular route was withdrawn after August 1916. Jordan's service from Broxburn and his Halley vehicles were taken over in February 1917, and it was proposed to buy up the Edinburgh & District Motor Company too, but this was deferred on account of the already difficult petrol situation.

Soon petrol supplies became even more scarce and further steps had to be taken to maintain services. The answer was found in fitting up all the Lothians to run on coal-gas. A shallow open box was built on the roof of the buses and a similar box, supported on stanchions, fixed over the charabancs, and into this box was lashed a large balloon which was charged with gas in Market Street and also at the outer termini in some cases. The gas was fed to the back of the engine casing by a tube of thin rubber, and on the charabancs this presented a temptation to schoolboys to try, unsuccessfully, to bring the vehicle to a halt by squeezing it. When returning with a diminished supply, the sagging gas-bag adopted a sort of

The Scottish Motor Traction Company's prototype Lothian bus of 1913. (*F. C. Inglis*)

One of the first Lothian buses put into service, No. 94.

A Lothian charabanc, No. 111.

wave motion from front to back as the vehicle ran through the breeze. There were occasional cases of gas-bags breaking loose altogether. The gas-bags were said to cost £50 each. Wear and tear was heavy and averaged 1¼d. per mile, and with gas at 2.17d. per mile, the total cost amounted to 3½d. per mile. The system served its purpose remarkably well with the fleet of about 35 vehicles, and was indeed slightly cheaper than running on petrol at its then price. It was alleged the buses ran better to Penicuik than back after refilling there.

In 1917 a few more of the Penicuik journeys were diverted through Loanhead, including one which already went via Roslin, and the Whitburn route was suspended at the end of the year. The Pumpherston route was also suspended in May 1918 but restarted on 1 April 1919. In early 1918 there was an old Albion bus on the Queensferry route, fitted with a gas-bag, and in the following summer this had a charabanc body still with gas-bag. The charabancs of the Edinburgh & District Motor Co. were eventually acquired in September 1918, but although roof boxes for gas-bags were partially built on them the job was not completed, and the vehicles soon disappeared. These vehicles are said to have been Commers and Albions. There was also a large W.D. type Maudslay charabanc with a wooden roof running on the Queensferry route shortly after the war, painted grey. The gas-bags were discarded as soon as possible, though some remained in use until 1921 and some of the boxes remained until there was an opportunity to remove them.

At this period traffic was brisk and the Queensferry route especially so. The last bus would stand at the Mound long before starting time already completely packed. No limit to the number of passengers was applied, and a conductor sometimes squeezed half a dozen passengers onto the steps alone, and hung on himself outside of that! Fares would then be collected on alighting. In those days a full load was indicated by repeating the starting signal, i.e. four bells. The later usual three bells came into fashion first on the Corporation vehicles; they had electric bells on which separate rings were less easily given. The charabancs were used on the Queensferry route in the summer, and they would be just as crammed with sailors sitting along both sides. The conductor collected his fares and punched tickets hanging on the footboard outside while the vehicle careered along, and clambered along from row to row while doing so, with a stride over the rear wheel arch. Today the whole procedure seems very precarious, though of course speeds were not so high and the roads quieter. S.M.T. conductors as well as drivers normally wore leggings, and very few women were employed during the war. Uniforms had green piping. Williamson's ticket punches were used and the tickets were now printed by Williamson's with all the stage names in fareboard layout, both sides being used. The colours were: 1d. white; 1½d. mauve; 2d. blue; 3d. green; 4d. brown; 5d. yellow; 6d. brown; 7d. green; 8d. white with a blue stripe; 9d. white with a green stripe; 10d. white with a blue stripe; 11d. white with a yellow stripe;1 shilling white with a red stripe. Some higher values cannot now be recorded, but 1 shilling and 8d. was pale brown

Scottish Motor Traction Company standard Lothian bus, running on coal gas 1917-18 at Waverley Bridge.

with a red stripe, and 2 shillings 2d. pale brown. No separate series was used for children etc., but three different sets were required for the lower values to cover the various groups of routes. The special Sunday fares had been given up. Return tickets were now issued for the higher fares and were surrendered for an exchange ticket of no face value with a red number printed sideways. Season tickets could also be obtained. Some one-way 1d., 1½d. and 2d. fares were also in vogue here and there, the uphill journey being a halfpenny dearer than downhill, or being offered inwards only within the city. These were printed right across the top of the ticket. The tickets were sometimes carried in a simple holder with two rows foot to foot and also back to back, giving sixteen positions, but often they were just made up into two or three bundles. The crews generally remained on the same route and became well known to their passengers. At Christmas time many a conductor decorated the inside of his bus with holly and coloured paper streamers. Although there were no fixed stopping places drivers were loth to stop on an up grade.

The timetables were now issued monthly, free, in a pocket-size booklet arranged alphabetically, and although the display sheet was still issued to parcel agents etc. for some years, it was abandoned about 1929, by which time three or four sheets were required to cover all the expanding services.

The Scottish Motor Traction Company expanded very considerably after 1919, and the story of its Edinburgh area activities will be continued in Volume 2. Meantime the company's rolling-stock up to 1919 may now be given, including all the Lothians, though much of it was built after that date.

The numbers of the Maudslays were as follows:

Some S.M.T. Co. tickets. Colours as in the text. Note the one-way fares across the top of the 1½d. ticket. (*Reinohl*)

52	bus – narrow body	S543	1906	60	bus – wide body	S551	1906
53	'' '' ''	S544	''	64	'' '' ''	S552?	''
54	'' '' ''	S545	''	65	'' '' ''	S781	1907
55	'' '' ''	S546	''	66	charabanc	S839	''
56	'' '' ''	S547	''	67	''	S840	''
57	'' '' ''	S548	''	51	''	S1378	1909
58	'' wide ''	S549	''	90	bus – wide body	S1379	''
59	'' '' ''	S550	''	99	charabanc	S1380	''

Two of them, S543 and S545, were later fitted with a larger type of radiator designed by Mr Thomson. S551 had a destination screen box mounted on stanchions on the front canopy.

The four Rykneild "R" type bought in 1910 were Nos. 61-3 and 87, S1687-90. Of the three double-deck bodies bought from Stagg & Robson of Selby at that time, one was put on a Rykneild and another on Maudslay S545, while another of the Rykneilds received what was probably S545's original body. The other two Rykneilds were provided with charabanc bodies. The Stagg & Robson double-deck bodies had top-lights to the windows.

The complete list of Lothians will, for convenience, be given next, although the last of them was not built until 1924.

It should be mentioned that prior to 1921 a registration number was not necessarily tied to a specific vehicle and a vehicle leaving a licensing authority's area normally had to be re-registered in its new area, while its old number would subsequently be reissued to another vehicle in the old area. In 1915-16 a number of Lothians were built and sold as lorries and buses to other firms. Most of the former were soon bought back again and provided with bus bodies to augment the S.M.T. bus fleet, and to these reissued Edinburgh registration numbers seem to have been applied. A total of 97 Lothians were built, 88 of them being in the S.M.T.'s fleet, and with three or four exceptions remained in service until 1929 and 1930.

S3057	95			S5916	60?	355	S9622	103	843	SG7202	229
S3597†	92?	55		S6423	61		S9707	104		SG7203	230
S3662	91			S6729	62		S9728	105	845	SG7680	227
S3703	94			S6761	63		S9830	106	846	SG7681	226
S3841	93		893	S7063	66		S7322*	107	97	SG7738	225
S4287	97?		78	S4068*	67?	66	SG 792	108		SG7985	224
S4288	98			S4963§	69		SG 887	109		SG7991	223
S4399	82			S4100*	72?	92	SG 888	110	850	SG8034	222
S4543	84			S4849*	73		SG1039	111	851	SF 226	215
S4617	85			S4770*	75		SG1890	140?	70	SF 227	216
S4654	88		889	S4813§	76	876	SG2106	230?	354	SF 228	217
S4655	89		891	S4400*	83		SG2107	231?	356	SF 229	218
S4716	96?	72	872	S5595*	87?	55	SG2128‡	65		SF 230	219
S4748	99?			S7618	86		SG2129	67		SF 253	242
S4836	51			S7715	90		SG2319	232		SF 254	256
S4846	52		852	S8461	71		SG2755	233		SF 274	257
S4851	53			S8533	74	874	SG3387	107		SF 275	258

S5224	54	S8594	77		SG3756	99	SF	330	259
S5496	56	S8668	79	879	SG4580	231	SF	365	260
S5550	57	S9102	81?	64	SG4581	234	SF	427	351
S5697	58	S9103	80	840	SG5639	101	SF	503	353
S5862	59	S9555	102		SG7201	228	SF	504	352

* Probably former lorry re-registered with reissued registration number.
‡ " " " "
§ " " S.M.T.Co.'s lorry, registration not changed.
† Destroyed by fire in 1920.

Changes in Edinburgh licence numbers arose in most cases after 1920 if the vehicle had been sent to the company's Dundee depot for a spell. Most of the Lothians carried bus and charabanc bodies at different periods; some were changed from one to the other several times. S4288 had solid tyred disc wheels for a time.

The numbers applied to the vehicles acquired from other firms at this period are not known.

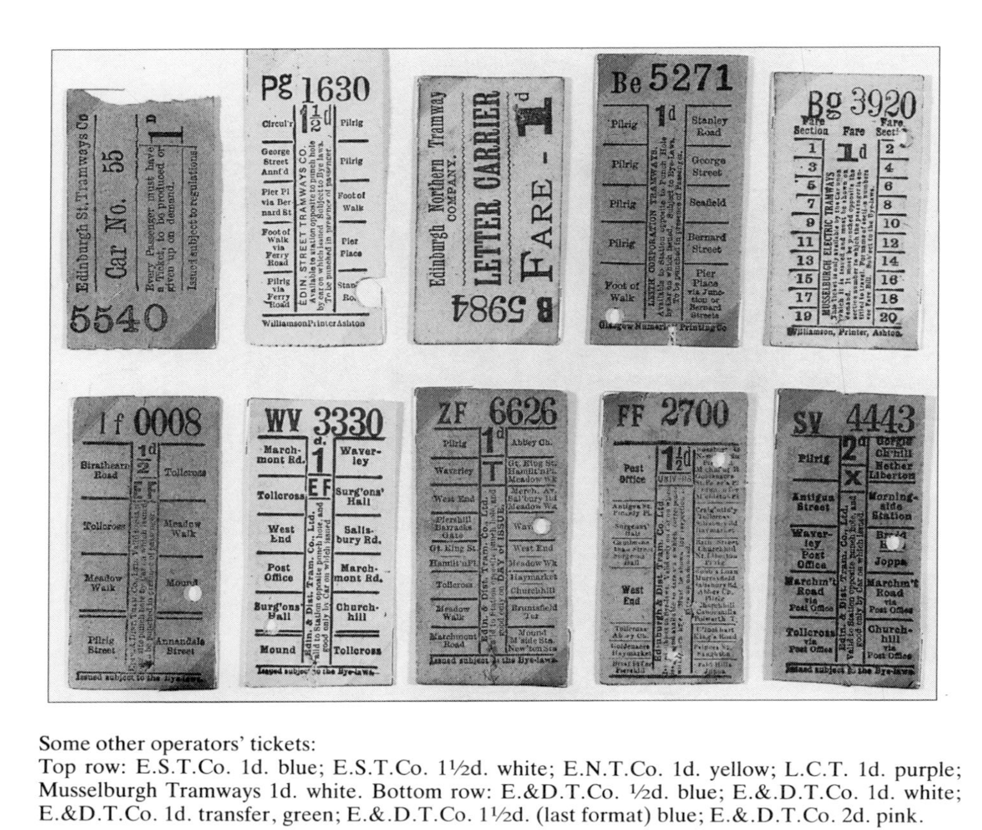

Some other operators' tickets:
Top row: E.S.T.Co. 1d. blue; E.S.T.Co. 1½d. white; E.N.T.Co. 1d. yellow; L.C.T. 1d. purple; Musselburgh Tramways 1d. white. Bottom row: E.&D.T.Co. ½d. blue; E.&.D.T.Co. 1d. white; E.&D.T.Co. 1d. transfer, green; E.&.D.T.Co. 1½d. (last format) blue; E.&.D.T.Co. 2d. pink.

5

The Advance of the Local Railways

We now return to 1870 when perhaps the weakest feature of the local railways was the premises which formed the main termini of the two companies. The Caledonian had, in 1870, diverted their tracks nearer to the west end of Princes Street where a new station was provided, opened on 2 May, but this was a somewhat makeshift affair and described by Acworth (*Scottish Railways*, 1890) as a wooden shanty. However, it suffered considerable damage in a destructive fire on 16 June 1890 and so a fine new station was then put in hand and opened piecemeal, with completion in 1894, though further alterations were entailed by construction of the hotel opened in December 1903. The easy level approach to the concourse and platforms from such a focal point as the West End was ideal. It had a vehicular entrance from Rutland Street and there was also a useful short flight of steps leading down to Lothian Road opposite Castle Terrace.

The N.B.R.'s Waverley station was less convenient of access and was also very inadequate for the traffic, but this also had to serve until the nineties, as related later.

The surrounding places which could be reached by rail at the beginning of the seventies have been recorded in Chapter 1. The main lines should need no description, though the N.B.R.'s "Waverley" route to Carlisle disappeared twenty years ago: the branch lines may be less well known.

The Peebles branch left the N.B.R. Carlisle main line at Hardengreen junction just beyond Eskbank, and climbed steadily upwards to its summit just beyond Leadburn whence it followed the Eddleston Water to Peebles. As it was single beyond Hawthornden, passing loops were provided at Leadburn and Eddleston, but not at Peebles station where the one platform was on the west side, as were the other platforms on the single line. The loop at Eddleston was later taken out leaving only the east side platform in use. The Dolphinton branch from Leadburn meandered down into the Lyne valley where it became flatter. The first small platform was on the down side, the others on the up, and at the terminus an end-on connection was made with a Caledonian branch from the west, that company's separate station being beyond an intervening road bridge.

The Polton branch left the Peebles line a short distance beyond Hardengreen junction, and climbed steeply through Broomieknowe,

CITY RAILWAYS

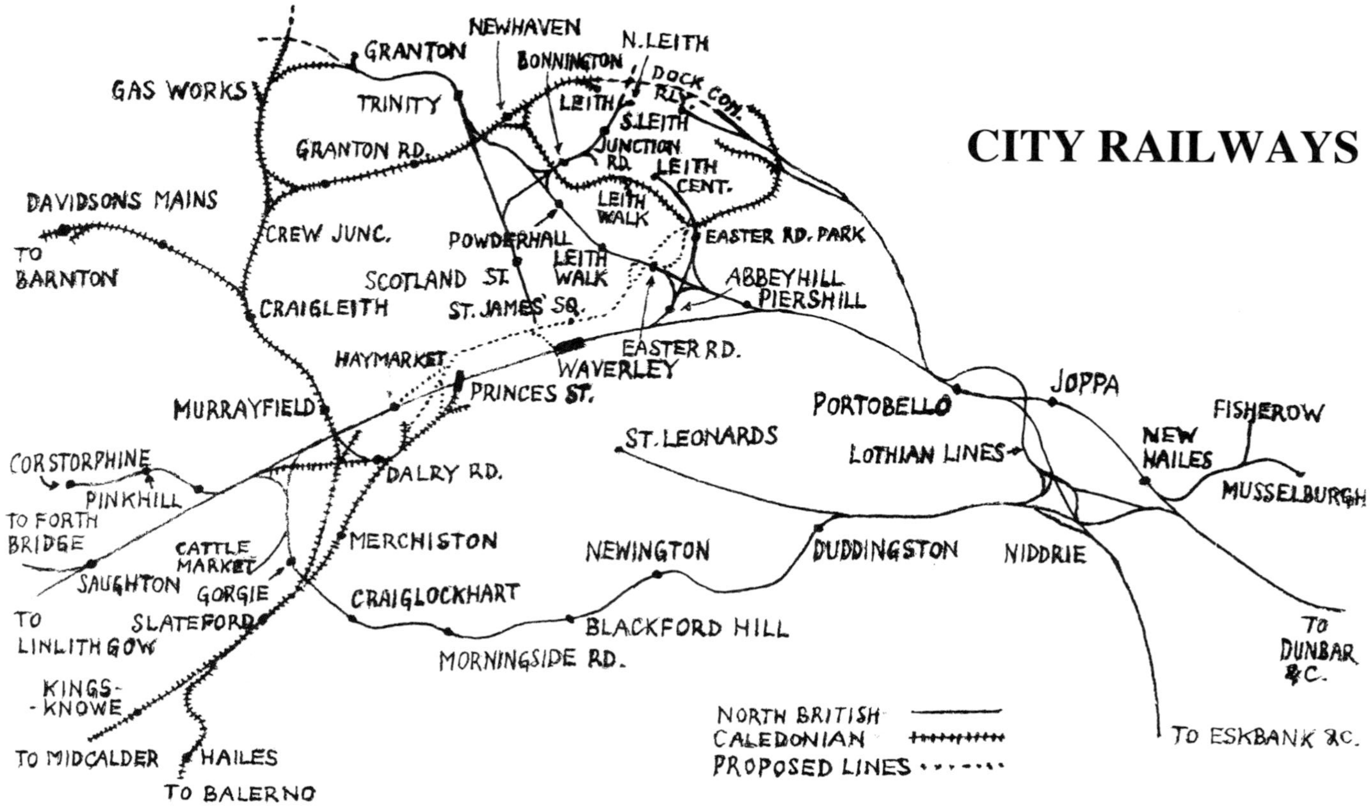

over its summit and down through a curved tunnel to immediately enter Lasswade station; then over a viaduct, and on down into the North Esk valley and its cramped little terminus. All platforms were on the up side of the single line. The Dalkeith branch was a short spur off the Carlisle main line just after it crossed the North Esk, the terminus having a single platform and a short roof.

The Haddington branch was far from flat but calls for no comment, the terminus with platform on the up-side being on high ground to the west end of the town. The North Berwick branch was similar, but had a more commodious two-platform terminus. There was a deep cutting before reaching the short platform on the up side at Dirleton.

Finally the Queensferry branch descended from the main line just before Ratho, at which it had its own adjoining platform at the lower level, on the down side. As the line curved away across the Almond valley, Kirkliston station, on the down side, was reached, after which there was much heavy cutting until it turned westwards to descend steeply down the hillside forming the shore of the Forth.

Much railway development was still taking place however. A branch to Macmerry, authorised on 3 June 1862, was opened on 1 May 1872. This left the East Coast main line at Monktonhall junction where it crosses the Esk, and climbed steeply on embankment to Smeaton from where it doubled back round into a reverse curve, still climbing, and now through a very deep cutting, eventually to emerge on more level ground at Ormiston, and on to the terminus, with another intermediate station at Winton. Platforms were on the down side except Smeaton which had an island platform. A goods branch from here linked with the Carlisle main line at Hardengreen junction until closed about the first war period.

The Caledonian Railway Princes Street station, opened in 1870. (*Dr. N. R. Ferguson*)

On 20 June 1870 a branch from Hawthornden to Penicuik was authorised and duly constructed. Passenger service from Waverley commenced on 2 September 1872. It was an interesting line, single all the way, with intermediate stations at Roslin Castle, Auchendinny, and Eskbridge. A short distance beyond Roslin Castle, the line ran through an artificial wooden tunnel erected at the behest of the Board of Trade on account of the proximity of the old gunpowder works in the valley below. Following some open country there was a substantial viaduct over the North Esk and the line immediately plunged into a lengthy tunnel emerging to pass through a paper mill with a siding. This was again immediately followed by another short but curved tunnel, at the other end of which lay Auchendinny station with another bridge over the river squeezed in between. The way onwards to Eskbridge was more straightforward, but thereafter the course followed the winding river, with several paper mill sidings, to its terminus at the south end of the town. All the station platforms were on the up side, except at Auchendinny.

A further Act on the same date had authorised another branch on the other side of the North Esk valley, to Roslin. This left the Carlisle main line at Millerhill, and had stations also at Gilmerton, some distance south of the village, and at Loanhead. The line, single with a passing loop at the latter station, was heavily graded and served several collieries. Beyond Loanhead, Bilston Glen was crossed on a massive girder viaduct. This branch was opened on 23 July 1874 and, in accordance with a further Act of 5 August 1873, was extended to Glencorse, the extension thereto being opened on 2 July 1877. The approach to Glencorse was over a graceful viaduct across the golf course, while beyond the station the rails continued for about another half mile to the gasworks on the northern outskirts of Penicuik. Station platforms were on the down side except at Gilmerton.

The Caledonian was also building its goods branch, authorised on 7 July 1862, from Crew on the Granton branch, down to Leith. A connection was also made from the Granton direction, and in order to be able to run trains between the Lothian Road station and the Leith and Granton branches, a line was built in 1864 from Dalry junction to Coltbridge junction. The Leith branch was a double line, the terminus being immediately west of the docks. An Act of 30 June 1874 authorised the West Dalry branch from this route to form a link for main-line trains down to the North British main line, and this was opened on 3 July 1876.

Another Caledonian branch of this period was the sharply curved but very picturesque single line up the valley of the Water of Leith to Balerno. Authorised on 20 June 1870 this left the main line beyond Slateford, and was provided with intermediate stations at Colinton, Juniper Green and Currie, the last having a passing loop. The branch was opened to passenger traffic on 1 August 1874. Its course took it first through Colinton Dell, then by a curved tunnel immediately beyond which lay Colinton station, on the north side. Scott's oatmeal mill and siding was then

The Caledonian Railway's approach to Princes Street station, from Grove Street bridge. The two tracks on the right led to the Lothian Road goods yard. Today this view would be of the Western Approach Road.

Lasswade station on the N.B.R. Polton line.

passed on the left, and the twisting line continued up the narrow valley to Juniper Green station, also on the north side. There was then a dip past Kinleith paper mill and siding before the line climbed again to Currie station with its two platforms. The rest of the route, though still tortuous, was more open. Balerno passenger station was situated immediately beyond the bridge under the main road, some distance from the village, with the platform on the west side. The branch then continued down to rejoin the main line again at Ravelrig junction where a number of sidings were provided. The goods station at Balerno was much nearer the village and reached by a spur leaving the passenger line before it passed under the main road. The main line station called Currie now became Curriehill.

The local railway services were very competitive despite the rather spartan carriages. Narrow four-wheel carriages were practically universal and three classes were usually provided, the third class being quite devoid of upholstery. The North British carriages might be described as a plum colour; those of the Caledonian a dark chocolate, the newer ones being relieved by cream upper panels. The engines, however, brought a touch of more vivid colour, the North British with their green-brown so difficult to describe, and the "Caley" with their beautiful blue. And in those days trains were really clean, at least on the outside.

The North British trains were mostly hauled by old main-line engines or in some cases by old saddle-tank engines, till the late seventies when Dugald Drummond, the company's locomotive engineer, introduced a class of very neat little 0–6–0 tank engines. Their wheels were 4ft. 6in. diameter and the cylinders 15in. x 22in. These engines were adorned with names chosen from the places on the branches which they normally served, and hence we had "Haddington", "Granton", "Bonnington", "North Berwick", "Polton", "Queensferry", "Dalkeith", "Leith" and "Musselburgh". In 1880 a rather similar 4–4–0 tank type appeared having driving wheels 5ft. diameter and solid bogie wheels 2ft. 6in. diameter. The cylinders were 16in. x 22in. The local names on this class were "Dirleton", "Roslin" and "Penicuik". Names such as "Haymarket", "Corstorphine", "Gogar", "Ratho", "Peebles" and so on were in use on main line engines. The use of names of this kind, however, had several disadvantages, and after Drummond had been succeeded by Matthew Holmes in 1882, they were all discarded.

The Caledonian trains were in the hands of old tank engines or the somewhat ungainly 0–4–2 tender engines with 5ft. 2in. diameter driving wheels and 17in. x 24in. outside cylinders. Names were not used. Some neater 0–4–4 tank engines were, however, appearing, with 5ft. 9in. diameter driving wheels and 18in. x 26in. cylinders, and for the Balerno branch J. F. McIntosh, the Caledonian locomotive engineer, produced a smaller version with 4ft. 6in. diameter driving wheels and 17in. x 24in. cylinders.

Much has been written elsewhere regarding locomotives and railway rolling-stock, and it is not proposed to deal with them in detail here.

Readers interested may refer to the usual works on the subject. However, let us have a look at the train services themselves, taking the 1876 summer timetable for our example.

There were stopping trains in the Dunbar direction, all with connections to Haddington and to North Berwick, at 7.05, 10.05, 3.55 and 6.30, also semi-fasts at 2.05 and 5.10, there being connections into these from South Leith at 10.00, 3.50, 4.25 and 5.55. Joppa and New Hailes were, however, generally served by the Musselburgh branch trains at 8.20, 9.35, 11.20, 1.10, 3.00, 3.45, 4.40, 6.00, 8.30 and 10.00. Macmerry had two trains only, viz. 7.15 a.m. and 4.40 p.m. Trains in the Galashiels direction ran at 6.20, 9.45, 1.45, 3.30 and 6.40, with connections from South Leith at 6.12, 9.25, 1.00 and 5.55.

Stopping trains from Waverley to the west ran at 6.50, 11.00, 3.00, 5.00 and 8.00. The Queensferry branch trains left Waverley at 9.10, 12.10, 4.45 and 7.15, all but the last connecting with ferries to Fife.

The Penicuik branch was served at 10.27, 1.30, 4.00 and 8.15, all but the last having a portion for Polton, which place also had trains at 7.40 a.m. and 9.45 p.m. The Roslin branch trains were at 11.00, 4.50 and 9.00 with connections also from the 7.40 and 1.30 trains. The Peebles line trains with connections on the Dolphinton branch were at 7.00, 10.40, 4.15 and 7.00. The middle two ran non-stop from Portobello to Hawthornden, the aforementioned branch trains providing connections from intermediate stations. The Dalkeith branch trains ran at 10.45, 12.20, 2.10,, 5.20, 7.35, 9.25 and 10.45.

To North Leith there were twenty-eight trains between 5.30 a.m. and 9.55 p.m., and to Granton eighteen trains between 6.05 a.m. and 10.20 p.m. Four of the five of the latter which connected with the ferry to Burntisland ran non-stop or called only at Leith Walk. The Granton and North Leith branch services were arranged to make connection between one another at Leith Walk.

The Caledonian had a few stopping trains on its main line, one of which each way on Wednesdays called at Ravelrig junction where platforms were provided, but this was not a public station. Other stopping trains ran to Midcalder or beyond, by way of the Balerno branch, at 6.20, 10.05, 2.00, 4.10 and 6.35, with another at 8.20 p.m. on Saturdays, while there was an 8.00 p.m. as far as Balerno only, Saturdays excepted, when it terminated at Currie.

The pattern on the return services was similar. On Sundays, only some of the main-line stations and the Haddington and Peebles branches were offered a service, though there were also two trains on the Granton branch to connect with the ferries.

During the seventies the horse-car services began to have their effect on the local railway traffic, but this was not taken lying down. The North British Company's frequent service to Leith in 1876 is worth noting and they also now offered very cheap fares between Waverley and/or any stations on the branch, as follows: first class 2d.; second class 1½d., third class 1d. (single). In addition third class return tickets available for specified trains at times suitable for workmen could be bought in advance at one shilling 3d. per dozen, and each half ticket could be used in either direction.

It will be remembered nevertheless that the public were not entirely pleased with the horse cars at that time, and the railway could still hold its own. It was cheaper and quicker, though the poor access to Waverley station gave cause for comment. The Caledonian, indeed, thought there was plenty of traffic to and from Leith for them too, and in 1878 set about laying separate passenger lines from Newhaven on their Leith goods branch to a new passenger station at the foot of North Junction Street. The passenger service of twelve trains a day between Princes Street station and the new Leith station was opened on 1 August 1879, and proved very popular. Extra trains had to be put on for the first Saturday's traffic. The fares charged were: first class 3d. single, 5d. return, third class 2d. single, 3d. return. Hitherto the Caledonian had catered for passengers to and from Leith by issuing through tickets valid on the Edinburgh Street Tramways Company's cars. The North British had already made a general reduction of their third class fares at the beginning of the year. The Caledonian Leith branch was a double line, and there was much deep cutting and embankment particularly between Murrayfield and Craigleith where passenger stations were provided. Other passenger stations were at Granton Road and at Newhaven, and at these and also at Craigleith the station offices were built on a bridge spanning the lines and adjoining a road bridge. The Leith station had an island platform with one track either side, and a short overall roof. There being no provision for the engine to run round its train after unloading, the coaches were pushed back up the grade out of the station: the engine then retired to a siding, and the coaches returned into the platform by gravity.

On the "Caley" main line a station which became very useful as the district became built-up was opened on 1 July 1882, named Merchiston, and was served of course also by the Balerno branch trains. Improvements in the approach tracks to the Lothian Road station were also prepared.

A bigger scheme was now afoot however: the Edinburgh Suburban and South Side Junction Railway, authorised by Acts on 26 August 1880 and 24 July 1882. This was really a North British scheme, and was amalgamated with its parent company on 1 May 1885. The route was double line and branched off the main line beyond Haymarket after crossing Russell Road. Diving under the Caledonian's West Dalry branch it joined a connection coming in from the west on the North British main line, and then climbed steeply around the south suburbs of the city with a summit just west of Morningside Road. On reaching Duddingston it joined the more level course of the old "Innocent Railway", which it used before curving northwards again to join the Waverley route main line just before it passed under Milton Road. The old "Innocent Railway" connections southwards and a new connection eastwards to the East Coast main line continued to be used for goods traffic and occasional passenger specials, and the line has thus always been a useful bypass for these. Passenger stations were provided at Gorgie, reached from either Gorgie Road or Slateford Road between which it lay; Morningside Road, Blackford Hill, Newington and Duddingston, and a circular passenger service from Waverley started on 1 December 1884. The rather circuitous route put Newington and Blackford Hill stations at some disadvantage for passengers to and from town. Nevertheless the line was popular and an additional station at Colinton Road, known as Craiglockhart, was opened on 1 June 1887. Much of the western end of the line lay in deep cutting, and except at Gorgie and Duddingston the station offices were on the adjoining road bridges.

A useful loop was laid by the North British eastwards from Abbeyhill to join the line from North Leith and Granton, and so reaching the main line just beyond the St. Margaret's locomotive depot. This was constructed under the company's Act of 22 July 1885, and came into use on 1 October 1886. A passenger station at the eastern end of this line, Piershill, was opened on 1 May 1891, and another at Easter Road on the North Leith and Granton line on 1 December 1891.

It should be mentioned that a station to serve the little village of Philpstoun, on the main line between Winchburgh and Linlithgow, had been opened on 12 October 1885; and a new goods station for the North British near the docks, at South Leith, on 2 February 1885. The passenger station at Portobello had long been criticised, but a fine new station with an island platform was completed in June 1887. The branch trains to South Leith continued to use their separate old platform however. For the International Exhibition in 1890 the Caledonian built a temporary station east of Slateford, just to the west of the bridge across the North British line. A small electric tramway operated in the exhibition grounds from this point to near the North British Craiglockhart station. The exhibition was also served by electric launches on the Union Canal, as well as by the tramways.

The Forth Bridge was now under construction. This was, of course, a most important development. Much has been written elsewhere about the bridge, and here it will be sufficient to record the incorporation of the Forth Bridge Railway Company, and its Act of 12 July 1882 to build the bridge and its immediate approaches, the interest being guaranteed by the North British, North Eastern, Great Northern, and Midland Railway companies. The North British built new main lines leading to it from the then Corstorphine station, and from the west beyond Winchburgh, the old Queensferry line from Kirkliston also joining them. A new station, subsequently called Dalmeny, was provided near the south end of the bridge. After some trial runs and tests the ceremony of the "last rivet" was performed in a gale by the Prince of Wales on 4 March 1890, and traffic commenced the following day, a passenger service being given from Edinburgh via Kirkliston and across the bridge to Dunfermline in place of the service on the old Queensferry branch which was then withdrawn. The new connecting lines on the south side and others in Fife were not opened until 2 June when through traffic commenced. A major change was thus effected in the whole pattern of the North British Company's operations. There was still some local traffic to Granton and one of the passenger ferry boats, the long remembered *William Muir,* continued to ply between Granton and Burntisland. The other three, *Auld Reekie, Thane of Fife* and *John Stirling,* were sold. The goods train ferries of course ceased and the special vessels *Leviathan, Balbirnie, Kinloch* and *Midlothian* were also disposed of. The goods and passenger traffic handled by the ferry boats had been very substantial. For example, the figures for the year to 31 January 1873 were:

Passengers (exc. season etc. tickets)	464,147
Parcels	58,732
Horses	675
Goods (tons)	232,782
Coal (tons)	90,033
Minerals (tons)	35,772
Livestock (wagon loads)	3,729
Fish (tons)	2,986

It should here be mentioned that in 1890 a Captain Arthur took over the Queensferry passage from the North British Railway, and the *John Beaumont* continued to ply until Arthur was succeeded in 1893 by D. Wilson & Son, who put the *Forfarshire* on the run. Further, in 1891, the North British Railway, through the North British Steam Packet Company, acquired a controlling interest in the Galloway Saloon Steam Packet Company, operating between Leith and various Forth resorts.

On 1 September 1897 a station was opened at Turnhouse on the new main line from Corstorphine. It is interesting to note that fares to stations on the Fife coast continued to be calculated on the shortest route, as was then the normal railway practice — in this case via the Granton-Burntisland ferry. Places such as Dunfermline were not so well off in this respect: the Forth Bridge counted as ten miles in calculating fares.

A disruptive railway strike broke out just before Christmas 1890 and lasted over the New Year.

We are now at a most interesting period of local railway development. Both companies had their eyes on Leith and the provision of increased facilities there, both passenger and goods. At the end of 1889 the two companies put forward their schemes.

The North British proposed a branch from Abbeyhill to a new station right at the Foot of Leith Walk, together with a connecting link onto the new Piershill loop towards Portobello. The Caledonian, being further away, had to be more ambitious in order to reach central and south Leith, and they put up two schemes. One was for a line from a point west of Newhaven on their existing Leith branch, which would curve away south and east, passing Bonnington Toll, then down beside the North British's proposed new station at the Foot of Leith Walk, whence to sweep up round Lochend and circle into a station near Salamander Street, with a spur leaving further out to cross over Seafield Road and the North British lines so as to reach the new Edinburgh Dock. There would be a triangular connection at Newhaven, and passenger stations on the new line at Newhaven, Leith Walk and Lochend.

The other scheme was more grandiose: no less than a line diving underground from outside the Princes Street station and proceeding under Charlotte Square, George Street and the Calton Hill, then out onto a viaduct and embankment over Greenside and Hillside, and sweeping on over Easter Road to join the aforementioned scheme at Lochend. A branch to a proposed station at the Waverley Market was included. Leith Town Council were agreeable to all the foregoing schemes. Edinburgh Town Council, not surprisingly, objected to this second "Caley" proposition, and the Act which the Caledonian succeeded in obtaining on 4 August 1890 did not include this part. The "Caley" expressed themselves as disappointed and brought forward a similar scheme next session.

This time the North British were brought into the plan, and spurs were proposed from the North British at Haymarket, and from the "Caley's" Morrison Street goods station as well as the original Rutland Street spur, all uniting under Charlotte Square. This time the line was proposed to join the North British west of Easter Road, and a new connecting line was to be built between a point east of there and the proposed new "Caley" South Leith line at Lochend. Instead of the branch station at Waverley Market, a larger one was proposed under St. James' Square. This Edinburgh and Leith Junction Railway was also rejected. Perhaps it was as well: it would have been a very expensive line to construct. Only the link from the N.B. at Easter Road to the C.R. at Lochend was authorised by the Caledonian Act of 3 July 1891, and it was never constructed.

The impact of the new route across the Forth was, however, calling for extensive improvement of the North British's facilities, and an Act was obtained on 5 August 1891 and work promptly put in hand for doubling the line to give four tracks in from Corstorphine, through Waverley and on to Abbeyhill junction. New tunnels at Haymarket, the Mound and Calton were necessary, and the Waverley station itself was also drastically rebuilt and improved. A separate long through platform on the south side was provided for the Suburban circle trains. The powers previously sought for the new Leith branch were now also granted by this Act.

The Caledonian, under an Act of 25 July 1890, built its double-line branch from Craigleith to Barnton with an intermediate station at Davidson's Mains. The summit of the line was just beyond this station. The terminus was provided with an unroofed island platform, the neat station buildings being behind the buffer-stops. This branch was opened on 1 March 1894, the terminus being called Cramond Brig until April 1903, while the Davidson's Mains station was known until then as Barnton Gate.

The North British added Powderhall station to their Granton branch at

A North British Railway train approaching Waverley station through Princes Street Gardens. The original two tracks were increased to four in the nineties.

Broughton Road on 22 April 1895. Further east the Aberlady, Gullane and North Berwick Railway Act of 24 August 1893 resulted in the single-line branch leaving the East Coast main line near Redhouse Castle and curving to within a half-mile of Aberlady, where a station was provided, before curving round again in a big sweep to reach Gullane. This branch was more or less at ground level, and the platforms were on the north side. The branch was opened by North British trains on 1 April 1898, and never got any further than its station at the east end of the village of Gullane, though the N.B.R. ran a "motor car service" in summer between Gullane and North Berwick for some years. This started on 14 June 1905 with two 23-seat Arrol-Johnston charabancs and continued in July, August and September of subsequent years until 30 September 1910. The original vehicles were very unreliable and the makers replaced them with better ones, using the original bodies, in 1907. A private platform between Aberlady and Gullane for use only by members of Luffness New Golf Club was brought into use in August 1903, certain trains calling there on members' request. The nominally separate company was amalgamated with the parent North British in 1900.

The North British Corstorphine station was too far from the village to be of much use, and on 12 August 1898 an Act was obtained for a short branch leaving the main line where it crossed the Water of Leith, and after running alongside for a short distance, curving northwards and westwards to a terminus in the village of Corstorphine. An intermediate station was provided at Pinkhill, which later proved convenient for the zoo. The new terminus had two long platforms either of which could be used for arrivals or departures, and a scissors crossover providing for engine release. The old station on the main line was renamed Saughton when the new double-line branch was opened on 1 February 1902.

In 1899 the Caledonian at last made a start with its South Leith line. There had been difficulty in acquiring some of the ground between Bonnington Toll and Leith Walk, and a further Act had been required in 1894 to cover a deviation at this part. In consequence the line crossed Leith Walk some little distance from the foot of the Walk, viz. immediately south of Manderston Street. The line crossed over Bonnington Toll diagonally, and here and at Leith Walk and at Easter Road massive lattice girder bridges were required. A double line was laid with goods stations at Bonnington, Leith Walk, Restalrig and South Leith and brought into use on 6 June 1904, but although the passenger station platforms at Newhaven were built they were not completed, and the ordinary passenger service never materialised. Nor were the rails laid on the east side of the triangle there. A similar connection at Crew from the Granton direction was abandoned soon after. In recent years this area has been partly covered by a housing scheme. A temporary passenger station was provided between Bonnington and Leith Walk for a military occasion in 1905. The whole branch was singled in 1917.

A useful new station on the Leith and Barnton branch was opened on 2 July 1900, at Dalry Road. This had an island platform and could be reached at either end from different parts of Dalry Road and also from Fountainbridge.

The North British were now building their new double-line branch down to the Foot of Leith Walk, where much property had to be acquired and some demolished, and also streets closed and altered, to make room for the large terminus which they called Leith Central. This was undoubtedly a convenient and worthy terminus with four platforms and high overall roof, but it is doubtful if such a large station was really justified. It was opened on 1 July 1903, and the south side suburban trains were run into and out of it on their journeys round the circle. Passengers on trains on the inner circle rails could change into a main-line train at Portobello for a direct run to Waverley, and similarly in the opposite direction. Some main-line trains to Glasgow or Dundee also started or terminated at Leith Central, and the then 8.05 a.m. from Polton ran direct there. With the opening of the new station, the service to South Leith was much curtailed, ceasing altogether in September 1904, by which time only three morning trips to South Leith were being run from Portobello.

Two North British country branches have now to be mentioned. In the east, an Act of 3 July 1891 provided for a twelve-mile branch from Ormiston to Gifford and Garvald, but a further Act of 24 August 1893 authorised instead an alternative line, seven miles long, to Gifford. Still nothing was done, however, till a Light Railway Order, under the new procedure for such undertakings, was obtained on 14 July 1898, and this resulted in a single-line railway with some steep grades and sharp curves from Ormiston as far as Gifford, with small intermediate stations at

Pencaitland, Saltoun and Humbie. The platforms of the first two were on the north side, those of Humbie and the terminus on the other. As built it was nine miles long, and was opened on 14 October 1901 by the North British, though the Light Railway Company remained nominally independent until the grouping of the railways in 1923.

To the south, the Lauder Light Railway was incorporated in 1898 and constructed under a Light Railway Order of 30 June 1898 as a single-line branch, ten miles long through the hills from Fountainhall to Lauder with an intermediate station at Oxton. It was very heavily graded and for much of the way sharply curved. The North British opened this line on 2 July 1901, though it also remained nominally independent till 1923. Both these lines were of course subject to the speed, weight and other restrictions of the Light Railway Acts, and crossed the public roads by unguarded crossings without gates, except where the Lauder branch crossed the main road just after leaving Fountainhall on its way up the hillside. Here the trains stopped while the guard opened and closed the gates. Both branches were worked by the small 4–4–0 tank engines and four-wheeled carriages.

A short branch line to Bangour Hospital was built under the Edinburgh District Lunacy Board's Act of 30 July 1900. This left the Bathgate line west of Uphall, and was opened on 1 July 1905, being worked by the North British. A new station was built on the Galashiels main line nearer the village of Newtongrange, replacing the old Dalhousie station on the other side of the South Esk on 1 August 1908.

Caledonian Railway train at Davidson's Mains station. Note the semaphore head code on the engine does not agree with the official code shown on page 172.

Leith Central station opened by the N.B.R. in 1903. The platforms were at the upper floor level with a carriageway entrance to the right at the end of the block. The direct entrance is seen behind the horses and there was another such entrance to the left further along Duke Street. (*F. C. Inglis*)

Returning to the Caledonian, a connection from the Granton branch was laid in to the new Edinburgh and Leith gasworks which had been built alongside the branch about a mile from its terminus. This was then open country, and as most of the gasworks employees would require transport to and from Edinburgh, a small station was built on the gasworks estate and a passenger train service, third class only, run at suitable times to and from Princes Street. This was started on 1 November 1902, but the trains were not shown in the public timetables beyond Craigleith. Nevertheless people from the few cottages in the vicinity of the gasworks occasionally made use of them. A private platform on the Balerno branch near Kingsknowe golf course opened on 16 November 1908 as Hailes platform, where trains stopped on request for members of Kingsknowe Golf Club, though members of the public used it too.

There were other proposals about this time for extending the Barnton branch to join the North British near Queensferry, or alternatively near Gogar, or by a loop back to Corstorphine, but nothing came of these.

For the Scottish National Exhibition at Saughton Park in 1908 the North British built a temporary wooden station on the Corstorphine branch where it crossed Balgreen Road. A fifteen minutes service was run on the branch at busy times during the period of the exhibition. A useful halt, Crossgatehall, was opened in the deep cutting between Smeaton and Ormiston on 1 September 1913. Another, on the East Coast main line between Prestonpans and Longniddry, called Seton Mains, was opened on 1 May 1914, but this was too far from Port Seton to attract much traffic.

About this time there was much development of coal traffic from the Lothians coalfields, particularly to Leith for export, and though we are really concerned only with passenger traffic, the resulting construction of new railways should be mentioned. The Lothians Lines of the North British, authorised by Act of 15 August 1913, comprised an additional single line from Monktonhall junction beside the river Esk on the East Coast main line, rising and curving westwards to join similar lines from the Millerhill and from the Duddingston directions near Niddrie junction, where the main lines passed underneath the new line. The new line then crossed over both the main lines again just west of Joppa station, and curving westwards again dropped down on a high embankment to join the Portobello-South Leith line where it left the main line at Portobello station. There were also improved facilities on the approaches to South Leith and the docks. A special signalling system was adopted for the new mineral line, instead of the unusual methods in use on single lines, and the lines were opened for the mineral traffic on 26 September 1915.

The unique route indicator used by the Caledonian should here be mentioned. This consisted of small white semaphore arms mounted on the front of the locomotive and set as shown on page 172. The system continued in use until about 1939.

After nearly a decade of competition with cable and electric tramways, and also with developing S.M..T bus services, it is opportune to

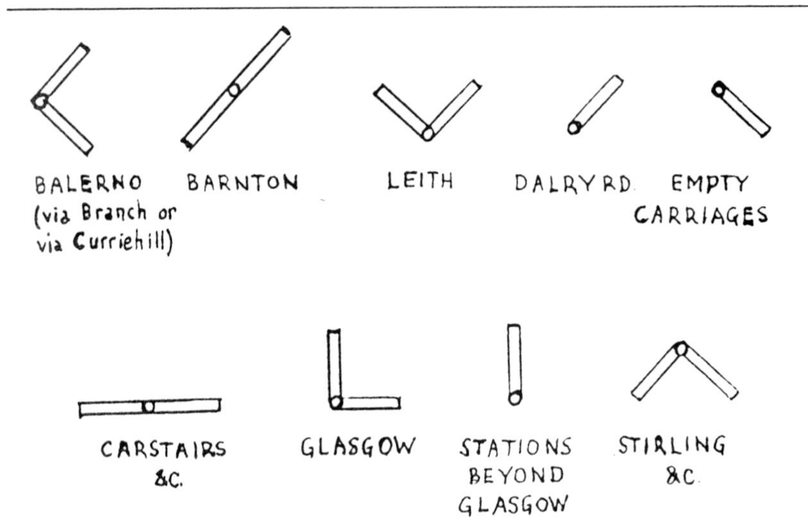

Caledonian Railways semaphore route indicators.

take a look at the railway timetables again. Let us take the summer of 1914 as exemplifying the services provided prior to the first war. These were as follows.

In the Dunbar direction, stopping trains at 6.43, 9.15, 2.02, 4.01, 5.18 and 6.30. There were Haddington, Gullane and North Berwick connections from most of the above and trains for these branches also at 9.07, 11.15, 1.34, 4.30 and 8.10, though not all three branches were served in every case. There were also certain Saturday only or Thursday only trains. Joppa and New Hailes were still served only by the Musselburgh branch trains and the Macmerry branch trains, the former having twenty-nine services between 4.58 a.m. and 10.07 p.m. with three more on Saturdays, and the latter trains at 7.03, 12.44(SO), 5.10 and 10.45(SO), all with portions for Gifford, to which place there was a further train at 9.32 a.m. In the Galashiels direction there were stopping trains at 6.15, 9.35, 1.05(SO), 3.25 and 6.50, with some Saturday extras as far as Gorebridge. Lauder was served by the foregoing except the 1.05, and also by a semi-fast at 4.25 p.m. which caught up the 3.25 connection. Peebles trains were at 6.58, 10.32, 1.00(SO), 1.34 (SO and non-stop to Leadburn), 2.17, 4.32, 5.31 and 8.35, most of them fast to Hawthornden. The 1.34(SO), and except on Saturdays the 5.31, took through carriages to Dolphinton which came from West Linton only at 8.50 a.m. Most of the other services provided connections to Dolphinton. Penicuik trains were at 7.40, 9.54, 1.28(SX), 1.40(SO), 5.06, 8.03 and 10.40(SO), and those to Polton at 7.13, 9.38, 11.30, 1.17(SO), 1.52(SO), 4.08, 5.53(SX), 6.51, 9.40(SO), 10.18(WSX) and 11.00(SO). Most of the Polton trains had portions or connections for Glencorse, though in the afternoon and evening and also around midday on Saturdays separate trains were run to the latter branch. Dalkeith had trains at 10.48, 12.13, 2.36 (with

Glencorse connection), 5.40, 7.21, 9.40 and 11.10, also one at 9.00 a.m. from Leith Central, to which station the 8.10 a.m. from Polton ran direct.

Stopping trains to Linlithgow ran at 6.15, 9.35, 10.42, 2.55, 5.25, 8.00 and 10.10(SO), to Bathgate at 7.45, 8.49, 10.35, 1.40, 4.29, 6.56, 8.38 and 10.30(SO), and on the Dalmeny line at 5.47, 10.15, 12.12(SO), 12.58, 2.25, 5.01, 6.04, 7.15, 7.55 and 11.00(SO). There were four trains on the Bangour branch, the first one inwards in the morning running forward to make connection at Drumshoreland instead of at Uphall. Six trains traversed the Ratho-Dalmeny line and the Corstorphine branch was served by twenty-four trains between 7.15 a.m. and 11.10 p.m. There were twenty-nine trains (one more on Saturdays) between 5.30 a.m. and 11.03 p.m. to North Leith, and eleven (one more on Saturdays) between 5.25 a.m. and 8.20 p.m. to Granton. The South Side Suburban circle line had fifteen trains each way with another four to and from Duddingston covering the western side of the line. The "penny jerks" between Waverley and Leith Central were provided by these and other trains totalling fifty-four daily, several of which did not call at Abbeyhill. The workmen's tickets to North Leith remained in operation and were available to Leith Central as well. A useful feature of the North British timetable was that the number of the Waverley departure platform was given for the various trains. Tickets for the Leith trains could be bought at the platform.

The Caledonian ran stopping trains on their main line at 6.30, 7.10 (as far as Curriehill), 7.55, 8.40, 9.40, 11.20, 1.20, 3.57, 5.00(SO), 5.10(SX and calling at Ravelrig on Wednesday) and 5.35, with two other evening

The Granton gasworks private station served by a workers' train to and from Princes Street at shift times. The line to the right led down to the foreshore and the North British at Granton Square.

trains missing Slateford and Curriehill. There were seventeen trains on the Balerno branch with three more on Saturdays, some of which continued on to Midcalder, but as most of the branch trains now terminated at Balerno an engine run-round loop had been provided there in 1899 to save proceeding to Ravelrig to run round. The Leith branch had thirty-four trains between 5.28 a.m. and 11.10 p.m. while Barnton was served by twenty-four with five more on Saturdays.

On Sundays the services were restricted to the main lines, one train each way on the Peebles line and the Haddington branch; and the Balerno and Barnton branches were added in the summer.

It will be seen that the railways were providing good services, and indeed they were carrying a fair proportion of the traffic. There had been some improvement in the rolling-stock too, though four or six-wheeled coaches were still almost universal on the branch line services. The motive power in use on the Caledonian had not changed to any extent, but on the North British new 0–4–4 tank engines similar to those on the Caledonian, and having 5ft. 9in. diameter driving wheels and 17in. x 24in. cylinders, had appeared on a few duties in the eighties. A new and neat 4–4–2 tank engine class was also appearing on the more important local trains. Driving wheels were again 5ft. 9in. diameter but the cylinders were 18in. x 26in. One of these was number one in the North British list, and as, at this time, the company commenced to paint the engine numbers in large figures between the initials N B for ease of identification with their new traffic control arrangements, this machine, familiar on the Corstorphine branch, became affectionately known as "nib".

Then came the war. Though there was not much change at first, coal and labour shortages began to have their effect and curtailment of service became necessary. On 1 January 1917 fares were increased, and a considerable number of stations throughout the country had to be closed to comply with a government order for release of men and materials for use in other directions. Those in the Edinburgh area were: Piershill, Crossgatehall, Gilmerton, Rosslynlee, Eskbridge, Broomieknowe, Blackford Hill, Craiglockhart, Saughton, Pinkhill and Kingsknowe, in addition to which services were also suspended on the North Leith, Granton and Dalkeith branches. After the war most of these were reopened in 1919 as follows: the Granton branch on 1 February, followed by the North Leith branch on 1 April except for Powderhall station, which was never reopened at all. Crossgatehall, Blackford Hill, Craiglockhart, Saughton, Pinkhill and Kingsknowe stations were also reopened on 1 February, followed by Piershill and Broomieknowe on 1 April; but Gilmerton, Rosslynlee and Eskbridge remained closed till 2 June, and Dalkeith did not get its service back till 1 October.

There was a railway strike from 27 September till 8 October in 1919, but thereafter services returned to the normal pattern. Road competition was, however, becoming keener, and the railways countered by offering reduced fares. Examples of cheap day return fares to and from Princes Street introduced at this time were: Craigleith 2d., Barnton 5d., Colinton

North British railway train of old four-wheel carriages with 4–4–0T engine at North Leith station.

5d., Currie 8d., Balerno 9d., third class. The weekly season ticket was popularised, becoming known as a "zone" ticket, of which the following sample third class rates may be quoted: Merchiston one shilling 4d., Murrayfield one shilling 4d., Leith one shilling 9d., Barnton two shillings 4d., Balerno four shillings, Musselburgh three shillings 1d.

In 1919 the North British resumed the working of the Queensferry passage, bringing in the *Dundee* which continued until Denny's took up the ferry in 1934. A halt was opened on 1 December 1919 at the east end of Queensferry on the old branch to Queensferry and Port Edgar, and a service of five trains daily was provided to it. Some pleasure steamer sailings were restarted from Leith in 1919.

6

Leith Corporation Tramways

The Schedule to the Provisional Order under the Leith Corporation Tramways Order Confirmation Act of 22 July 1904 empowered the Corporation to purchase the whole of the Edinburgh Street Tramways Company's lines in the burgh, to use mechanical power with Board of Trade consent and to construct additional tramways. The clauses covered the usual variety of matters, including the question of junctions with other systems including that of Edinburgh, and Edinburgh's interest in their side of Pilrig Street; parcels, workmen's cars and fares, which were not to exceed one penny per mile; and safeguards concerning the use of electric or steam power. The work was to be completed in five years and there was permission to run buses over the routes while construction was proceeding, and over contemplated extensions. Such buses were not to be electrically driven unless by batteries. Apart from the reconstruction and doubling of the existing lines, the new routes authorised were: from Pilrig by a junction facing upgoing cars in Leith Walk, down Pilrig Street to join the existing route in Newhaven Road; from Pilrig by another junction facing into the foregoing, by Iona Street and Easter Road, to a triangular junction with the Seafield route; a link across the Foot of Leith Walk from Junction Street to Duke Street and to Constitution Street; a line along a proposed new road from Pier Place to Annfield, to bypass Newhaven, which road in fact was not built until 1971! The Iona Street and Easter Road route was never constructed.

At the end of July 1904 the Corporation appointed a subcommittee to consider the form of traction to be adopted, and this committee thereupon inspected the tramways operating in several other cities and towns. Stirling's Motor Construction Company hoped their petrol- driven tramcar would be adopted. On 11 October it was resolved to adopt the overhead electric system, and that the work be carried out by direct labour. Mr James More was appointed consulting engineer. Leith Walk, Junction Street and Commercial Street were to be provided with centre poles to facilitate the movement of ships' boilers through them.

The Edinburgh Street Tramways Company handed over their system to the Corporation at 2.00 p.m. on 23 October 1904, though their activities officially ceased at the end of the previous day. Mr Adam retired and their traffic superintendent, Mr J. Wilson, was appointed interim manager for the Corporation. The staff were issued with new uniforms and Bell Punch ticket punches. The Corporation continued the horse car services as before except in Craighall Road, where the "Outer Circle" cars were turned back at the top and bottom of the hill. The half-hourly horse bus service from Newhaven to Granton also continued.

The committee and officials were now busy with estimates, designs and tenders for rolling-stock etc., and proposals for routes, frequencies and fares. On 10 January 1905 the council decided to order thirty open-top and six closed-top cars, half from the B.T.H. Co. and half from the Brush Co. The cost of the whole conversion, and equipment including rolling-stock, was estimated at just under £122,000.

At the beginning of February 1905 Mr Relph was appointed construction superintendent and work on the new Pilrig Street route was commenced on 6 February. During subsequent reconstruction of the other routes single-line working with temporary crossovers was adopted on the double-line sections, but service had to be temporarily suspended over the single-line sections. An "instruction car" for training drivers was ordered at the end of March, and a sprinkler car in April, both from the B.T.H. Co. A ratepayers' plebiscite declared in favour of Sunday services being run, though there was some high feeling about it. Mr Wilson was confirmed as manager on 11 May.

Work proceeded quite rapidly. The town council and Col. von Donop for the Board of Trade inspected the Pilrig Street route on 7 June 1905 and it was passed for use by horse cars which commenced to run on 15 June, giving a seven-minute headway from Pilrig Street to Stanley Road. The new electric cars were now arriving from the B.T.H. Co., but acceptance of some was deferred as they did not have the specified type of controller. It was proposed to start the first electric section on 21 July but this had to be postponed. There were difficulties with the new depot being built near Smith's Place and its access tracks, and it seems that some of the new cars had to be left out in the street. However, an electric car was tried over the line to Stanley Road at 3.00 a.m. on 28 July. A certain baillie, having heard of the intended expedition, turned up and was said to have driven the car part of the way, his unofficial taking of precedence causing some ill-feeling among his colleagues!

At last the Leith Walk, Pilrig Street, Newhaven Road and Stanley Road sections were duly passed for electric cars by the Board of Trade on 12 August, and a service of eight electric cars was run over the route from 18 August 1905. The fare was 1½d., with a 1d. fare from Foot of Leith Walk to Bonnington Terrace, or from Pilrig to Stanley Road. There was also a ½d. stage from Foot of Leith Walk to Pilrig. Four B.T.H. and four or five Brush open-top cars were used, and the latter did not escape some criticism of details of their equipment either.

The remainder of the circle round to the Foot of Leith Walk by Newhaven and Junction Street, and also the Ferry Road link, were completed and inspected by the Board of Trade on 14 September, and the service was operated round the circle from two days later. The circular

Some railway tickets.

fare was 2d. Ferry Road was catered for by a service between Pilrig and Stanley Road via Foot of Leith Walk.

By October, all but the Brush Company's closed-top cars had been delivered, and the remainder of the system was ready except for the Seafield line and the equipment on the Bernard Street swing bridge. The Bernard Street and Commercial Street sections were inspected by Col. von Donop on 19 October and services commenced the following day.

An official opening ceremony was arranged for 3 November 1905, and at 4.30 p.m. that day five cars, the leading one (believed to be No. 6) decorated with yellow, white and pink chrysanthemums, laurel and holly, and with palms on top, left the depot for a trip over the main parts of the system. The other four cars were top-covered ones. The official party of some 150 persons, led by Provost Mackie who drove the first car along with Mr Relph, included the Leith Town Council and officials, representatives from Edinburgh Town Council, the Edinburgh and District Tramways Company, the Chambers of Commerce, Merchant Company and other public bodies, and all the various contractors concerned. After proceeding via Pilrig, Pilrig Street, Newhaven, North Junction Street and Foot of Leith Walk to Bernard Street, the party returned to the Foot of Leith Walk, where the provost addressed a large crowd from the top of the leading car and declared the tramways open. The party then repaired to a celebration dinner in Smith's rooms followed by speeches in the usual congratulatory vein, and also a plea for through electric cars to Edinburgh. The employees were also entertained to supper at the same establishment, after finishing duty early at 10.30 p.m.

The remaining horse cars running on the Seafield route were withdrawn after 2 November as they had been sold; but unfortunately, due to

Leith Corporation open-top car, built by "Brush", on trial run at Bonnington Toll. Showing also the Caledonian Railway's massive girder bridge.

The Official Opening of Leith Corporation Tramways. Decorated car at the depot, 3 November 1905.

Leith Corporation top-covered car supplied by B.H.T.Co. with half opening roof (nos. 31-33).

a hitch, the route was not ready to take the electric cars and so there was no service to Seafield for eighteen days.

A trial over Bernard Street bridge took place on 10 November, and this and the Seafield line were inspected and passed by the Board of Trade on 21 November 1905, services commencing at once. The circular route was altered to proceed to and from Newhaven via Bernard Street, and new services run between Pilrig and Caledonian Station via North Junction Street and between Seafield and Stanley Road via Pilrig and Pilrig Street. Extra cars ran from Pilrig to Bernard Street, and to Bonnington Terrace via Ferry Road. A range of halfpenny fares was then introduced, followed on 26 November by penny transfer through tickets from Foot of Leith Walk to Post Office or St. Andrew Street over the Edinburgh system, with a similar 1½d. transfer between Bernard Street, Seafield, Junction Bridge or Bonnington Terrace (later Stanley Road), and Hanover Street or Tron Church. The maximum speed authorised was 12 m.p.h., subsequently increased to 15 m.p.h.

The Corporation were fortunate in obtaining their materials at very favourable prices, and the system was well constructed. The gauge was of course the standard 4ft. 8½in., and 45ft. rails of a special section weighing 106.7 lbs. per yard were used. They were obtained from the North Eastern Steel Co., Middlesbrough, and rested on a 6in. bed of concrete. Points and crossings were of Hadfield's "Era" manganese steel. The layout at the Foot of Leith Walk was quite a complicated piece of work but as it was preassembled by the makers was duly installed in twelve days. The system was double line throughout except for a short length in Duke Street, the curves at either end of Stanley Road and the junction at Bonnington Terrace.

The overhead trolley wire was of 4/0 gauge grooved section, which was then still a novelty. Apart from the centre poles already mentioned they were used also in Bernard Street and Craighall Road. Side bracket-arm poles were used in Ferry Road, part of Newhaven Road, Stanley Road, Duke Street and at certain other locations. Elsewhere span wires were provided. Quite elaborate wrought-iron scroll-work was added together with a short ball-and-spike shape finial, and a tall fluted cast-iron base bearing the burgh coat of arms. Overhead fittings were by S. Dixon & Sons Ltd., Leeds, who also provided six sets of automatic point controllers and automatic signals for the three single-line curves. Guard wires to prevent telephone wires falling on the trolley wire were installed where required. Current for the system was supplied from the Corporation's electricity generating station near Junction Street, by p.i.l.c. cables pitched in troughing to feeder pillars in Leith Walk near the depot entrance, Newhaven Road near Bonnington Toll, Lindsay Road, Junction Bridge, Constitution Street and Leith Links. The first two were 0.5 sq. in. section, the remainder 0.25 sq. in. There was also an extension feeder of 0.25 sq. in. section from the Newhaven Road pillar to another at Stanley Road. The side-feed cables to the line were taken through a short conduit into the base of the pole and out through holes near the top, making a neat arrangement. Negative feeders were laid to Foot of Leith Walk, Lindsay Road and Bonnington Terrace. Pilot cables for testing and telephone circuits were also provided, and were run overhead where suitable. The price of current was initially 1¼d. per unit. A horse-drawn tower-wagon was provided, there being also a second temporary one during the construction period.

The swing bridge across the harbour at Bernard Street involved some interesting problems. The bridge in those days was owned by the Leith Dock Commission, and was operated by hydraulic power. Before swinging, it was arranged so as to lift on its centre pivot with a tilting action, whereby the attachments above the ends of the 2/0 gauge bridge trolley wires supported from girders spanning the bridge dropped out of complementary spring-loaded forks on the fixed land girder at one end. The other end was similar, the spring-loaded forks being on the bridge girder and lifting upwards off the attachment on the fixed girder. The trolley wire attachments were thereby kept in alignment when the bridge was in position, and were clear for swinging when it was tilted. The approach tracks on either side were provided with trap points electrically controlled from the tilting movement of the bridge, and the position of these was indicated by a semaphore signal arm mounted on the adjacent pole. The trolley wire over the approach track in each case was fed from the line on the other side through the bridge trolley wire, so that it also became dead by the disengagement of the attachments when the bridge was tilted prior to opening. This equipment was also provided by S. Dixon & Sons Ltd.

The car depot had eight lyes (i.e. tracks) fanning from trailing connections to each track in Leith Walk. A two-lye repair shop was provided on the south side.

Leith Corporation open-top car supplied by the B.T.H.Co. No. 13 at Newhaven before the Granton extension was built. The horse bus then plying between Newhaven and Granton is seen on the right.

The electric system was now in full operation. The remaining 22 old cars and most of the 37 horses had been disposed of. The old Morton Street premises had been given up. There were suggestions for extending the Seafield line to connect with the Musselburgh system, for replacing the Newhaven-Granton horse bus by a motor bus (though a tramway extension was also being mooted) and for running a bus to Easter Road, but none of these materialised. The "Brush" closed-top cars were at last delivered. The "instruction" car was no longer of use as such, and it was proposed to convert it to a toast-rack car for summer service. Instead a further open-top body by the Brush Co. was obtained for it.

Mr Relph resigned in May 1906 and was replaced by Mr F. A. Fitzpayne as engineering superintendent. For the summer of 1906 services were given as follows: the Newhaven circular via Bernard Street and via Pilrig Street every ten minutes; Pilrig to Stanley Road via Ferry Road every five minutes; Seafield to Stanley Road via Pilrig Street every ten minutes; Pilrig to Pier Place via Bernard Street every ten minutes part day, except on Saturday afternoons when these cars ran via North Junction Street. A workmen's ½d. fare and certain 1d. transfer fares were introduced and on 12 November 1906 the Seafield-Stanley Road 2d. fare was reduced to 1½d. and nearly all the 1½d. fares reduced to 1d. The ½d. fares had proved unremunerative, however, and though some additional ones had been tried, they were at this time all withdrawn except Foot of Leith Walk to Pilrig or Junction Bridge, which survived till August 1907. A parcels service was started on 10 June 1907.

The undertaking was proving successful. By 1911 the operating expenses had been reduced to 4.5d. per car-mile, the lowest figure attained by any tramway undertaking in the kingdom. In the last half-year of horse operation the cost had been 8.32d. per car-mile, and the average speed only 6 m.p.h.

It was not long before extensions were being proposed, and Portobello, Granton and Davidson's Mains were considered. It was agreed that Newhaven to Granton, and also a line along Ferry Road to Goldenacre and Granton, would be justified and powers were obtained for these in the Leith Burgh Act of 1908. As in the case of the Pilrig Street line, one track in Ferry Road and Granton Road lay in Edinburgh, the boundary being in the centre of the road. Negotiations resulted in Leith owning the pair of tracks, Edinburgh retaining a right of purchase, as had been arranged in the earlier case. A suggestion that sidings be laid into the C.R. and N.B. railway stations and the Newhaven fish market and thus to carry fish to the trains was not proceeded with.

In April 1908 the platform staff were provided with new cap badges showing the burgh coat of arms instead of the intials L.C.T. as previously. Another through booking was arranged the following month in connection with the exhibition at Saughton Park that year. At a fare of 2½d. this was available from any part of Leith, and Leith Corporation's share was ¾d.

Two new crossovers were provided in Commercial Street early in 1909 and work on the Granton extension also started then. Commencing with a junction in Pier Place there was a double line by Lower Granton Road to Granton Square, thence by (High) Granton Road and Ferry Road back to Bonnington Terrace, where single-line junctions were formed onto the existing lines leading to Junction Bridge and to Pilrig. The "S" bend under the railway bridge at Trinity Crescent had to be a short single-line section and was provided with automatic signals. These were also fitted up at the Bonnington Terrace junction in the summer of 1911. The overhead was span wire construction throughout, and there were feeders to pillars in Ferry Road near Clark Road, in Granton Road near Wardie Crescent, and in Lower Granton Road. A junction was laid in Ferry Road at the top of Granton Road ready for the proposed extension to Davidson's Mains. Thermit welding and chilled blocks were used, the latter preventing wear of the setts adjacent to the rail by cart traffic. There were crossovers at Granton and Granton Road station, and a facing one at the top of Granton Road too.

The low road is mostly narrow, and while construction was proceeding the bus from Pier Place was started from Stanley Road and proceeded to

F. A. F. Fitzpayne, manager Leith Corporation Tramways 1909-1920. Manager Edinburgh Corporation Transport 1929-1935. (*E. R. L. Fitzpayne*)

Granton by East Trinity Road, a transfer ticket being made available from Pier Place. This diversion lasted from 18 February till early in May.

Mr Wilson the manager died suddenly on 6 April and Mr Fitzpayne was put in charge meantime, being confirmed as manager on 27 July 1909.

The low road to Granton was ready first. The council had a trial run on 14 April and then on 11 May 1909 the bus was withdrawn and the Pilrig to Pier Place via Bernard Street car service was extended to Granton. This now ran via North Junction Street in the evenings as well as on Saturday afternoons. A twenty minutes service was run between Pilrig and Caledonian Station via North Junction Street during the day. The fare from Pilrig to Granton was 2½d.

Col. von Donop inspected this part of the route for the Board of Trade on 2 June, and came back and passed the next section from Granton up to Goldenacre on 2 July, the car service being immediately extended accordingly. A formal opening of the new circle was proposed for 22 July, but the portion between Bonnington Terrace and Goldenacre was not ready, and it was 3 August when this was passed by the inspector and the new circular service commenced. The speeds authorised were: Trinity Bridge-Granton, Trinity Road-top of Granton Road and Bonnington Terrace-Craighall Road 12 m.p.h.; elsewhere 15 m.p.h. except the usual 4 m.p.h. for curves. The cost of the extension was put at £50,390.

The Granton Circle via Bernard Street and via Pilrig Street operated on a ten-minute headway each way, the fare for the circle being 4d. The old "Outer Circle", now a misnomer, was run during the morning rush and afternoon only, on a ten-minute headway. Seafield to Stanley Road via Pilrig Street, and also Pilrig to Stanley Road via Ferry Road continued to provide ten-minute services. At certain times of the day the latter was increased to a five-minute service while the former was extended via Newhaven, Bernard Street and back to Pilrig, a curious working causing it to be known as the "figure nine car". Additional cars worked Pilrig to Bernard Street. Another part-day service was started from Pilrig to Goldenacre via Junction Street, but this only lasted a few weeks till 2 September. The Pilrig and Caledonian Station via North Junction Street service was also dropped on account of poor receipts.

Meantime the old Granton bus was experimentally put on between Seafield and King's Road from 15 June 1909, at a fare of 2d. with transfers available also. But a horse bus was by now an anachronism and the service was withdrawn at the end of October. The bus was put up for sale and all but one of the twelve horses disposed of. The Fire Department took five for £100, viz. "Yankee", "Willie Watson", "Duncan", "Soldier" and "No. 1". The Cleansing Department paid £15 for "Kirky". Who bought the other five is not recorded, and one wonders what other intriguing names we might have learnt. The one horse retained was for the tower-wagon, but the poor animal went lame within a year and was replaced by an "outsider", hired while the council made up their minds about a motor tower-wagon.

Some fares were revised from 11 November, and additional transfers introduced: the age for half-fare was also reduced from 16 to 12. From time to time pressure was brought to bear for the reintroduction of ½d. fares, and after several refusals these were conceded again from 15 August 1910.

For the winter of 1910 the Granton Circle was reduced to a twenty-minute headway during the slack periods, although the ten-minute service was maintained to Granton via Bernard Street. Certain early morning cars ran to Granton via North Junction Street as did a Saturday afternoon service, and some early morning cars ran via Junction Street and Ferry Road. The council kept a very close watch on the services and their earnings, and it is interesting to note that the Granton extension was provided with services without any additions to the rolling-stock. The Bernard Street-Pilrig part-day cars were experimentally extended to Stanley Road for a month or so, and the old Outer Circle completely dropped. Then the full ten-minute Granton Circle service was restored from 1 April 1911. The pattern of the regular services was now set for some years, viz. Granton Circle; Pilrig-Stanley Road via Ferry Road; Seafield-Pilrig-Stanley Road-Bernard Street-Pilrig, "figure nine"; and Pilrig-Bernard Street. There was thus no regular service on North Junction Street.

Further extensions were considered in 1911. Seafield to at least the burgh boundary, or to the top, or the foot, of King's Road, and the Easter Road route were reported upon; but the question was complicated by Edinburgh's current thoughts on rail-less traction (trolleybus) routes in the district including Easter Road and Bonnington Road. Nothing came of these proposals, however. They were again under active consideration in 1913-4, when meetings were held with the Edinburgh authorities, and the use of motor buses, possibly as a joint undertaking, was discussed. Then of course the war ended all such schemes.

In 1912 it was felt that there should be more top-covered cars, and tenders were called for twelve top covers to be fitted to existing open-top cars. These were duly received from the Brush Co. at the end of the year and cost £111 each. Vestibule screens for the driver were also proposed and a car was fitted with these the following year. Two forms were tried, an orthodox wood-framed screen above the ordinary rounded metal dash panel at one end, while the other end was provided with a new angular dash as well, having a flat front and two flat corner sections, all built up with vertical wood matchboarding. This latter type was adopted when it was eventually agreed to equip further cars.

The motor tower-wagon was finally decided upon and a Halley machine ordered. It was received and registered WS194 in March 1914, whereupon the horse was sold — for £8. The disadvantages of the centre poles in the narrower streets were being felt, and it was proposed that those in Junction Street and Commercial Street be replaced by span wires using rosettes where possible, and this was eventually done.

In the spring of 1914 restoration of the North Junction Street service was requested and also a five-minute service to Seafield. Although the manager reported adversely, a ten-minute service in rush hours from Pilrig to Pier Place via North Junction Street, and an increased service between Pilrig and Seafield, were instituted on 13 April. In the summer an early morning service to Seafield was run for golfers! A 3d. fare for the Granton Circle was also proposed. Traffic continued to be heavy at times and trailers were proposed but turned down. Eight more top covers were, however, ordered from the Brush Co. at a cost of £968. It was now realised that the equipment, though well maintained, would not last for ever, and a renewals fund was started. A windscreen device was tried on car No. 20 but was found unsatisfactory, and the drivers asked that complete vestibule screens be fitted to the platforms of all the cars. They also asked that the front destination boards be dispensed with, believing the roller blind screens to be sufficient. After some consideration it was agreed to fit a further six cars with vestibule screens. A full drop window was provided in these in place of a circular shutter in the first one.

In December 1914 an experimental "island" was installed at the Foot of Leith Walk. This was of wood and in the following February it was agreed to extend it and make it permanent. Complaints of noise due to rail corrugation called for investigation, and the watering car was fitted with grinding blocks to deal with the problem.

The war was now on, and the curtains on the car windows served a real purpose in the partial blackout. As they suffered from passengers' attentions, however, other methods of shading had to be tried. Workmen's fares were granted to the Forces except on Sundays as from 16 May 1915. In July a decorated car toured the system for a fortnight to stimulate recruiting. Its furnishing was carried out by Sir Robert Maule. One of the minor effects of the prevailing conditions was the inability of the uniform contractors to provide brass buttons, and the old ones had to be re-used! Of more importance was the decision in October to recruit women as conductresses. The first eight started on the Ferry Road service in December, which was increased to a five-minute headway. The through tickets to the Edinburgh system were withdrawn on 11 November, at the instigation of the Edinburgh & District Tramways Company.

Traffic was still increasing, and so were costs, though Leith still boasted the lowest figure in Scotland, viz. 5.65d. per car-mile. The ½d. fares were abolished on 15 March 1916. To deal with lunchtime crowds two conductors were carried on the 1.02 p.m. journey from Bernard Street to Pilrig. The Caledonian Railway found it necessary to renew the girders of the bridge at Lindsay Road, necessitating single-line working, so the old temporary crossovers used during the horse car conversion were laid down in April.

The crews again complained of the nuisance of changing the front destination boards, and this time a compromise solution was found. The coloured boards, lettered according to the route, were to be replaced by coloured boards without any lettering and this was tried first on the Granton Circle cars in the summer of 1916. As the scheme proceeded some changes were made to the coloured boards and they then became: Granton Circle, outer rails green; inner rails blue; Pilrig and Bernard Street yellow; Pilrig and Granton via Junction Street white and blue; Pilrig and Stanley Road via Ferry Road white (another source quotes red); Seafield and Stanley Road via Pilrig blue and red. With new screen blinds showing both destination and via . . . introduced in 1917, the problem was resolved. At the end of 1916 it became necessary to train women as drivers, or motoresses as they were termed. Small folding seats were provided on some cars for conductresses.

On 27 October 1916 a subsidence occurred in Duke Street and for the next week Seafield was served by one car left beyond the obstruction. Early the next year single-line working had to be introduced between Pier Place and Trinity Bridge during repairs to the sea wall. Signals were provided. About this time the Corporation contracted with the Post Office to convey the Granton mails to and from the Foot of Leith Walk for 3d. per bag. As many Post Office telephone wires were replaced by underground cables a start was made in removing the guard wires which were redundant.

Traffic continued to increase, particularly in the industrial parts of the burgh and to Granton, and early in 1917 the Bernard Street-Pilrig cars were extended to Bonnington Terrace, and later, at the other end, to Caledonian Station. There were complaints of overcrowding and poor timekeeping aggravated by the partial blackout. To improve matters the Stanley Road-Pier Place-Bernard Street-Pilrig leg of the "figure nine car" was abandoned, and a five-minute service run from Pilrig to Granton via Bernard Street instead. This carried a yellow board. The service via North Junction Street now ran on Saturday afternoon only. These changes took place on 15 March 1917 and resulted in there being then no service in Craighall Road.

At the beginning of 1918 the war effort was pressing still harder. The authorities asked if Leith could spare any rails, poles or cars, but there were only a few rails and twelve poles in stock and certainly no cars could be spared. On the other hand, Leith managed to buy ten Brush controllers and four motors second-hand from Belfast. Staffing was difficult and women were appointed as inspectors. The last car times were brought forward from 11 April, and several stopping places were eliminated in July, while by September an effort had been made to reduce the services where possible in order to save coal at the power station.

With the war over many difficulties remained, especially relating to costs, and a new faretable was introduced on 16 May 1919. The child's minimum fare rose to 1d., and other concessions were withdrawn. Early next year another increase was called for and a 2d. transfer introduced. A trip round the Granton Circle now cost 6d. Some of the stopping places were being restored, and in July an evening service by North Junction Street was again tried. The King's Road extension was discussed once more but other events were pending, and powers for this line were included in Edinburgh Corporation's Act of 1920 which also provided for the amalgamation of the Burgh of Leith and the City of Edinburgh.

So on 20 November 1920, after much negotiation and considerable opposition, amalgamation was effected and the Leith tramways merged with the Edinburgh undertaking. The Leith manager, Mr F. A. Fitzpayne, was appointed deputy manager in the combined undertaking.

The "Bell-punch" type tickets used on the Leith system showed the stage names in "fareboard" layout, the colours of the various values being: ½d. bright brown; 1d. pink; 1½d. pale brown; 2d. white (at another time yellow); 2½d. blue; 3d. mauve; 4d. green; 6d. brown; 1½d. transfer to Edinburgh pale brown with blue stripe. The corresponding transfer ticket issued by the Edinburgh & District Tramways Company had a red stripe. A blue 1d. ticket was used for the Newhaven-Granton bus. In earlier years the tickets had been printed by the Glasgow Numerical Printing Co. and carried an advertisement on the back, but after the Granton extension was opened both sides of the tickets were used for the stage names. Latterly printing was by Auto Ticket of Liverpool.

The electric rolling-stock remains to be mentioned in more detail. The open-top cars from the B.T.H.Co. and the Brush Co. were similar, though the latter had only three windows whereas the former had four. The B.H.T. cars, which were actually constructed by the United Electric Car Co. Ltd., were 27ft. 6in. long and ran on four-wheeled trucks of the Brill 21E type with a six-foot wheel-base and 32in. diameter wheels. The two motors were GE54 type, and B18 controllers with provision for rheostatic braking were supplied. There were 22 seats inside and 36 outside. The British cars were 6in. longer and seated two less outside. Their trucks were the Brush AA type with 1002B motors and 3A type controllers. The top-covered cars were similar, the top deck seating being two less in each case. The Brush cars had a more domed roof, but the B.T.H. cars on the other hand were provided with an opening portion down one side of the roof, the panels sliding under the other half. All the cars had longitudinal wooden seats in the lower saloon and the usual transverse reversible seats upstairs. The stairs were of the ordinary pattern. There was a headlamp in the centre of the dash panel and a roller blind destination screen was mounted above the upper deck rail. Later these were removed to below the canopy, No. 29 being the first car so altered in December 1909. A coloured board lettered according to the route was carried on the upper deck rail, and side destination boards were also carried on the windows. The conductor's bell was of the cord type. Platform gates were originally proposed, but these were cancelled. The folding steps, originally of metal, were replaced by wooden ones when they wore out. Curtains were provided for the lower saloon windows. The colour scheme was "Munich Lake" and white, similar to that in Edinburgh, but the gold lettering "Leith Corporation Tramways" on the rocker panels and the car number on the dash were shaded in blue.

The B.T.H. open-top cars were numbered 1-15 and the Brush ones

16-30. The three B.T.H. top-covered cars were Nos. 31, 32 and 33, while the three Brush top-covered cars were Nos. 34, 35 and 36. The "instruction car" previously mentioned was originally numbered 61, but when converted to a normal Brush open-top car became No. 37. The sprinkler car was numbered 60 and painted green. It had a tank for 1,000 gallons of water, together with sprinkler pipes, two revolving brooms and a snowplough. GE58 motors and B18 controllers were fitted. The Brush top covers obtained in December 1912 were fitted to twelve B.T.H. cars, as were three of the further eight obtained in December 1914, so that all the B.T.H. cars became top-covered, though most of them hybrids. The other five of the eight obtained in December 1914 were fitted to Nos. 16, 17, 18, 19 and 37. The top-covered cars were also fitted with Peacock brake gear. The windscreen obtained from the Equipment & Engineering Co. in May 1914 was tried on No. 20, while the experimental vestibule screens of 1913 were fitted to No. 35. In 1917 this car was provided with new truck side frames with a seven-foot wheelbase. New wooden dash panels and vestibule screens were subsequently fitted to No. 29 in March 1915, followed by Nos. 10, 8 and 11 during the next two months, when it was decided to cancel the other two sets authorised on account of the war difficulties. No. 29 was the only open-top car so fitted. In 1919 Nos. 2 and 15 were provided with new 7ft. 6in. wheelbase trucks fitted with magnetic track brakes.

The places shown on the destination screens after 1916 were: Pilrig via Junction Street; Pilrig via Pilrig Street; Stanley Road via Junction Street; Stanley Road via Pilrig Street; Newhaven; Dock Gates; Bernard Street; Seafield; Foot of Leith Walk; Granton via Pilrig Street; Granton via Bernard street; Granton Circle; Nth. Junction St.; Depot Only; Special.

7

The Musselburgh Electric Tramways and Three Other Proposals

In preceding chapters several proposals for tramways outside the city have been mentioned, most of which never materialised. Let us now deal with one that did, and some which at least got to the length of securing statutory powers.

About the turn of the century the Drake and Gorham Electric Power and Traction Company Ltd. were active in promoting electric tramways in various parts of the country. One of the schemes they pursued was the oft mooted proposal for the extension of the tramway from Joppa to Musselburgh.

The Portobello and Musselburgh Tramways Order 1900, confirmed 6 August 1900, authorised this company to construct a tramway to be worked by electrical or mechanical power, but not by steam or by animals, from the Joppa terminus of the Edinburgh system, through Musselburgh to a point in what we now know as the "Coast" road, four chains east of the public house at Levenhall. The route was to be a single line with seventeen passing loops. A spur from each direction was to give access to a depot and generating station on the south side of the High Street in Musselburgh, east of the Town Hall, while a branch thirteen chains long with a triangular junction at the Mall was to run to Inveresk Road. The gauge was not stipulated but there were all the usual provisions and safeguards. Cars were to be run at least every half-hour on weekdays between 8.00 a.m. and 10.00 p.m., and in connection with the last car from Edinburgh. Sunday services had to have the consent of the local authority, as also had the carriage of goods and animals. Maximum fares were 1d. per mile and for workmen ½d. per mile. The portion within the Edinburgh boundary was not to be constructed for twelve months unless the Corporation agreed, and they had the right to buy it from the Company if they wished.

Matters moved slowly, however, and later the Board of Trade gave a special direction extending the time for completion of the system, except for the portion within the Edinburgh boundary which the Corporation thought of building itself.

By 1903 there was still no progress, and the position was retrieved by the Portobello and Musselburgh Tramways Order 1903, confirmed 11 August 1903, which authorised a subsidiary company, the Pioneer

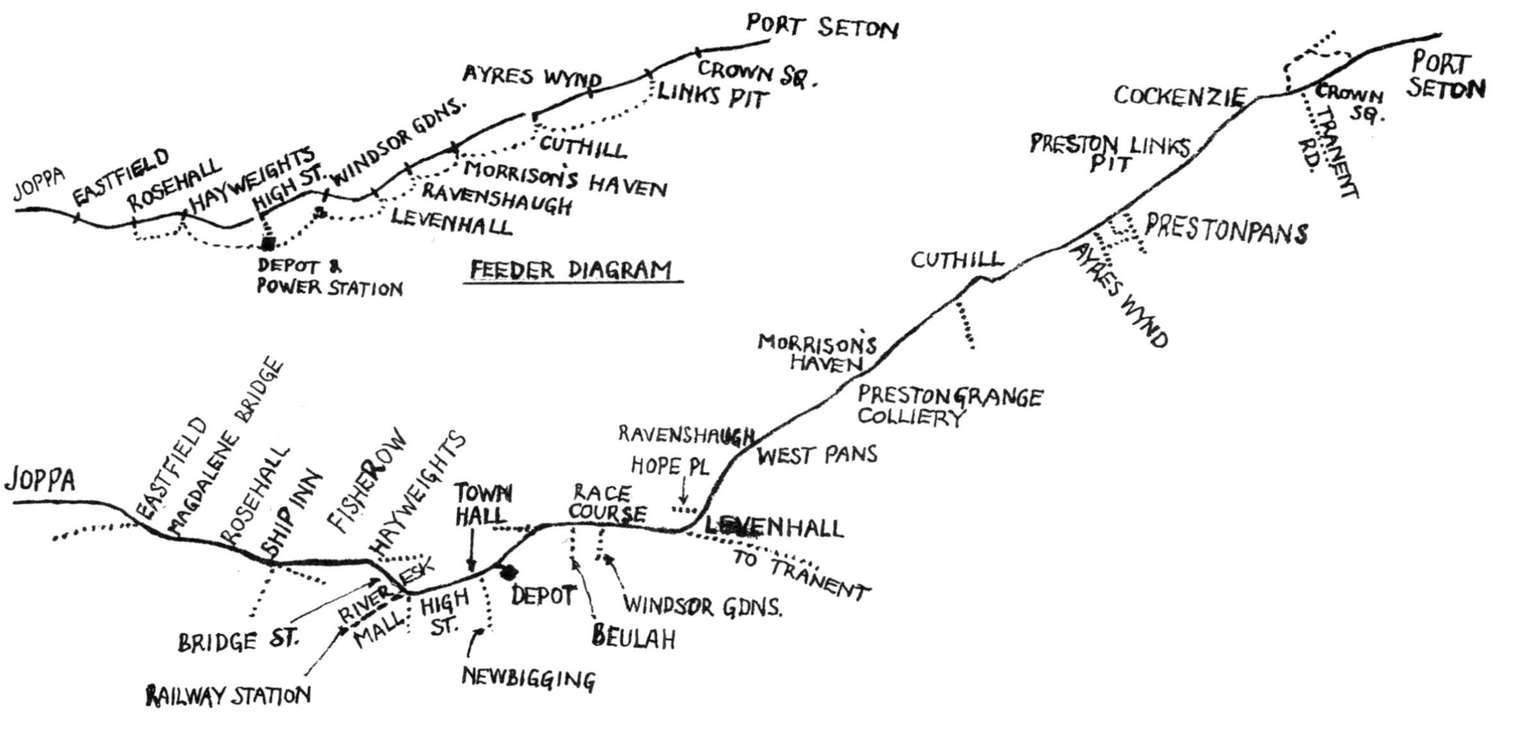

MUSSELBURGH TRAMWAYS

Electric Company Ltd., to construct the portion of the route between the Edinburgh terminus at Joppa and the city boundary at the Brunstane Burn. Edinburgh now had no veto except in respect of an actual connection to its system. An extension of time until 6 August 1904 was given for the remainder of the Musselburgh system and the name of the new company brought in. In September 1903 the company changed its name to the National Electric Construction Company Ltd.

There was still no move to build, however. The company were interested in trying the "G.B." surface contact electric system, and in January 1904 got Edinburgh and Musselburgh to agree. In March this plan was abandoned. Time was running out, and so at last construction was started about a month or so later, the orthodox overhead electric system being adopted. The line was not complete by 6 August 1904, however, and it was 2 December before the first trial was run. Access to the depot was by a trailing connection towards Joppa only, and the branch down the Mall to Inveresk Road was never built. The depot itself was a corrugated iron shed with four tracks in a yard behind the buildings on the south side of the High Street, the single line connection leading through a high arched gateway. The steam generating station was at the back of the car shed and consisted of three water-tube boilers and three Davey-Paxman engines driving 100KW dynamos, boosters and batteries being incorporated in the installation.

In later years the steam power was shut down and the rotaries driven by a high-tension supply from Portobello through the associated Lothians Electric Power Company's network.

The gauge was of course 4ft. 8½in., and 45ft. rails weighing 90lbs per yard were used. From Joppa to Bridge Street a double line was laid, the bracket-arm poles being on the north side. From there on to Levenhall the poles were on the south side. A double track was also laid from the Town Hall past the depot to Loretto Corner. 2/0 gauge trolley wire was used with the usual section insulators and feeder cables, as shown on the diagram. The permitted speed was 10 mph, but 12 mph was allowed on the "country" portions.

After a trial run to Levenhall on 2 December and to Joppa four days later, the Board of Trade inspection took place on 9 December 1904, and the public service commenced after a ceremonial trip on 12 December. The weather was most inauspicious. There was already two inches of snow on the ground and it was still snowing heavily. Nevertheless a large company gathered in the dynamo room, where the wife of Musselburgh's Provost Simpson switched on the machines. Edinburgh's Lord Provost Cranston expressed the hope that electric cars would be extended to the GPO, but no further! Thereafter some of the party braved the elements for the inaugural run in four cars to Joppa. An entertainment was provided in the evening, but the snowstorm prevented several guests from attending.

A ten minutes service was run, increased to five minutes on Sunday afternoons, Musselburgh Town Council having agreed to the running of

One of the Musselburgh Electric Tramways' first lot of open-top cars 1904, outside the depot and about to turn back to Portobello, or more precisely Joppa. The line into the depot can be seen trailing in on the left.

Sunday cars. The horse bus which the North British Railway ran from Musselburgh station to Levenhall was, consequently, withdrawn after 22 December. The full journey cost 2d., and ½d., 1d. and 1½d. fares were offered. Cheap fares for workmen were available in the early morning. The tickets carried the stage names in fareboard layout with the title Musselburgh Electric Tramways in the centre column, and the colours were: ½d. pink(?); 1d. white; 1½d. pale brown; 2d. blue. Williamson punches were used, that firm supplying the tickets too. The intermediate stages were lengthened on 1 January 1906, and half fares for children introduced in the following month.

William Bain, who had been the construction engineer, was interim manager, becoming manager and engineer in May 1905. The promoters now formed a local company which took over the system by agreement and also its local electricity supply interests. This was the Musselburgh & District Electric Light & Traction Company Ltd., incorporated in August 1905, with authorised capital of £120,000. The car service proved popular, and the company started to think about extensions to Tranent, Port Seton and Newcraighall. The Tranent route was tried by starting a bus service from Levenhall. This commenced on 23 December 1905, every half-hour on Saturdays and Sundays. It was operated by two new Wolseley double-deckers seating 18 inside and 18 on top, the fare being 3d. with a 5d. through fare from Joppa. The registration number of one of them was SS4. One of the vehicles was destroyed by fire on 2 April

1906. Hitherto Tranent could only be reached by a horse bus service from Prestonpans station run by James Young at a fare of 6d.

For the Port Seton route the company promoted the Portobello & Musselburgh Tramways (Port Seton Extension) Order 1906. This sought a single-line route, with twelve passing loops, from the Levenhall terminus to Port Seton at Barracks House. Musselburgh Town Council, however, raised objections to the short length between the Levenhall terminus and the burgh boundary. Road widening at three points was asked for, and when the company agreed to this the council threatened to restrict Sunday services and asked for a substantial proportion of the receipts. The company urged that this issue be discussed separately, to which the council first agreed, then reversed their decision in favour of submitting the dispute to the Board of Trade. When the representatives of the council and the company arrived there they found a telegram from the council cancelling the mandate. So the 1906 Order had to go forward without the opposed portion within the Musselburgh boundary, and was confirmed in this form on 4 August 1906. The same provisions were included, and the local authorities were to use the poles for lighting.

Meantime, on 11 August 1906, an 18-seat Thornycroft toast-rack charabanc with wood roof was put on the route between Levenhall and Port Seton, again half-hourly on Saturday and Sundays only, the fare at first being 4d. but increased to 6d. three weeks later. The fare on the Tranent bus was also then increased to 5d. Negotiations for a tramway to Tranent were in hand but, although East Lothian County Council were co-operative, agreement with Midlothian County Council could not be reached, and this scheme was therefore dropped. However, an additional bus, this time a Napier, was obtained for the Tranent route which was operated daily from 1 May 1907.

The Burgh of Cockenzie and Port Seton had also objected to the line through their area as proposed in the 1906 Order, but had been persuaded

Thornycroft charabanc used by the Musselburgh & District Electric Light & Traction Company between Levenhall and Port Seton in 1906 before the cars were extended to Port Seton.

to give their assent on the company promising to endeavour to obtain power for the alternative route the council wanted. Eventually this resulted in the Portobello & Musselburgh Tramways (Port Seton Deviation) Order 1907, confirmed 29 April 1907, which provided for the route being taken northwards at the Tranent Road corner, along Main Street, Red Row and past Rose Cottage to join the original route. There was also a formidable list of road widenings to be carried out, though in a few cases these were not to be done until the extension was connected to the existing line at Levenhall. In the event this deviation was never carried out.

The company also went ahead with another Order to get their two lines connected before proceeding with construction, and at the Inquiry at the Justiciary Court in Edinburgh on 29 April 1907 the difficulties with the 1906 Order were related. The Musselburgh Town Council were now agreeable if the three road widenings were carried out, and the company, as before, were willing. The Portobello & Musselburgh Tramways (Levenhall Extension) Order 1907 was therefore confirmed on 26 July 1907, and authorised the 34.47 chains of line between the existing terminus and the previously authorised tramway starting at the burgh boundary. Four years from the date of the inquiry were allowed for completion, and all the provisions of the earlier Orders applied.

Construction of the new line was now started and the Levenhall-Port Seton bus withdrawn after the summer of 1907, the Tranent one becoming Saturdays and Sundays only again at the same time. Thomas Hunter replaced William Bain as manager in May 1906.

There was much trouble in Musselburgh in the summer of 1907, however. Drivers were being paid 4¾d. per hour with an extra ½d. after six months' service and a further ½d. after eighteen months if free from accidents. Conductors earned ¼d. less. The men demanded an increase of ½d. throughout this scale (conductors to get the same as drivers), a fifty-six-hour week, and some minor alterations. This not being granted, they came out on strike on 1 August. Three cars were taken out by inspectors but were attacked and damaged in Bridge Street, and they had to be replaced. This time each carried two policemen, and the trolley ropes were wound round the booms to prevent interference. But the crowds were hostile, windows were smashed, and the crews roughly handled. Passengers would not risk travelling and the cars went in early. New drivers were obtained from allied companies in the south, so a few cars were run next day too. The rioters appeared in court and were duly fined, but they seem to have had much public support. On the following day, Saturday, only one car was left with any glass in its windows. They were taken into the depot in the early evening, after some derailments. The manager was stoned and injured. On the Sunday the progress of the cars was blocked by large crowds lingering on the track. During the following week an increasing number of cars continued to run, still accompanied by police, and still subjected to rowdyism. Twenty police were sent from Edinburgh. Musselburgh Town Council tried to mediate

The car terminus at Port Seton: car No. 5 approaching. This car was destroyed in a collision in 1917. (*J. Stevenson*)

and met the company, but new men were signing on and the company refused arbitration or reinstatement. The strikers held meetings at which public enthusiasm gradually waned, though rowdyism and obstruction continued, including the use of detonators and, on one occasion, a flock of sheep! A strikers' opposition motor service was well patronised, but ran only for a few days. After the next weekend conditions became normal again: it was all over. The company had won, but some Musselburgh councillors wanted to ban Sunday services as a reprisal. Later the company claimed £220 from the town council for damage done, and eventually recovered about half.

A passenger shelter at Joppa was proposed towards the end of 1907. Edinburgh at first considered a joint building, but in the end left the company to provide it on their own. In 1908 A. A. Watkins was appointed manager.

On 5 August 1909 the new extension was opened as far as Tranent Road, Cockenzie, and to the Port Seton terminus on 31 December following. A twenty minutes service was given to Port Seton, increased to ten minutes in the summer. The last few hundred yards of the route were laid on a reservation raised slightly from the south side of the roadway. Most of the route lay along narrow roads. The way through Prestonpans in particular was very narrow, and there were some sharp curves and scanty clearances from buildings. Bracket-arm poles were used for the overhead, and due to the considerable offset between wire and track in places, trolley ropes had to be abandoned. Manually operated signal lights were provided at some locations.

The fare from Joppa to Port Seton was 5d., using a yellow ticket. Tickets for intermediate fares were: 3d. pink, and 4d. green. At this time the ½d. and 1½d. fares were withdrawn, but in response to public complaint the latter were restored on 15 November 1909. The company's operations were no goldmine, though they had managed a 2 per cent dividend.

In 1911 the service was still every ten minutes to Levenhall and every twenty minutes to Port Seton, reduced to thirty minutes in the evening, but increased to ten minutes for the summer months, when the company also intimated "a more frequent service is run on Sundays and holidays". On such occasions it was necessary to run the cars in groups of two or three, they having to shunt round one another on the shorter passing loops. The bus service to Tranent ceased in 1913 and the Thornycroft was sold to the Mexborough & Swinton Traction Co., while the Napier became a tower-wagon.

In 1913 C. W. Bentley was appointed manager, but he resigned in January of the following year and was succeeded by R. Watson who had been secretary since the company's inception. D. L. Winter was appointed engineer.

There was another strike of car crews on Saturday 20 February 1915, but the men went back after an hour. It was an uneasy truce, however, wages and overtime being the issue, and following the sacking of three crews a fortnight later, only a skeleton service could be run by inspectors. The Industrial Commissioners held an inquiry on behalf of the government on 19 March, at which Mr W. B. Cownie, the company's managing director, declined to reinstate the six men. However, reinstatement of the others was offered, together with payment of a war bonus, and on 22 March the services were running normally again.

In June 1915 the timetable for Port Seton listed a service till "11.20 p.m. which stops at Levenhall if no passengers beyond that stage, and 11.45 p.m. provided passengers board car at Joppa". By the end of the year the Joppa-Levenhall cars were extended to Prestongrange Colliery.

The company had seen several managerial changes and more were to come. The engineer joined the forces in February 1916 and E. J. Walsh came to succeed him, but four months later the manager resigned whereupon Walsh became manager and engineer. He in turn resigned in December 1919 and was succeeded by H. C. Babb, who was still in command when the company's transport operations ceased.

The rigours of the war made maintenance difficult, and it is said that the service became even less reliable than the Edinburgh cable system. Women were employed on both driving and conducting and also on track work. As so much of the route lay along the seashore the car windows on that side were painted over to screen them from the sea at night. There was of course no means of turning cars end for end. Miners' traffic called for additional cars. Here the rolling-stock may be dealt with.

The initial fleet consisted of ten orthodox open-top cars, seating 22 inside and 32 on top, with three windows and reversed stairs. They were built by the British Electric Car Company and ran on 6ft. wheelbase trucks. The electrical equipment was by B.T.H. with G.E.C. motors.

Numbered 1 to 10, the cars were painted red with ivory pillars and rocker panels, and bore the name Musselburgh Electric Tramways, but after the war this was gradually altered to M. & D.E.L. & T. Coy. Ltd. Roller-blind destination screens were mounted above the top rail, and it may be noted that the Joppa terminus was called Portobello on these first ten cars. In the summer of 1905 four further cars, Nos. 11 to 14, were obtained, the order being sublet by the B.T.H.Co. to the Brush Company. These were similar but had ordinary stairs and seated 35 on top. Later, in 1909, these four cars were fitted with closed tops with the usual open balconies. The trolley bases were fixed to the side of the roof nearest the shore, to assist in reaching the overhead wire, and the destination screen boxes were later refitted below the platform canopies. The places shown on the blinds were now: Joppa, Hayweights, Musselburgh, Levenhall, Ayres Wynd, Port Seton, Miners Only, Depot Only, Special. Two more similar closed-top cars were also obtained from the Brush Electric Co. in 1909, and numbered 15 and 16.

There were several collisions and derailments during the war period, mostly due to the prevailing conditions. One of the worst occurred in the dark near Windsor Gardens early in 1917, when the last car returning to

Musselburgh Electric Tramways top-covered car No. 13 at Joppa. This was the other car involved in the collision in 1917. After a complete rebuilding it returned to traffic as a new No. 5.

the depot crashed into the preceding car which was standing disabled and unlighted owing to the collapse of its trolley. The cars involved were Nos. 5 and 13, and the former was so badly damaged that it was scrapped. The latter, however, was eventually repaired, and repillared for five windows each side of the lower saloon. In September 1918 it was turned out painted brown and renumbered 5. During the war not much could be done with the rolling-stock which soon became rundown. In September 1917 Musselburgh Town Council complained of this, and as the cars were licensed by the Edinburgh magistrates for running within the city to Joppa, asked Edinburgh to take action in the matter. An inspection was made early one morning, apparently without warning, a tactic at which the company protested. Only one car, No. 14, was reported in good order, and in May 1918 renewal of Edinburgh's licences for the Musselburgh cars was on a three-monthly basis, several being withheld pending repairs with which Hurst Nelson & Co. Ltd. were called in to help. Some of the old cars lost their destination screens. After the war an overall green livery was adopted. A metal skate in place of the trolley-wheel was tried on one or two cars.

As has been mentioned, additional cars were required, and three old single-deckers with 28 seats on Brill trucks were acquired from Sheffield Corporation in 1918. Two of them had been built by Sheffield Corporation in 1903 and one by Brush in 1900. These were numbered 17, 18 and 19. Called "Tanks" by the men, they were not repainted for a year or two. On occasions such as Musselburgh race days and during the summers of 1917 and 1918, one or two of the Slateford electric cars were borrowed from Edinburgh. All the cars were decorated for the Riding of the Marches celebrations in August 1919.

As might be expected, fares had to be increased. On 14 March 1920 the Joppa-Port Seton fare went up to 7d. and the minimum fare became 1½d. Only five months later there was a further increase when the fare all the way became 9d., but in April 1922 fares were reduced, all the way becoming 7d. again, and 1d. stages were restored. Because of these fluctuations in fares the stage names on the tickets were abandoned in favour of numbers, varying between 1 to 10 and 1 to 20, odd numbers on the left-hand column and even numbers on the right-hand column. The wording in the centre column was now: "Musselburgh Electric Tramways. This ticket is only available by the car upon which it is issued and must be shown on demand. It must be punched opposite the section number to which the passenger is entitled to travel. For name of section numbers see Fare Bill. Subject to the Bye-laws." The colours were now: 1d. white; 1½d. pale brown; 2d. blue; 3d. mauve; 4d. green; 4½d. purple; 5d. red; 6d. brown; 7d. white with red stripe; 9d. yellow with blue stripe; 1d. child, brown. There was also a brown ticket headed "Luggage or Dog Ticket 3d. Musselburgh Electric Tramways"; beneath, a wide centre column contained the conditions of issue with "Dog" and "Luggage" in each outer column headed Out and In. This ticket was overprinted in blue "L. & D.". The tickets were carried in a long single-row holder.

The Musselburgh single-deckers at Joppa en route for storage at Gorgie depot in January 1928. The Musselburgh top-covered cars continued in service for a few more weeks and one of the three ex-Sheffield ones is seen on its outward journey.

In 1923, with electrification of Edinburgh's Portobello route nearing completion, an agreement was drawn up for a through service between Waterloo Place and Port Seton, with both Corporation and company cars participating. For this new era, which commenced on 24 June 1923, the Musselburgh closed-top cars were smartened up with two shades of green, the upper-deck sides of some enjoining passengers to "Enjoy the sea breezes" of "11 miles ride beside the sea", and destination screens refitted where missing, although the single-deckers never had them. Edinbh. G.P.O. and King's Road were added to the blinds. The crews were fitted out with new uniforms. Three more cars were bought from Sheffield Corporation, this time closed-top double-deckers with short top saloons, open stairs and very short platform canopies. One of them was originally built by G. F. Milnes & Co. in 1901, another by Craven's in 1902 and the third, which differed slightly in having top-lights to the lower saloon windows, at Sheffield Corporation's own works in 1905. This one had a Brush truck and 30 seats upstairs. All three seated 22 in the lower saloon. They entered service in November 1923 as Nos. 20, 21 and 22. At this time all the closed-top cars and several of the open-top ones were fitted with magnetic track brakes for use over the Edinburgh tracks. Those without them were not normally used up to Waterloo Place, and the single-deckers remained restricted to service over their own company track.

In 1924 two additional passing loops were constructed between Levenhall and Prestonpans, and the track doubled over the Esk Bridge, then being widened, and into the High Street in Musselburgh. Much track repair work was also put in hand.

In 1926 one car, No. 11, was rebuilt and repillared, giving it five windows each side to the lower saloon, in which upholstered transverse seats were fitted. No. 5 was fitted with these new seats also.

However, by 1927, the financial situation was becoming unsatisfactory and, as will be recorded in Volume 2, the company ceased normal tramway operation after 25 February 1928, though miners' special cars continued to run at shift-changing times between Hayweights and Prestongrange Colliery for about a further month. From 23 February a fleet of buses took over the route to Port Seton, starting from the top of Waterloo Place, but were diverted around Portobello by Baileyfield Road and Milton Road. To make room for them in the depot, the open-top and single-deck cars were cleared out at the end of January and driven via London Road and George Street to Edinburgh's Gorgie depot for storage. When the company finally decided to cease operating any cars, the whole fleet was sold for scrap. Those stored on the outside lye at Gorgie depot had been badly vandalised, and in August had to be towed back one by one to Musselburgh for breaking up. The fate of the tramway route thereafter will be related in Volume 2.

A route which attracted tramway promoters over many years was that to Queensferry. It was a popular drive in summer and thirty "brakes" were in use on the route. The National Electric Construction company brought forward a scheme in 1905, proposing a Dolter surface-contact system from the West End and with a connecting line from Goldenacre to Davidson's Mains. Capital was to be £150,000. Linlithgow County Council and others objected at the inquiry in April 1905, and so the necessary authority did not materialise.

At the same time Mr Colam of cable car fame was interested in a competing concern, the Edinburgh Suburban Electric Tramway syndicate, who proposed to lay their lines by Belford Bridge, and to have two other connecting lines, one from Comely Bank, and another from Bonnington Terrace via Ferry Road. This scheme did not go forward either, but the idea of a tramway to Queensferry came up from time to time, until, towards the end of the First World War, Edinburgh Corporation themselves sought powers to build such a line. At this time there was heavy traffic in naval personnel to and from the bases at Port Edgar and Rosyth, and this was expected to continue. Although warned that a tramway of this nature was unlikely to pay, the Corporation went ahead with a Provisional Order in 1918.

The scheme envisaged a double line from the West End at Hope Street, and also another from the Comely Bank terminus, to Cramond Brig, which would be widened. Over the widened bridge and onward to beyond Burnshot the tracks were to be laid on the south side of the road. Thereafter a reserved track to the south of the roadway was to be built, diverging around the small wooded plantations, as far as Chapel Gate, from where the south side of the roadway was to be used again for a short distance before resuming the reserved track around the next plantation, and on to the top of Hawes Brae. The roadway was to be used down the brae, and after passing the pier the line would become single through the town to Hopetoun crossroads, with six passing loops. A double line reserved track would then continue south of the Hopetoun road, which was joined a short distance before the proposed terminus at the west gate of Port Edgar naval base.

The proposals also included an alternative line from a point near the top of Hawes Brae, cutting across the fields to a point east of Dalmeny station, from where a single line would be laid along the road, including a passing loop under the station bridge. From there a double-line reserved track south of the road was to be laid as far as Kirkliston Road, which it would cross and then cut through the fields to join the first route beyond Hopetoun crossroads.

Although the plans covered the laying of tracks, it was proposed that the portion of the route between New Halls pier and the terminus be constructed as a trolley-vehicle system.

Many objections were lodged, and to placate some, the alternative line by Dalmeny station was dropped. There was much public opposition to the project, which was regarded as a waste of money, and a ratepayers' petition was drawn up. The Admiralty then insisted on the Dalmeny line and also reduced fares for naval personnel as the price of their support, whereupon the town council held a special meeting on 20 September 1918 and decided to withdraw their Order and abandon the scheme. An alternative route from the authorised Corstorphine extension to Queensferry via Kirkliston was then suggested in the town council, but got no further than a suggestion, and that was the last heard of tramways to Queensferry.

To revert to 1905, the Edinburgh Suburban Electric Tramways Company proposed to build an electric line from the Nether Liberton terminus via Gilmerton and Eskbank to Bonnyrigg, terminating along the Lasswade Road, with a branch from Eskbank to Dalkeith terminating near the Palace Gates. The company secured their powers by the Edinburgh Suburban Electric Tramways Order Confirmation Act 1906 (passed 21 December 1906). The route was to be a single line with passing places and with a triangular junction at Eskbank. The usual provisions were included: the gauge was to be 4ft. 8½in. or as approved; the overhead or other system as approved; poles to be lighted and painted, though not oftener than three-yearly, as required by the local authority. Five years were allowed for completion. A fifteen minutes service to Dalkeith and a thirty minutes service to Bonnyrigg were stipulated, and the company were to carry all the passengers off the last car from Edinburgh, though if these averaged less than twelve over six months the company need not run after 11.00 p.m. The fare to Dalkeith was to be 4d. and to Bonnyrigg 5d.

The company had already thought it better to get their line right into the city if they could and to this end proposed to extend from Nether Liberton by way of Lady Road, Dalkeith Road, Pleasance and Jeffrey Street to a terminus at the Waverley Bridge. They also proposed a branch along Melville Drive to Tollcross, and suggested to the Corporation that they be allowed to provide the Craiglockhart route, about which the Corporation were then deliberating. The surface-contact system was proposed for these new lines within the city, and the conversion of the Mound route to work in conjunction with the Craiglockhart route was also suggested. Edinburgh Town Council were interested but as we have seen they preferred to hold with their existing lessees, and did not support the new company.

So nothing further transpired. Dalkeith Town Council asked the company about starting, but there appear to have been financial difficulties. The company obtained another Act in 1911 (passed 18 August 1911) extending their time for construction until two years after 21 December 1911. Nevertheless nothing was ever done and the powers lapsed. A similar trolley-bus route had been proposed by the Dalkeith Railless electric Car Company in 1908.

One other concern has to be mentioned. About 1909 the War Office had decided to build the new barracks at Redford. This led to a company known as the Colinton Tramways Company seeking powers for a line from Craiglockhart terminus to the Loan, Colinton, with a branch to Slateford station and along Slateford Road, Angle Park Terrace and Fountainbridge to East Fountainbridge. At the inquiry in July 1909 there were objections from Midlothian County Council and from Edinburgh Corporation, who had an eye on the route themselves. Nevertheless the Order was passed on 25 November 1909 as the Colinton Tramways Order Confirmation Act 1909. This authorised a line through the fields between Craiglockhart and the barracks site, with the branch to connect with the line the Corporation were now projecting to Slateford station, and another branch to the Caledonian Railway sidings behind Slateford station. The contractor for the barracks buildings was to have the right of using the line for materials. Steam power could be used for this purpose for four and a quarter years: thereafter the line was to be electrically operated and a generating station allowed for. Later, power from Edinburgh Corporation was agreed. The gauge had, of course, to be 4ft. 8½in., and five years were allowed for completion. As with the Edinburgh Suburban Company, buses were authorised within five miles of the line over contemplated extensions.

In April 1910 a contract was let to William Jackson, Edinburgh, to make the formation through the fields and construct the bridge over the canal near Slateford. Temporary railway track was laid the following month for use by the contractor building the barracks, and two steam locomotives were used on it.

By 1913 the company had made no effective progress, only the reserved track formation being made, from which the barracks contractor's rails were now removed. The company then sought powers for a line from Angle Park Terrace via Dundee Street and Fountainbridge to a terminus just west of Earl Grey Street, with running powers over the Corporation line along Slateford Road. Edinburgh Corporation objected to this and considered electrifying their own line inwards from Ardmillan to

Haymarket and the east end of Morrison Street. The company's Provisional Order failed, and so they then suggested the Corporation might build the line from Craiglockhart to Colinton themselves, offering, in March, to sell their rights to the Corporation for £10,200. The town clerk drew up a report on the matter, suggesting the Corporation should accept in the public interest, as a service would be required by the War Office, yet such could not now be provided by the company.

The town council deliberated and thought of building the line through the fields from Craiglockhart for operation by a self-propelled car. No action materialised, however, and in November the company sought an extension of time for the compulsory purchase of a certain field at Slateford between the canal and the station, belonging to the Corporation, without which they would not be able to complete their route to Slateford. This was refused though continued temporary access across the field to the railway bridge was agreed.

The company then obtained the Colinton Tramways Extension Order Confirmation Act 1914 (passed 8 July 1914) which granted them a three years' extension of time from 25 November 1914, and also power to sell their concern to the Corporation at any time if the latter secured Board of Trade approval to purchase. In 1915 the Corporation again refused to buy up the company, as already mentioned in Chapter 3, and consequently failed to secure powers to build a line to Colinton themselves. Nevertheless the company secured extensions of time annually until 25 November 1920. It was now evident the Colinton company would have to be liquidated to clear the way for the Corporation to serve the expanding city, and so at last, early in 1920, the Corporation agreed to purchase the concern for about £5,000. The Corporation found the bridge over the canal useful for carrying some new water mains.

The old formation through the fields remained for several years until building was developed in the area. Part of the route then became Craiglockhart Road, including the spur to the old Craiglockhart terminus. The other portion northwards towards Slateford station and the bridge over the canal can still be seen, and is now in use as a footpath leading to Allan Park Road.

Index